I0125460

AGAINST EXCLUSION

AGAINST EXCLUSION

DISRUPTING ANTI-CHINESE VIOLENCE
IN THE NINETEENTH CENTURY

Audrey Wu Clark

THE OHIO STATE UNIVERSITY PRESS

COLUMBUS

Copyright © 2024 by The Ohio State University.
All rights reserved.

Library of Congress Cataloging-in-Publication Data

Names: Clark, Audrey Wu, 1980– author.

Title: Against exclusion : disrupting anti-Chinese violence in the nineteenth century / Audrey Wu Clark.

Other titles: Disrupting anti-Chinese violence in the nineteenth century

Description: Columbus : The Ohio State University Press, [2024] | Includes bibliographical references and index. | Summary: "Traces the discourses of the model minority and the yellow peril back to the nineteenth century and examines the activist efforts and writings of Ah Toy, Mary Tape, Wong Chin Foo, Yan Phou Lee, and Yung Wing, who sought to prove their humanity and their right to citizenship amid the exclusion and dehumanization of Chinese Americans"—Provided by publisher.

Identifiers: LCCN 2024019147 | ISBN 9780814215623 (hardback) | ISBN 0814215629 (hardback) | ISBN 9780814283745 (ebook) | ISBN 0814283748 (ebook)

Subjects: LCSH: Ah Toy. | Tape, Mary McGladery, 1857–1934. | Wong, Chin Foo, 1847–1898. | Lee, Yan Phou, 1861– | Yung, Wing, 1828–1912. | Chinese Americans—Social conditions—19th century. | Race discrimination—History—19th century. | Chinese Americans—Crimes against—United States. | Racism against Asians—History—19th century. | Violence—United States—History—19th century. | Model minority stereotype. | China—Emigration and immigration—History—19th century.

Classification: LCC E184.C5 C575 2024 | DDC 305.8951073—dc23/eng/20240712

LC record available at https://lccn.loc.gov/2024019147

Other identifiers: ISBN 9780814259269 (paperback) | ISBN 081425926X (paperback)

Cover design by Susan Zucker
Text composition by Stuart Rodriguez
Type set in Minion Pro

Finally, for Char

CONTENTS

ACKNOWLEDGMENTS

This book about rampant physical and epistemic violence was not an easy one to write. But it is a book that celebrates survival. I owe a debt of gratitude to my editor, Ana Maria Jimenez-Moreno, my two anonymous readers, and the board at The Ohio State University Press for their enduring support and impactful edits. I also greatly appreciate the feedback I received from Cathy Hannabach, Rachel Fudge, Micha Rahder, and Michelle Velasquez-Potts as this book developed. I am forever in debt to my advisors, Colleen Lye and Richard Cándida Smith. I could not have gotten through this difficult project without my writing groups: Mimi Khúc, Mai-Linh K. Hong, Caroline Kyungah Hong, Leah A. Milne, Julia H. Lee, Jennifer Ho, Megan Geigner, Calina Ciobanu, Emily Alianello, Shirley Lau Wong, Alyssa Quintanilla, Jane Wessel, Michael Wagoner, Gabriel Bloomfield, Mike Flynn, and James Cobb. I thank Michelle Allen-Emerson, Shirley Lin, Sharika Crawford, Eileen Tess Johnston, and Mike Parker for mentoring me at USNA. I thank my students for helping me persevere through the most difficult of times. I also thank the Volgenau Fellowship, the Faculty Development Fund, and the Olmsted Fellowship for the great support as I developed and finished this project. I thank the workers and librarians at Bryn Athyn College, Haverford College, Smith College, Harvard University, Yale University, the University of California, the National Archives at San Francisco, and the San Francisco Public Library. My dear friends in and out of academia have continued to inspire me: Christine

Hong, Lawrence-Minh Bùi Davis, Sarah Townsend, Jesse Costantino, Brendan Prawdzik, Marlon Moore, Mike Major, Naida García Crespo, Derek Handley, Joan Shifflett, Melody Wukitch, Mary Senoyuit, Nicole Uchida, Theresa Rosenthal, Sarah Slye, Kristi Petree, Mindy Lo, and Dara Kao. I thank my local friends for their gifts: Kelly Sweeny, Raima Carpenter, Liz Cash, Stephanie Martin, Brenda Salsman, Chelsea Barzal, Abby Meckes, Dawn Morgan, Susan Bausum, Maria Gannon, Jack Ryan, Keisha Holt, Julia Huang, Jhena Sword, Michelle Cable, Evelyn Lunasin, Loretta Lamar, Denise Boucher, Cindy Winnick, Kristin Murrell, Leslie Davis, Brenda Novak, Jess Samaras, Valerie Leitzel, Gloria Cramer, and Aparna Srinivasan. I thank all of my relatives stateside and beyond. I am always thankful to my siblings: Connie Cheng, Alan Cheng, Michael Wu, Nancy Wu, Karen Karyshyn, Bobby Karyshyn, Tony Clark, and Gina Clark. I thank my parents, Dick Clark, Candy Clark, Hen-Vai Wu, and Serena Wu, for showing me how to survive. And for growing up alongside this arduous book, I thank Quentin and Dashiell. Finally, I thank my one and only, Charles Clark.

"Violence and the Sacred"

THE DRIVING-OUT ERA

This book seeks to revise the ways in which we assess Asian American resistance. In addition to rehabilitating early Chinese American historical and literary figures, I demonstrate that they perform the exceptional minority stereotype that led to what historians Beth Lew-Williams and Jean Pfaelzer have called the driving-out era of Chinese Americans in order to critique the liberalism that created the state of exception in the first place. In contrast to twentieth-century Asian American approaches to resistance in defying stereotypes, these early Chinese American figures deployed the earliest traces of the model minority and the yellow peril stereotypes in order to make themselves visible during a period of rampant anti-Chinese violence and legal exclusion. In this way, this book contributes to prevailing scholarly conversations about the dual stereotypes but contextualizes them in the nineteenth century during the period of exclusion and the liberal state of exception that led to the Chinese American driving-out era.

On October 24, 1871, a mob of five hundred white American and Latinx men lynched eighteen Chinese people by rope in Los Angeles's Chinatown.[1] The Massacre of 1871 began with the assimilative act of an American church

---

1. Zinn Education Project.

wedding of two Chinese people, and to which white Americans took offense:[2] Pfaelzer writes, "Perhaps most threatening to whites was that the 'Melican' wedding contradicted the myth that the Chinese were in the United States as temporary sojourners."[3] Scott Zesch, through his archival research, provides some of the lynch mob's comments after the mass hanging: the shoemaker A. R. Johnston, the head of the mob, stated, "The cheap labor is done away with now. The sons of bitches are hanged!"[4] Less than two hours after the massacre occurred, an unnamed member of the lynching party stated, "I am satisfied now. I have killed three Chinamen."[5] This shocking event was one of many Chinese American lynchings during the driving-out era that took place during the 1870s and 1880s in the United States; this era is not well documented in US historiographies, in part because of the dominant narrative of legislated and social racism against Black Americans during this period and because, historically, Asian Americans have not often been thought of as victims due to the model minority stereotype. As the archives of the Massacre of 1871 demonstrate, the mass lynching of the seventeen Chinese men and one Chinese woman suggests that their discursive subjectification as "cheap labor" reduced them to objects that were disposable.[6] The mob's inhuman reactions to the lynching, too, rendered them objects, however superior.

The asymmetrical objectifications of the lynched victims and the lynch mob exemplify theorist Giorgio Agamben's claim about the objectified, "killed but not sacrificed" homo sacer; in other words, the sacred figure that must be killed or driven out through lynching in this specific instance, "without penalty of murder" but preserved as the sacred exception to consolidate the sovereign in a way that the sovereign, too, is exceptionally exempt from the law and objectified.[7] Whether actually killed or not, Chinese Americans in the nineteenth century existed in a state of exception in which they were stripped of their natural and legal rights, or what Lisa Marie Cacho has termed "a social death,"[8] a term she borrows from Orlando Patterson. Patterson famously defines social death for slaves as "natal alienation," or "the loss of ties of birth in both ascending and descending generations" and "general dishonor" within a structure of power.[9] Asian American critics such as Jodi Kim have since applied Patterson's term social death to orphaned transracial GI babies during

---

2. J. Yung, 22.
3. Pfaelzer, 51.
4. Zesch, 144.
5. Zesch, 148.
6. I thank Calina Ciobanu for introducing me to the concept of disposable lives.
7. Weheliye, 33; and Agamben, 17.
8. Cacho, 7.
9. Patterson, 7, 13.

the Cold War in Asia.[10] In her critical text, *Death beyond Disavowal*, Grace Kyungwon Hong links Agamben to Cacho's and Patterson's notion of "social death" when she states, "Giorgio Agamben extends this idea [of Foucault's theory of biopolitics] to argue that, by creating a category of political life that is different from the simply biological or physical state of life, the modern state produces a new form of 'bare life,' in which one is physically alive, but one's life is politically unprotectable."[11] Although the figures of my study were not driven out of West Coast cities during the Chinese driving-out era of the 1870s and 1880s, many of them were not US citizens or, like Yung Wing, were stripped of their citizenship and thus experienced social death.[12] As Alexander Saxton has famously pointed out, all Chinese Americans were the "indispensable enemy" or, in Agamben's terms, the *exceptional* scapegoats of a contradictory but sovereign US liberalism during the nineteenth century.[13] *Against Exclusion: Disrupting Anti-Chinese Violence in the Nineteenth Century* excavates the exceptionalism with which Chinese Americans were racialized and subject to death—whether by lynching, other forms of driving-out, or loss of citizenship or rights—and the ways in which some of the earliest canonical figures of Asian American studies used the very stereotype of exceptionalism in their activism to expose and dismantle the contradictory exceptionalism of nineteenth-century US liberalism that both required and "disavowed" the death of Chinese Americans.[14] Although this study focuses on the asymmetrical Chinese exceptionalism and the exceptionalism of nineteenth-century liberalism, rather than neoliberalism, as Hong argues, that required Chinese American[15] death for its existence, I argue that nineteenth-century liberalism specifically operated through the disavowal of its exceptionalisms.

The driving-out murders, specifically lynching, to which the Chinese fell prey, is a specific kind of racially motivated murder that spectacularly draws attention to the body—however fragmented—against which Black people, Indigenous people, and people of color have not been legally protected and which liberalism has historically both required and disavowed. Although the term has historically referred to the "form" of a racially motivated murder with a noose, lynching, particularly since the Black Lives Matter movement and the 2022 Emmett Till Antilynching Act, has come to signify any racially "motivated," spectacularly objectifying death, not necessarily but inclusive

10. J. Kim, 169.
11. Hong, 25.
12. I thank Alyssa Quintanilla for pointing this insight out to me.
13. Saxton, 105.
14. Hong, 7.
15. I consider any Chinese living in the US as Chinese American.

of murder by hanging.[16] People do not often know that coincident with the proliferation of African American lynchings during the postbellum era, Chinese Americans were also spectacularly driven out, often by lynching, during the 1870s and 1880s. This is partly because, even in the nineteenth century, Americans often cast Asian Americans as the hyperbolically submissive, law-abiding, economically efficient minority exceptions, even before the term "model minority" was coined in the 1960s.[17] This nineteenth-century stereotype of the minority exception thus hides the history of driving-out and public discipline that is often forgotten or left out of historiographies. I recognize the deep and fraught history of African American lynching and am not conflating African American slavery and segregation with Asian exclusion. In this study, I deploy the term "lynching" to contribute to Colleen Lye's theorization of the "Afro-Asian Analogy"—that Black-Asian comparative racializations make possible a triangulation between Black, white, and Asian and that their "association with substitution lies the potential for Afro-Asian antipathy as well as unity."[18] Frank B. Wilderson III, who coined the term Afropessimism, meant to describe the lack of progress in African American history, has importantly argued: "Anti-Blackness is its own beast—a conceptual framework that cannot be analogized to capitalism, or any other ism." Furthermore, he claims that it is a mistake to "disguise Black suffering as 'exploitation of the working class' or as a kind of suffering that's common to all people of color."[19] At the same time, Lye, whose work I build upon, *triangulates* Black, white, and Asian instead of making a one-to-one, comparative analogy. In this book, Chinese American exceptionalism and its corollary of driving-out is part of the triangulation with the specificity and non-exceptionalism of anti-Black violence (the history of lynching) and whiteness. Still, Chinese Americans were lynched by rope during this period, which contributes to the possible alliances between Blacks and Asians which Lye posits in her "Afro-Asian Analogy." I am intervening in the Afro-Asian analogy by suggesting that, while both African Americans and Asian Americans were lynched in the late nineteenth century, Asian American lynching and driving-out differently, asymmetrically mirrored and exposed the liberal state of exception to which both Asian Americans and African Americans were dissimilarly subject (the former as exceptional, the latter quotidian); moreover, the exceptional minority stereotype of the nineteenth-century model minority and yellow peril helped to construct the liberal state of exception.[20]

16. See UPM staff, "Ersula J. Ore on Lynching."
17. Lye, *America's Asia*, 8.
18. Lye, "Afro-Asian Analogy," 1735.
19. Wilderson.
20. Weheliye, 11.

Driving-out, of which lynching is a part, is thus part of the liberal state of exception; that is, it is as exceptional as it is spectacular regardless of whether the driven-out victim is racialized as exceptional or not, since it is and has been part of liberalism's exceptionalism from whose consequences it is exempt. Saxton cites the beginning of this Chinese American driving-out era in the 1860s when "San Franciscans [. . .][21] in the winter of 1867 drove a gang of Chinese laborers from their work on the Potrero Street railway [and] were functioning as an anticoolie club." He further notes that "Chinese were stoned, beaten, run down on the street. And there were hints of more ominous actions. In April a stocking factory belonging to the firm of Goldstone and Sharp, employers of Chinese, burned for a total loss. [. . .] Boycotting continued as the major public weapon of the anticoolie clubs."[22] The other exceptional and spectacular forms of violent expulsions of Chinese Americans in the driving-out, which included the lynchings on the West Coast of the United States in the 1870s and 1880s, encompassed civic death in which Chinese Americans were stripped of their rights. Although not always murdered during these expulsions, many Chinese Americans died during these forcible removals from "exposure" to the outside elements.[23] The lynchings of Chinese Americans continued in the 1880s when a Chinese laundryman was lynched in Denver, Colorado.[24] In 1875 in Trout Creek, Nevada City, Nevada, white employees of the Central Pacific Railroad committed arson and then shot and killed Chinese laborers as they exited their burning cabin.[25] In 1877 white working-class mobs murdered Chinese in both Port Madison, Washington, and on the Lemm Ranch, which was followed by the burning of Chinatown, in Chico, California.[26] The Rock Springs Massacre in Wyoming Territory in 1885 claimed the lives of twenty-eight Chinese people.[27] Dozens of Chinese people were murdered by white miners in the Snake River Massacre in Oregon in 1877.[28] En masse, the Chinese were spectacularly driven out of Tacoma and Seattle, Washington Territory, and Eureka and Arcata, California, in 1885 and San Jose, California, the following year[29]—to name only a few expulsions by white mobs. The driving-out era exploded in the 1870s and 1880s.[30]

---

21. Throughout the book, bracketed ellipses are my own, indicating text elisions.
22. Saxton, 72, 73, 74.
23. Lew-Williams, 124.
24. Pfaelzer, 54.
25. Pfaelzer, 173.
26. Lew-Williams, 17; and Pfaelzer, 69, 71.
27. J. Yung, 22; Lew-Williams, 169; and Pfaelzer, 215.
28. Lew-Williams, 180.
29. Lew-Williams, 1; Pfaelzer, 219; Lew-Williams, 103, 105, 106, 113, 114; and Pfaelzer, 192.
30. Saxton, 268.

During the Massacre of 1871, the Chinese attempts to assimilate by putting on an American wedding demonstrated the exclusive inclusion of the Chinese in liberal American society even before they were legally deemed "aliens ineligible to citizenship" by the 1882 Exclusion Law; their efforts to assimilate fulfilled and threatened the egalitarianism and exclusiveness of liberalism, respectively. This book contextualizes the earliest Chinese American voices and autobiographies, which critics have often dismissed as assimilationist, during the driving-out era of the 1870s and 1880s—to highlight the importance of these writers and activists and their efforts to humanize and "enflesh"[31] (to be discussed below) themselves when, they, too could fall prey to driving-out. In his autobiographical essay, "Why Am I a Heathen," in which he criticizes the hypocrisy of Christianity, Wong Chin Foo acknowledges the contemporary driving-out period: "[God] has created this and other worlds to effectuate beneficent, not merciless, designs, and that all that He has done is for the steady, progressive benefit of the creatures whom He endowed with life and sensibility, and to whom as a consequence He owes and gives paternal care, and will give paternal compensation and justice; yet His voice will threaten and His mighty hand chastise those who deliberately disobey His sacred laws and their duty to their fellow man."[32] Here, he imagines the "beneficent" "other worlds" of Chinese Americans and their "life and sensibility" during a period in which they were being violently objectified while Christians were "deliberately disobey[ing] His sacred laws and their duty to their fellow man." Here, Wong powerfully gives humanity and agency to his fellow Chinese Americans as they faced the violence of being driven out of West Coast cities. The historical people I discuss in this book all perform the important work of what Alexander Weheliye has theorized as "enfleshment": "The flesh, rather than displacing bare life or civil death, excavates the social (after)life of these categories: it represents racializing assemblages of subjection that can never annihilate the lines of flight, freedom dreams, practices of liberation, and possibilities of other worlds."[33] Responding to the "bare life" of being, the homo sacer of nineteenth-century liberalism, the historical people I discuss in this book all perform the important "(after)life" of the driving-out era—specifically their own agency of belonging to the US. The liberalism that was sovereign during the nineteenth-century was indeed complex but also a contradictory ideology, which believed in freedom and equality but denied minorities civil rights. Nineteenth-century liberalism empowered Chinese Americans by giving them (low-paying) work but disempowered them

---

31. Chin et al., *Aiiieeeee!*, xxvii; Chin et al., *Big Aiiieeeee!*, xii, 8; E. Kim, 25; and Weheliye, 2.
32. Wong Chin Foo, "Why Am I a Heathen?," 11–12.
33. Weheliye, 2.

through violence; we see this contradiction with other minorities as well: liberalism gave women the power to enact social reforms but denied them suffrage and also emancipated African Americans and gave African American men the right to vote but perpetuated a racially segregated society. The activism of the five figures of my study that was based on a "state of relationality" "in creative acts of political formation, reading, writing, and voracious organizing" in an "unstable" liberal "hegemony" in this case—or what Wendy Cheng has coined the *infrastructures of activism* (combining Raymond Williams's "structure of feeling" and Ruth Wilson Gilmore's "infrastructures of feeling")[34]—fought against the exclusions of liberalism and, in doing so, dismantled the contradictions and expanded the hegemonic notion of liberalism. At times the figures of my study engaged with their exceptional minoritization to gain traction in the political sphere. Their exceptional minority stereotype was composed of both the model minority—which, in the nineteenth century, was economic efficiency, submission, and hyperbolization of character traits rather than the wealth it has been assigned in the twentieth century—and the yellow peril—the discursive notion that the Chinese were filthy, diseased, and insidiously out to imperialistically take over other nations. In deploying these stereotypes to point out the contradictions of liberalism for all Americans, these figures demonstrated that the collapsible stereotypes of the nineteenth-century model minority and the yellow peril were part of the liberal state of exception. This phenomenon also recenters race in Agamben's theory of the homo sacer—a lack for which Weheliye has criticized it:[35] the contradictions of the exceptional minoritization of Chinese Americans as model minority and yellow peril reflected and exposed the contradictions of the liberal sovereign state. Unfortunately, the minimal reception, even in Asian American studies, of the figures of my study demonstrates the ways in which their efforts have been unacknowledged and were merely absorbed by liberalism as assimilationist.

Ah Toy, Mary Tape, Wong Chin Foo, Yan Phou Lee, and Yung Wing were part of the first wave of Chinese immigration in the United States and consequently witnessed and responded to the driving-out era of the 1870s and 1880s. Chinese immigrants began arriving in the mainland US, specifically the West Coast, in the late 1840s seeking to capitalize on the Gold Rush in the Sierra foothills. The number of Chinese immigrants grew from 2,716 in 1851 to 20,026 in 1852. By 1867, 12,000 Chinese were working for the Central Pacific Railroad, a necessary structure following the Gold Rush. Liberals viewed

---

34. W. Cheng, 3, 3.
35. Weheliye, 4.

the Chinese in the nineteenth century as exceptional minorities—"admired for their industry and frugality" and their "economic efficiency,"[36] and their hyperbolic submission in the 1850s. As cheap labor, the Chinese composed 90 percent of the railroad's workforce. When the railroad was completed in 1869, Chinese railroad workers migrated to the nearest major city, San Francisco, with hopes of finding further employment. Other Chinese were already working in big West Coast cities. By 1870 the number of Chinese living in San Francisco was over 12,000, and by 1882 the number was around 30,000. Joan Trauner writes, "By the 1870s, the racist argument had broadened in scope, and the Chinese were viewed as 'a social, moral and political curse to the community,'"[37] or the yellow peril. The Chinese were the largest racial minority group in California at the time, and during these latter decades of the century, San Francisco had the largest population of Chinese in California, about 24.4 percent of the state's total population of Chinese.[38] Although the driving-out occurred mostly on the West Coast, all of the figures of my study—some of whom lived on the East Coast—were affected by and responded to the driving-out era.

The discourse of Asian exceptionalism, which led to the driving-out era, was circulating well before the Civil War when the Chinese first began to arrive in the mainland US, as Ah Toy demonstrates. However, following the emancipation of enslaved persons and the specific kind of social death that slavery created, liberalism required for its contradictory existence a new social death or general dishonor of Chinese Americans through the racial exceptionalism in the Chinese American driving-out era, the Page Act, and the Chinese Exclusion Act. As I mentioned, lynching, which was a significant part of the driving-out era, is a form of racial violence and death that centers on the spectacle of the body that has been maimed or disfigured in its display, which for the historically fragmented Asian American body poses both a challenge and a precise image. As critic Rachel C. Lee has argued citing Eric Hayot and Colleen Lye, the bodies of Asian Americans have often been presented as bodies that are fragmented or "de-anthropomorphized."[39] Rachel C.

---

36. Trauner, "Chinese as Medical Scapegoats"; and Lye, *America's Asia*, 5.

37. Trauner, 2.

38. Shah, 25; and Trauner.

39. In *The Exquisite Corpse of Asian America: Biopolitics, Biosociality, and Posthuman Ecologies*, Rachel C. Lee writes, "'De-anthropomorphization' becomes the neologic mouthful Hayot coins to refer to Lye's approach: Lye's forceful de-anthropomorphization of the concept of race [. . .] thus leads us to a broader theory of disappointments of what one might call anthropomorphic desire, that is, of the disappointments produced by the awareness that an originary fantasy of the body's personal and human simplicity can only be thought in relation to such larger and more inhuman concepts as transnationalism, diaspora, globalization or the history of the means of production" (14–15).

Lee closely ties her analysis of fragmentation to Kandice Chuh's well-known conceptualization of Asian American studies as a "subjectless discourse" "to create the conceptual space to prioritize difference by foregrounding the discursive constructedness of subjectivity."[40] The relative lack of general knowledge surrounding the driving-out era of Chinese Americans during the 1870s and 1880s and its context for the publication of the first Chinese American autobiographies reaffirms the exceptionalism with which Asian Americans have historically been stereotyped as a racial minority group—that is, as the yellow peril that contains and is part of the model or exceptional minority—and their related fragmenting disembodiment or de-anthropomorphization. *Against Exclusion* argues that to expose the contradictions of liberalism and to track the progression of reform in the Gilded Age and Progressive Era, the first Chinese American public figures, Ah Toy, Mary Tape, Wong Chin Foo, Yan Phou Lee, and Yung Wing, responded to and memorialized the driving-out era by asserting their bodily selves during a period in which Chinese Americans were objectified, fragmented, and de-anthropomorphized through lynching and being driven out that was not and has not been of historical remembrance.

The focus on the Chinese American driving-out era of this study is inspired by Lisa Lowe's *The Intimacies of Four Continents* (2015), in which she "aim[s . . .] to be more specific about what I would term the economy of affirmation and forgetting that structures and formalizes the archives of liberalism, and liberal ways of understanding. This economy civilizes and develops freedoms for 'man' in modern Europe and North America, while relegating others to geographical and temporal spaces that are constituted as backward, uncivilized, and unfree."[41] In her genealogy of liberalism and "affirmation" of post-"man" or postliberal humanism, influenced by Sylvia Wynter's countering of liberal humanism or "man" through her work on "human as praxis," Lowe seeks to give voice—that is, "affirmation and presence"[42]—to those who have historically been excluded from the universal equality of liberalism. In her genealogy, she writes of the contradictions of classical liberalism: liberalism, she writes, "includes at once both the universal promises of rights, emancipation, wage labor, and free trade, as well as the global divisions and asymmetries on which the liberal tradition depends, and according to which such liberties are reserved for some and wholly denied to others."[43] Elissa Zellinger writes, US liberalism "championed the contradictory ideals of individualism and democratic union—all the while actually restricting these supposed

---

40. Chuh, *Imagine Otherwise*, 9–10; and Rachel C. Lee, 11–12.
41. Lowe, 3.
42. See McKittrick. Lowe, 40.
43. Lowe, 3–4.

universals, and the subjectivity that subtends them, to white men. Liberal subjectivity was not a universal right; rather, such autonomous individualism was created by excluding women, the enslaved, and Native peoples, and denying them the political and social freedoms enjoyed by those identified as full liberal subjects."[44] In the nineteenth century, US liberalism was philosophically inclusionary but, in practice, excluded women and racial minorities. Thus, the contradictions of the exceptional minority stereotype—the model minority and the yellow peril—mirrored and exposed such contradictions of exceptional, sovereign liberalism in the nineteenth century.

THE EXCEPTIONAL FIRST CHINESE AMERICAN VOICES

On the one hand, the murders and the spectacular expulsions of masses of Chinese people from West Coast cities in the 1870s and 1880s stemmed from and perpetuated the exceptionalizing objectification of the Chinese as what we might term now the yellow peril / model minority in the US. On the other hand, white sovereignty exposes itself in all these instances as an example of theorist Walter Benjamin's concept of "divine violence," which differs from sovereign violence insofar as it "dissol[ves] [. . .] the link between violence and law" and "deposes [violence]."[45] I argue that through the contemporary white American renunciation of the lynch mob, exemplified after the Massacre of 1871 when newspapers were quick to renounce the lynch mobs' actions, the revelation of the parallel objectifications of Chinese Americans as the exceptional minority and white Americans as liberalism and its nineteenth-century subset, white supremacy, is a form of divine violence insofar as it deposes violence to expose, equally, the "sacredness of life."[46] The first Chinese American writings and voices were born out of these violent events; that is, they responded to and documented the driving-out era. The sacred "bare life," or the "sacred life" of the homo sacer that the spectacularizing act of driving-out, of which lynching is a part, underscores the exceptionalism of Chinese Americans insofar as "bare life" must be killed but not symbolically sacrificed, as encapsulated by the California Supreme Court case *People v. Hall* (1854), which publicly determined that "Asiatics" were objects, rather than subjects, that could not testify against whites.[47] Exceptionalism was the way in which "bare life" could be exterminated but not sacrificed. Although this decision was overturned by *People v. Elvea* (1859), the exceptionalism of the sacred

---

44. Zellinger, 5.
45. Agamben, 65.
46. Zesch, 169; and Agamben, 83.
47. Agamben, 83; and Pfaelzer, 39.

Chinese body in the nineteenth century endured and culminated in the spectacularly objectifying forms of anti-Asian violence, in the 1870s and 1880s. The
enfleshed narratives of Ah Toy, Mary Tape, Wong Chin Foo, Yan Phou Lee,
and Yung Wing reframed Chinese Americans as complex humans espous-
ing ideas and emotions; they did so to combat the discursive, objectifying
"bare" and "sacred life" of Chinese Americans that was mutually reinforced
by the exceptional minority stereotypes and contemporary Chinese often fatal
driving-out.

Chinese American, and broadly Asian American, literature began with
the publication of newspaper biographies, and autobiographical essays and
books. The newspaper accounts of the sex worker Ah Toy's court cases from
1849 onward and of Mary Tape's open letter to the San Francisco Board of
Education in her Supreme Court case against segregating Chinese students in
Tape v. Hurley (1884), Wong Chin Foo's "Why Am I a Heathen?" (1887), Yan
Phou Lee's *When I Was a Boy in China* (1887), and Yung Wing's *My Life in
China and America* (1909) all historically coincided with the driving-out era
of Chinese Americans in the 1870s and 1880s. Whereas few criticisms of these
figures and authors historicize them, *Against Exclusion* contextualizes the first
Chinese American court cases and autobiographies within this period of grave
anti-Chinese sentiment and fatal violence. Continually susceptible to driving-
out as Chinese Americans during this period,[48] Ah Toy, Mary Tape, Wong
Chin Foo, Yan Phou Lee, and Yung Wing were survivors of the driving-out
era and, with the exception of the sex worker Ah Toy and the earliest activist
Yung Wing, were published as the "good Chinese" or the assimilated Chinese Americans in the late nineteenth century. Due to the stereotype in the
nineteenth-century of Chinese being an exceptional minority, liberals often
presumed Chinese assimilation, particularly in the case of Ah Toy, Mary Tape,
Wong Chin Foo, Yan Phou Lee, and Yung Wing. Assimilation in itself implies
exception—an exception from the general mass of Chinese Americans who,
as what would soon be understood as yellow peril, cannot assimilate. It also
suggests the exception that liberalism, in praxis, made to incorporate Chinese
Americans (even in death) into its national body through newspaper accounts
and publication of their autobiographies and other writings. Thus, these figures performed two kinds of work: (1) enfleshing or humanizing their fellow
Chinese American homo sacer victims of the driving-out era through their
own activism and autobiographical work, and (2) mirroring and exposing the
exceptionalism of nineteenth-century liberalism to Chinese and whites, alike,
that structurally depended on Chinese American exceptions or other spectacularly killed but not sacrificed homo sacer.

---

48. Lowe, 13.

THE EXCEPTIONAL MINORITY DISCOURSE

The Chinese American driving-out era took place during and because of the liberal state of exception in which liberals exceptionalized and killed Chinese Americans or stripped them of their rights. Chinese exclusion—the dominant Asian American term for the period—and exceptionalism share the same prefix of "ex-" or out, exclusive of, which suggests that they were both part and not part of the liberal state. Liberals stereotyped Chinese Americans as the *exceptional* minority, which encompassed specific nineteenth-century notions of the model minority and the yellow peril, and unlike any other minority in the liberal landscape of the US. Despite its exceptionalism, the seemingly laudatory and innocuous model minority stereotype of economic efficiency and submission historically wreaked a great deal of damage on Asian Americans in the US during the nineteenth century. I trace the model minority stereotype through the nineteenth century: from tropes of economic efficiency, subservience, and other hyperbolic character traits to the driving-out era of the 1870s and 1880s in which Chinese Americans were not only excluded by the Page Act and the Chinese Exclusion Act (1882) but also systematically murdered and spectacularly and violently driven out of West Coast cities, the exceptionalism of the model minority stereotype systematically dehumanized and took rights from Chinese Americans. In this way, the exceptionalism of the model minority stereotype contributed to Chinese exclusion and anti-Chinese violence. This book contributes to recent studies by James Kyung-Jin Lee, erin Khuê Ninh, and Ellen D. Wu on the stereotype's historical toxicity to American life and its psychic damage to the first Chinese Americans and eventually all Asian Americans by racial association and a shared history of legal exclusion.[49]

Since the 1960s, when the term "model minority" was first coined, it has been used to describe the achievements in education and wealth of Asian Americans to the detriment of other racial minorities in the US. In his famous 1966 *New York Times Magazine* article, "Success Story, Japanese-American Style," Berkeley sociologist William Petersen began circulating the notion of the "model minority" based on the resilience of the Japanese American community after their World War II internment.[50] Since the influx of professional-class Asian immigrants in the US after the 1965 Immigration Act,[51] the model minority stereotype has been used to discipline other minority groups such as African Americans, Latinxs, and Native Americans. Decades after Petersen's

---

49. See James Kyung-Jin Lee; erin Khuê Ninh; and Ellen D. Wu.
50. Petersen, 20–43.
51. Ong, Bonacich, and Cheng, 4.

groundbreaking article, many magazines followed suit with *Newsweek on Campus*'s 1984 cover, "Asian Americans: The Drive to Excel," and *Time* magazine's 1987 cover of Asian American students entitled, "Those Asian-American Whiz Kids." Today, besides disciplining other minority groups, the model minority stereotype denies the historical and contemporary victimization of Asian Americans by discursively imagining them as inhuman superheroes who are nevertheless crafty and insidious and thus racially inferior to white Americans. It also banefully places undue pressure on Asian Americans to perform even when they have exceeded their inherent talent. As sociologists Rosalind Chou and Joe R. Feagin have pointed out, because of the model minority stereotype, Asian Americans are at a higher risk for mental health issues among people of color.[52] The model minority stereotype, as they point out, continues to obviate the long history of Asian American racism, oppression, and activism in the US.[53]

The inevitable collapse of the model minority into the yellow peril stems from, as critic Eric Hayot points out, the common view of Chinese Americans in the nineteenth century as untrustworthy, "inscrutable," "mechanical" "automatons" who threateningly represented the "past and future, animal and superman."[54] Throughout history, the model minority myth decontextualizes the efforts and achievements of Asian Americans by pretending that there is no racial hierarchy in which Asian Americans are perceived of as inferior to white Americans. Asian Americans' attempts to assimilate into white American culture are often viewed in isolation from their struggles for racial and social equality. In contrast with present-day perceptions of the model minority in which Asian Americans are seen as "besting" white Americans by amassing financial and cultural capital, the nineteenth-century model minority signified mechanistic economic efficiency while Chinese Americans attempted assimilation[55] as Americans. As a result, the exceptional minority in the nineteenth century stereotyped, enfranchised to a certain extent, and at the same time undermined people such as Ah Toy, Mary Tape, Wong Chin Foo, Yan Phou Lee, and Yung Wing; these figures aligned themselves with the driven-out victims of the era and sought to prove their humanity and their right to citizenship amid Chinese exclusion and allegations of Chinese as menacing automatons. That is to say, even as their performance of exceptionalism as the "good Chinese" who evaded driving-out and gained public notice reflected the exceptionalism and exclusions of nineteenth-century US

---

52. Chou and Feagin, 2, 3.
53. Chou and Feagin, 3, 5.
54. Hayot, 122.
55. Ninh, 17; and Chu, *Assimilating Asians*, 4.

liberalism, their performances were taken as the essence of who they were and their efforts were folded back into the sovereignty of liberalism. Although these figures were certainly accomplished in the ways in which the exceptional minority currently denotes, they sought achievements to underscore their humanity and rights to citizenship during a period in which they were systemically dehumanized or de-anthropomorphized through exclusion laws and anti-Asian violence.

Different from the model minority of the 1960s in its de-emphasis on wealth and academic achievement, the exceptional minority of the nineteenth century can be traced to the early era of US exclusion legislations and violence directed toward Chinese Americans and the concurrent achievements by the aforementioned Chinese American figures and radical and liberal activists in the late nineteenth century. Exemplifying the discourse of the exceptional minority, Tacoma's probate judge James Wickersham stated the following before the expulsion of Chinese from Tacoma, Washington Territory, in 1885:

> The fear I have always had was not that the Pacific coast would be overrun by [Chinese] criminals and a foreign race of base and immoral character [. . .] but that we would be confronted by millions of industrious hard-working sons and daughters of Confucius who, if given an equal chance with our people, would outdo them in the struggle for life and gain possession of the Pacific coast of America.[56]

The discursive, yellow peril fear of the model minority economic efficiency and hard work ethic, which would conquer white America, was common in the nineteenth century. In fact, Rudyard Kipling argued before 1890 that "the Orientals would one day march upon the Caucasians. [Kipling] also declared that the Chinese were the only people in the world who could 'swarm.'"[57] Even the Chinese perpetuated the exceptional minority myth of model citizens: in 1881 China's minister to the United States, Zheng Zaoru, "praised New York's Chinese, pointing out that only eight of them had been convicted of crimes during the previous decade, and that not one had been guilty of intoxication, disorderly conduct, burglary, or highway robbery."[58] The exceptional minority stereotype during the nineteenth century was a pervasive discourse.

During this period, white Americans perceived Chinese Americans as both the yellow peril "enslaved coolies"—who were likened to the recently emancipated African Americans—and the model minority, which threatened

---

56. Lew-Williams, 119–20.
57. Thompson, 3.
58. Seligman, 120.

the efficiency of white labor. Liberalism documented the exceptional, in tandem stereotype of the yellow peril and model minority through the establishment of the Anti-Coolie Association in 1869, the slough of anti-Chinese violence during the 1870s and 1880s, the Page Act of 1875, which prohibited the immigration of Chinese women based on the hyperbolic assumption that they were all prostitutes, and the Chinese Exclusion Act of 1882, which prevented the immigration of the Chinese because they were deemed "aliens ineligible to citizenship."[59] These laws and acts of violence were symptoms of white Americans' ambivalence toward Chinese Americans.

The model minority is inherent in the yellow peril, as Colleen Lye and Robert G. Lee have claimed; that is, the yellow peril and model minority are binary discourses which emerged historically in tandem with each other. Examining late nineteenth- to mid-twentieth-century literature, Lye works against the longstanding historical interpretation that the yellow peril emerged separately in the nineteenth century whereas the model minority came about during the Civil Rights era of the twentieth century; instead, she argues, they emerged together in the nineteenth century.[60] Likewise, Lee diagrams the trope of Asian American economic efficiency.[61] According to Lee and Lye, the "Oriental" or the "Asiatic," respectively, contributed to white supremacy by contrast.[62] The enduring, mutually constitutive discourses of the model minority, yellow peril, and white supremacy have had and continue to have value in American society. This study builds on the groundbreaking work of Lye and Lee by situating the binary stereotypes of the model minority and the yellow peril specifically in the nineteenth-century liberal state of exception.

Thus far I have talked at length about the model minority in the United States; however, the beginnings of its binary term, the "yellow peril," are less clear.[63] Nevertheless, critic Richard Austin Thompson argues that anti-Asian sentiment was circulating in the United States as early as the 1850s,[64] immediately after the Chinese began to arrive in the mainland US. Moreover, Chinatowns throughout the United States have historically been associated with disease and urban quarantines. Both scientific and common sense discourses of the era labeled Chinatown as a space of uncleanliness and

---

59. Takaki, 14.

60. Lye, *America's Asia*, 5.

61. Robert G. Lee, 8.

62. Lye, *America's Asia*, 20.

63. Some scholars argue that it was generated by the fear of Mongolian invasions of Europe from 1236 to 1291. Various sources trace the term "yellow peril" to Russian sociologist Jacques Novicow (*Le Péril Jaune*, 1897). Thompson, 3.

64. Thompson, 7–8.

contagious disease.[65] In 1867 the San Francisco Board of Supervisors began to quarantine the Chinese living in the cities because they were supposedly "public health intrusions."[66] Five years later, California legislators restricted the entrance of Chinese people with disabilities—legislation that paved the way for the Chinese Exclusion Act of 1882.[67] Chinatown in Los Angeles was also the site of quarantining disease in the early twentieth century.[68] Likewise, in the nineteenth century, Chinatowns and Chinese immigrants were conflated as sources of contagion as well as spawning spaces of illicit drugs and activities such as opium, gambling, and interracial affairs.[69] Disease was reportedly from quarantinable, ethnic enclaves such as the "Mexican quarter," Chinatown, and Little Italy.[70] In other words, the point of quarantining the discursively diseased Chinese in ethnic ghettoes like Chinatown was to bolster white supremacy—to reassure white Americans that the "Chinese" foreign disease could not become native to the whites in the United States. In particular, Yung wrote about his exemplary life in *My Life in China and America* in response to the yellow peril stereotype that the driving-out era and the contemporary and proceeding plague period both perpetuated. The smallpox epidemic of 1868, eventually blamed on the Chinese in San Francisco, is one such historical accident that gave rise to the yellow peril panic in the nineteenth-century US. San Francisco experienced smallpox outbreaks in 1868, 1876, 1880, and 1887, and the disease was discursively believed to racially originate with the Chinese and Chinese Americans: "After the 1869 smallpox epidemic, the San Francisco Board of Supervisors required the quarantine and physical inspection of passengers and cargo from Asia."[71] For this reason, the Chinese became what Trauner calls easy "medical scapegoats." Organized in 1867, the Anti-Coolie Association replicated the discourse of Chinese disease from the 1868–69 smallpox outbreak by publicly delineating the threat the Chinese laborer posed to the working force and health of white Americans.[72] Likewise, shortly after the Massacre of 1871, which I discussed earlier in the introduction, native white Americans of Los Angeles organized an anti-coolie club. Finally, after the recession of 1875, the white Workingman's Party of California rose as an anti-Chinese labor organization that blamed the

---

65. Shah, 20.
66. Schweik, 28.
67. Schweik, 167.
68. Schweik, 170.
69. Urbansky, 79.
70. Schweik, 170.
71. Shah, 58.
72. Shah, 28.

Chinese for the recession and rising white poverty rates. These anti-Chinese or anti-coolie groups formed largely in response to the stereotype of the yellow peril. Liberals loved Chinese for being the economically efficient, model minority and hated them as the yellow peril for their competitive industry and foreignness. In the nineteenth century, liberalism, which encompassed progressive thought and white supremacy, was, and continues to be, a form of discursive power. The emergence of the binary yellow peril / model minority stereotype coincided with this ideological contradiction. That is, the Chinese American stereotype of exception was the antipode of sovereign nineteenth-century US liberalism.

Because it was perceived as a threat to white supremacy and liberalism, even as it was constitutive of it, the model minority was always part of the yellow peril in the nineteenth century. Contemporary historians attribute the anti-Chinese sentiment among white laborers in the 1870s to the conclusion of the continental railroad in May 1869, when Chinese laborers began to filter into other sectors of labor and were exploited for their cheap labor by capitalists to the disadvantage of competing white laborers.[73] Chinese immigrant willingness to work harder for lower wages generated Chinese competition with white workers, which led to anti-Chinese hate crimes. Historian James D. Hart states, "white workers attempted to burn the San Francisco docks of the Pacific Mail Steamship Co. (1877)—said to be the major importer of 'coolies'— and the agitation headed by Denis Kearney, who made famous the rallying cry, 'The Chinese must go!' in the 1870s, resulted in such actions as a riot in San Francisco in which twenty-one Chinese were killed and much property in Chinatown was destroyed."[74] The anti-Chinese riots in San Francisco in 1877 were so explosive that the National Guard, the State Guard, and the San Francisco Guard were needed to quell the violence.[75] While white Americans feared contamination by Native Americans and African Americans, they feared that Asian Americans would conquer them.[76] Thus, in addition to economic efficiency, Chinese Americans were discursively known for being hyperbolically submissive, smart, and capable, even dangerously "industrious, cunning, and resilient."[77] Nineteenth-century liberalism continually collapsed the yellow peril stereotype and the exceptional model minority stereotype, and undermined the humanity and talent of many in the Chinese American community.

---

73. Jerome Alfred Hart, 42–43.
74. James D. Hart, 94.
75. Jerome Alfred Hart, 58, 62.
76. Lew-Williams, 5, 6.
77. Lew-Williams, 5.

A HISTORY OF NINETEENTH-CENTURY US LIBERALISM

Nineteenth-century liberalism is often known as classical liberalism insofar as it relied on laissez-faire and conservative individualism. What is most important to my study is the contradictions of racial (in)equality of nineteenth-century liberalism. However, liberalism has many different definitions. It is often thought of in broad terms such as what Lowe calls a history of freedom for some and unfreedom for others.[78] She also defines it as "the universal promises of rights, emancipation, wage labor, and free trade" that are allowed to some and denied to or available through the sacrifice of others.[79] Relatedly, Chuh defines the term as meaning "model/criterion of being of the globally dominant Western/Eastern bourgeoisie" and the kind of humanism that espouses "the falsity of and damages done by its claims to universality and resoundingly decried its uses and dissemination towards the end of imperialism and colonialism, white supremacy and capitalism, environmental devastation, patriarchy, and compulsory normativization of multiple kinds."[80] It also means, according to Chuh, the "promise of the good life at the core of the ideal of social mobility through educational investment" and "displacing the lamentability of the production and dispossession of Indians with the grievability of Indigenous peoples continues to claim sovereignty within the concretizing structures of settler colonialism."[81] Other critics, including Peter C. Myers, have defined liberalism as individual rights, including those to private property, universalism, a do-nothing or laissez-faire government, and self-reliance.[82] Of laissez-faire as the defining factor of liberalism, Stephen Skowronek writes, "at the start of the 19th century, it implied the liberation of individual entrepreneurship; by the end, it had become a defense of overweening corporate power."[83] Critic Robert Yusef Rabiee focuses on the hierarchy of nineteenth-century US liberalism in his book *Medieval America*. In it, he states that liberalism is "imperfectly defined as a political ideology emphasizing belief in free market capitalism, the 'one man, one vote' vision of universal suffrage, and the defense of individual liberties (however those liberties may be defined)."[84] He argues that nineteenth-century US liberalism was a "synthesis" between liberalism and feudalism, which operates on the principles

---

78. Lowe, 3, 27.
79. Lowe, 3–4.
80. Chuh, *Difference Aesthetics Makes*, 2, 3.
81. Chuh, *Difference Aesthetics Makes*, 11, 20.
82. Rabiee, 12, 19, 113, 147.
83. Skowronek, 388.
84. Rabiee, 6.

of "structure of nature," "property structure," "family structure," "managerial style," "political structure," and an "aesthetics."[85] While the definitions of liberalism are diverse but coincident, its genealogies are just as varying.

Richard Cándida Smith traces the term liberalism to the seventeenth and eighteenth centuries.[86] By the nineteenth century, liberalism in the US became full of ideological contradictions, and most people in the United States were liberals, or children of the republic, with the exception of very few outliers.[87] In other words, liberalism critiqued and promoted critical political issues such as slavery and imperialism. Asserting less of a contradictory definition of nineteenth-century US liberalism, Elissa Zellinger traces it to the writings of John Stuart Mill: "The self that Mill envisioned in *On Liberty* (1859) was defined by self-sovereignty and liberty, two closely connected concepts. [. . .] Here the public/private distinction, a crucial premise for the formation of liberal ideology, begins to develop: Mill's nuisance-free private space of self-rule has a clear end in a society where this self interacts with others."[88] According to Zellinger, Ralph Waldo Emerson's credo of self-reliance became a crucial underpinning to liberalism, which also bisected the private and public spheres of individual life.[89] In this division, as she argues, liberalism excluded social minorities such as women, Black slaves, and Indigenous peoples.[90] Cándida Smith likewise states that with the exception of very few conservatives at society's "fringes," everyone in the nineteenth-century US, as descendants of the American Revolution, were liberals—including those who were for and against slavery.[91] There were also disagreements among liberals about whether the writings of John Locke were liberal or conservative.[92] Some liberals also believed in the right to be vigilantes: liberals "associated [vigilantism] with 'rule of men,' by which he meant formal democracy but in practice autocracy by wealthy demagogues. Vigilantism grew rapidly through the first half of the 20th century, as small proprietors who dominated local communities fought against centralizers, economic, political, [and] cultural."[93] Although it reached its height in the twentieth-century US, liberal vigilantism was certainly functioning in the lynch mobs of the nineteenth century.

85. Rabiee, 16.
86. Cándida Smith, correspondence with the author, May 18, 2023.
87. Fitzmaurice, 125; and Cándida Smith, correspondence with the author, May 18, 2023.
88. Zellinger, 13.
89. Zellinger, 15, 21.
90. Zellinger, 5.
91. Cándida Smith, correspondence with the author, May 18, 2023.
92. Cándida Smith, correspondence with the author, May 18, 2023; and Bell, 698–99.
93. Cándida Smith, correspondence with the author, May 18, 2023.

In the early to mid-nineteenth century, the US was split by conservative and progressive liberalism, particularly over Black slavery.[94] On the other hand, economist Mark Kanazawa discusses the infighting among liberals specifically about Chinese exclusion as early as the 1850s: "On the one hand, miners favored Chinese exclusion as a means of reducing competition for the available gold. On the other hand, Chinese miners contributed significantly to state and local tax revenues while adding relatively little demand for public services such as schools and hospitals, being mostly adult males."[95] However, both Kanazawa and Saxton argue that some liberal opposition to Chinese exclusion included "altruistic" defenses of Chinese human rights.[96] The ideological contradictions of US liberalism in the nineteenth century are thus illuminated by Agamben's theory of sovereignty and its constitutive paradox of inclusionary exclusion, or being above the law it has constructed. It is in this way that sovereignty, once exposed, is dialectically reconstituted by a new homo sacer.[97]

The historical figures of my study trace the dialectical progression of liberalism in the nineteenth-century US from the liberalism of the Gilded Age (1865– or 1877–96) to the Progressive Era (1890s– or 1896–1917). Nancy Cohen writes that after Reconstruction, Gilded Age liberals faced "the first real confrontation with the implications of universal suffrage and mass democracy, the transformation of the majority of the citizenry into wage earners, the rise of the corporation as a new type of property, the devastating fluctuations of the international market economy, and the growth of the administrative capacity of government."[98] That is, she argues that liberal reform began in the Gilded Age rather than the Progressive Era, to which it is often attributed. However, for Cohen, Gilded Age liberals were ineffective in guaranteeing the rights of others; she writes of Hofstadter's labeling of "the Gilded Age 'Mugwump type'" who was "'a conservative in his economic and political views' and a 'liberal' in the classic sense. Ignoring 'the serious abuses of the unfolding economic order,' he was 'dogmatically committed to the prevailing economics of *laissez faire.*' Progressive reform was born out of the revolt against the outmoded ideas of the mugwumps by their successors."[99] The Progressive Era, on the other hand, was characterized by mass social reform:[100] "Even as the

---

94. Howe, 4.
95. Kanazawa, 781.
96. Kanazawa, 802–3; and Saxton, 133.
97. Agamben, 15, 9.
98. Cohen, 4.
99. Cohen, 9.
100. Gerstle, 1049.

basic institutions of the capitalist economy and representative, constitutional government were preserved, the minimal state of an earlier liberalism was abandoned in favor of one with the power to intervene in the market and to promote social welfare. The progressives' new liberalism, most historians conclude, was fundamentally reformist; it sought to use state power to regulate the capitalist economy to improve the living conditions and 'security' of the citizenry, without abolishing private property or revolutionizing liberal-democratic political institutions."[101] Despite Progressives' emphasis on "moral regeneration," Jim Crow, Chinese exclusion, and the suspension of women's suffrage still persisted during this era.[102] Nevertheless, as I argue in this book, Ah Toy, Mary Tape, Wong Chin Foo, Yan Phou Lee, and Yung Wing took part in and reflected the transition between the classical liberal Gilded Age and the reformist Progressive Era. However, the liberal absorption of their enflesh-ment as homo sacer or racially exceptional demonstrates the ways in which liberalism, in all its ideological contradictions, has shapeshifted and endured. Although these historical figures critiqued the social and legal exclusions of nineteenth-century liberalism, they employed its means of self-individualism and self-reliance to fight them and, in this way, perpetuated some of liberalism's foundational tenets.

In response to such discourses of the yellow peril and Chinese disease and despite their disparate beliefs, Toy, Tape, Wong Chin Foo, Yan Phou Lee, and Yung still embraced the liberal universal humanism that embraced such discourses. Liberal universal humanism was gaining traction in the United States in the nineteenth century and promoted by Transcendentalists and popular literary figures such as Mark Twain, whom Wong and Yan Phou Lee knew, and who helped coin the term "Gilded Age."[103] Likewise, insisting on the primacy of God in universal humanism,[104] the industrialist Henry Rogers, who was close friends with Mark Twain, Helen Keller, and Booker T. Washington, wrote, "Whether they arrive at truth or error, men have nothing else from which to philosophize than the constitution of their minds and faculties, and you may as well 'bay the moon' as strive to alter the convictions normally founded on them. If wrong, the error arises from the constitution of humanity, and must still be supposed a truth."[105] In this way, universal human-ism opposes the injunction of the mutual exceptionalism that constructs the "*homo sacer* (sacred man), who *may be killed and yet not sacrificed*" and the

---

101. Cohen, 5.
102. Gerstle, 1051.
103. Cohen, 18.
104. Peden, 45.
105. Rogers, 356.

sovereign who can kill without penalty.[106] In other words, liberal humanism did make progressive gains for Chinese Americans, as evidenced by the publications of the figures of my study, despite legal exclusion. Arguing for their democratic, "human" freedoms as Chinese Americans and often "postulating God"[107] through their work, Tape, Wong Chin Foo, Yan Phou Lee, and Yung Wing define their humanity through revealing their vulnerabilities in contrast to the exceptional, superhuman model minority stereotype but also their anger at injustice; they fought for racial equality and democracy, differing opinions about religion, accomplishments in activism and education, sympathy with others, and against white supremacy—all contradictory constituents of nineteenth-century US liberalism.

EXCEPTIONALISM AND BARE LIFE

Nineteenth-century US liberalism was a state of exception that required a scapegoat or a homo sacer for the integration of its contradictions. As I mentioned earlier, Giorgio Agamben's theorization of the exceptional homo sacer or the person who represents politicized (*bios*) bare life (*zoē*) of Western politics,[108] who cannot be sacrificed but may be killed without charge of murder, illuminates the liberal exceptionalism of the yellow peril / model minority stereotype in the nineteenth-century US. That is to say, as Saxton has argued, the Chinese were the "indispensable enemy" or the scapegoats of nineteenth-century US liberalism, which encompassed proslavery and antislavery sentiments, and were philosophically inclusive and legislatively exclusive of racial minorities and women. The division of Chinese Americans into both "good" model minority and "bad" yellow peril reflected the contradictions of nineteenth-century US liberalism. Following Foucault's theorization of biopolitics and biopower, Agamben argues that sovereign power itself is a kind of exclusion that is lawmaking but also banned or excluded from the law: Agamben writes that the sovereign is both law and exempt from it.[109] He clarifies, "Sovereignty is always double because Being, as potentiality, suspends itself, maintains itself in a relation of ban (or abandonment) with itself in order to realize itself as absolute actuality (which thus presupposes nothing other

---

106. Agamben, 8.
107. Peden, 45.
108. Agamben, 7, 8, 10, 73, 113.
109. Agamben, 17–18.

than its own potentiality)."[110] That is, sovereignty cannot know itself as having abandoned the law nor as requiring the homo sacer for its existence.[111] Like the sovereign, the homo sacer is ambivalent or "double" insofar as it cannot be sacrificed but can be killed and that he is included in society for the purposes of exclusion: "Exception and example constitute the two modes by which a set tries to found and maintain its own coherence. But while the exception is, as we saw, an *inclusive exclusion* (which thus serves to include what is excluded), the example instead functions as an *exclusive inclusion*."[112] Whereas the sovereign is privileged by an "*inclusive exclusion*"—being above the law—the homo sacer or bare life is relegated to "*exclusive inclusion*"—or, not protected by the law. This asymmetrical state of exception between the sovereign and the homo sacer is a dynamic which Agamben calls "symmetrical" but which is actually *asymmetrical* in power.[113] Likewise, both nineteenth-century US liberalism and Chinese Americans are discursive exceptions that structurally rely on and mirror each other; in other words, the contradictions of nineteenth-century US liberalism are symmetrical or analogical to Chinese American racialization as the model minority and yellow peril, or the exceptional minority. And thus, the Chinese American exception risks exposing the contradictory foundations of sovereign liberalism.

Since, in a state of exception, the exceptionalism or the exemption of sovereignty from law cannot be represented, the contradictions of freedom and unfreedom of nineteenth-century US liberalism remained intact. Agamben writes that the sovereign must be unrepresentable in its singularity—it cannot be known that it relies on the homo sacer—and is, in this way, exceptional.[114] It is the symmetrical mirror of the homo sacer that poses a threat to the exceptionalism of the sovereign and, in the case of this study, nineteenth-century US liberalism. Calling attention to and memorializing the otherwise publicly dismissed victims of the Chinese American driving-out era, the historical figures of my study act as social "troublemakers": as Agamben claims, "The troublemaker is precisely the one who tries to force sovereign power to translate itself into actuality."[115] That is, the visibly violent driving-out of Chinese Americans through the references and representations of Chinese American public figures lays bare the exceptional sovereignty of nineteenth-

---

110. Agamben, 47.
111. Agamben, 24.
112. Agamben, 21.
113. Agamben, 55, 84, 102, 134–35, 84.
114. Agamben, 24.
115. Agamben, 47.

century US liberalism that is, in practice, above its own law of equality and freedom. Otherwise, as Hong argues, liberalism *disavows* the actual and social deaths it requires for its maintenance. Ah Toy, Mary Tape, Wong Chin Foo, Yan Phou Lee, and Yung Wing also "make trouble" by surviving the violent driving-out era and writing about themselves and the other driven-out victims of the era as the exceptional homo sacer—thus enfleshing themselves and those who were lynched or driven out in other ways in their racial community. Agamben gives examples of when the homo sacer refuses to die, even though he experiences a social death, and causes embarrassment and the potential dissolution of the sovereign power.[116] In order to preserve the exception of sovereignty, what must be constructed instead of the corpse is a statuesque "colossus" that represents the sacrificial death of the homo sacer.[117] The living, human figures of my study thus represent the colossus—social death memorials of the driven-out homo sacer—that expose the dual exceptionalisms and "untie"[118] the symmetrical and requisite knot of the sovereign power and the homo sacer or the other excluded exceptions who refuse to die. This "untying" is what Agamben and Benjamin refer to as "divine violence"[119]: "divine violence is not one kind of violence among others but only the dissolution of the link between violence and law. [. . .] Benjamin can say that divine violence neither posits nor conserves violence, but deposes it."[120] By surviving being literally lynched or driven out in other ways and through their representations of themselves through court cases and autobiographies, the historical figures of my study enact a sort of divine violence by exposing the exceptionalizing violence of liberal sovereignty in the US. However, time and again, we see their performative efforts misinterpreted and absorbed by liberalism, as proving their exceptionalism as homo sacer.

---

116. Agamben, 97.

117. Agamben, 98.

118. Agamben writes, "The sovereign tie is more originary than the tie of the positive rule or the tie of the social pact, but the sovereign tie is in truth only an untying. And what this untying implies and produces—bare life, which dwells in the no-man's-land between the home and the city—is, from the point of view of sovereignty, the originary political element" (90).

119. Agamben claims, "In this sense, sovereign violence, like divine violence, cannot be wholly reduced to either one of the two forms of violence whose dialectic the essay undertook to define. This does not mean that sovereign violence can be confused with divine violence. The definition of divine violence becomes easier, in fact, precisely when it is put in relation with the state of exception. Sovereign violence opens a zone of indistinction between law and nature, outside and inside, violence and law. And yet the sovereign is precisely the one who maintains the possibility of deciding on the two to the very degree that he renders them indistinguishable from each other" (64).

120. Agamben, 65.

AFTER AGAMBEN

Although it seems somewhat anachronistic and politically asymmetrical to compare the structures of sovereignty and bare life of Roman antiquity and the Nazi concentration camp to nineteenth-century US liberalism, they were all, as Agamben would argue, based on a "state of exception."[121] Agamben writes that "it is not the city but rather the [Nazi concentration] camp that is the fundamental biopolitical paradigm of the West."[122] Although influential, Agamben's theory of homo sacer has had critics and detractors. As my study does, Achille Mbembe situates sovereign power in modern, democratic liberalism: "I start from the idea that modernity was the origin of multiple concepts of sovereignty—and therefore of the biopolitical. Disregarding this multiplicity, late-modern political criticism has unfortunately privileged normative theories of democracy and has made the concept of reason one of the most important elements of both the project of modernity and of the topos of sovereignty."[123] However, whereas Agamben views the racial other as simply an example of homo sacer, Mbembe recenters race by framing the exceptional, symmetrical structure of the sovereign power and the homo sacer in the slave plantation instead of the Nazi concentration camp.[124] Like Mbembe, I refocus race at the center of the state of exceptionalism by framing my study with the Chinese American driving-out in the sovereign liberal nineteenth-century US. Alexander G. Weheliye also critiques Agamben's treatment of race as a symptom or merely an example of the homo sacer by building on Mbembe's insistence on the centering of race in the theorization of sovereignty; in doing so, he contributes to Wilderson's notion of "Afropessimism," powerfully arguing that the Black body has historically been figured as anything but exceptional: "Because black suffering figures in the domain of the mundane, it refuses the idiom of exception."[125] Likewise, Saidiya Hartman has famously argued that the discipline of and violence against the Black body has historically been a "terror of the mundane and quotidian."[126] On the other hand, Chinese American exceptionalism in the nineteenth century was spectacular and, in this particular way, contributed to exposing the antinomies of liberalism. However, exceptionalism highlights the ways in which Asian Americans and African Americans have both been racialized as exploited laborers but differently as

---

121. Agamben, 58.
122. Agamben, 181.
123. Mbembe, 13.
124. Mbembe, 21, 39–40.
125. Weheliye, 11.
126. Hartman, 4.

"free" and unfree. Lowe writes of the intimacy of the four continents that "it means revealing the proximity of the geographically, and conceptually, distant sites of the Caribbean and China, and appreciating together settler practices with the racialized laboring figures of the slave and the 'coolie.'"[127] As "free" and exceptional, economically efficient labor, the Chinese, conceptualized as coolies, were neither slave nor free: as Moon-Ho Jung has influentially argued, "Coolies confused the boundary between slavery and freedom, black and white, causing the mass demand for Asian migrant laborers as well as appeals for their exclusion in the postbellum United States."[128] In contrast with African Americans whose bodies and sufferings were thought of as "mundane" but who were legally emancipated even though they remained socially and legislatively "unfree" after the Civil War, the Chinese were socially and legally excluded from US citizenship and characterized as the in-between model minority and yellow peril—that is, neither slave nor free—and were thus racial exceptions in the nineteenth-century US. By deploying Agamben's theory of the state of exception and the exceptionalism of sovereignty in understanding the Chinese American place in the political landscape of nineteenth-century US liberalism, this study intends to recenter race—specifically the nineteenth-century model minority and yellow peril stereotypes that are particular to Asian Americanness—in the state of exception.

As many critics and theorists influenced by Hortense Spillers and Sylvia Wynter, such as Weheliye, Hartman, Lowe, Kandice Chuh, and Rachel C. Lee, have argued, the assertion of the enfleshed body that has been excluded from the rights and "universal" equality of liberalism fights this inequality, exposes the contradictions of liberalism, and articulates an alternative humanity that is not premised on the Western liberal "man." In *Habeas Viscus*, Weheliye theorizes "enfleshment" as a form of Wynter's "human as praxis" instead of the liberal and exclusionary Western Man: "the flesh thus operates as a vestibular gash in the armor of Man, simultaneously a tool of dehumanization and a relational vestibule to alternate ways of being that do not possess the luxury of eliding phenomenology with biology."[129] Weheliye clarifies, "Building on Hortense Spillers's distinction between body and flesh and the writ of habeas corpus, I use the phrase *habeas viscus*—'You shall have the flesh'—on the one hand, to signal how violent political domination activates a fleshly surplus that simultaneously sustains and disfigures said brutality, and, on the other hand, to reclaim the atrocity of flesh as a pivotal arena for the politics emanating

---

127. Lowe, 18.
128. Jung, 6.
129. Weheliye, 44.

from different traditions of the oppressed."[130] The flesh, for Weheliye, carries a history of oppression and remembrance but also ways of relating to others that are not reliant on the exclusion of Western Man. In this way, those who have historically been considered by the West as "not-quite-human" speak back to Western liberalism.[131] Like Weheliye, Wynter does not consider homo sacer as a sufficient enough theoretical unit of analysis of the Black body. In addition to Agamben's decentralization of race and focus on the camp as the site of exception as rule, Wynter does not necessarily envision a spatial difference between sovereignty and homo sacer. Instead, liberal man is the collapsed sovereign and homo sacer, that is the *homo oeconomicus*, which is "a uniquely secular liberal monohumanist *conception* of the human."[132] All liberal *homo oeconomici*, Wynter argues, enter the symbolic realm of society through "a *nongenetically* determined, origin-mythically chartered symbolically encoded and semantically enacted set of *symbolic life / death* instructions. *At the same time*, at the level of *bios / the brain*, the above second set of instructions are genetically (neurochemically) *implemented*. This implementation occurs according to the 'laws of nature' first set of instructions, with the second set of instructions, thereby, being alchemically *made flesh!*"[133] According to Wynter, it is such mythical "storytelling" that "charters" the "brain" and exclusions of the liberal homo oeconomicus.[134] Wynter's emphasis on storytelling as the chartering origin myth of homo oeconomicus inspired Weheliye's theory of enfleshment, which is a storytelling that combats the exclusionary myth of the liberal homo oeconomicus. Shaping contemporary Black studies, Agamben's and Wynter's works have, in turn, influenced contemporary Asian American studies, such as Lowe's suggestion of "new narratives of affirmation and presence"[135] by those racialized others excluded in her genealogy of liberalism; Chuh's theorization of "illiberal humanism," or humanist practices that work "toward the protection and flourishing of people and of ways of being and knowing and of inhabiting the planet that liberal humanism, wrought through the defining structures of modernity, tries so hard to extinguish"; and Rachel Lee's theorization of the Asian American "exquisite corpse" or "assertions of open-endedness" which "contains a dispositional, affective charge—the practice of scholarly analysis and art in a spirt of intense, but also generous, engagement that is distinct from an 'odious control [that] does not work all

130. Weheliye, 2.
131. Weheliye, 3.
132. McKittrick, 21.
133. McKittrick, 27.
134. McKittrick, 29, 34, 72.
135. Lowe, 40.

that well."[136] The historical fragmentation of the Chinese American body during the largely unacknowledged driving-out era made *enfleshment* through legal or autobiographical narrative all the more urgent for Toy, Tape, Wong Chin Foo, Yan Phou Lee, and Yung during their contemporary era.

I recognize that the application of *enfleshment*, a theory meant for the Black body that has historically been fetishized by white Americans who "don, occupy, or possess blackness or the black body as a sentimental resource and/ or locus of excess enjoyment"[137] in chattel slavery and after, to Chinese Americans in the nineteenth century may seem problematic, conflationary, and comparatively minimizing of the specific Black experience in the US. However, as both Weheliye and Lowe point out, we must recognize both the allying similarities and the different "genres"[138] of humans that have been excluded from the narrative of liberal humanism: Weheliye states, "For the flesh provides a stepping stone toward new genres of human, in which we finally begin to honor the long-ago issued expiration date to the 'materialized scene . . . of female flesh "ungendered"' in its roles as a deviation from Man and instead begin to concentrate on how flesh 'offers a praxis and a theory, a text for living and for dying, and a method for reading both through their diverse meditations' (Spillers, 'Mama's Baby,' 207)."[139] Likewise, Lowe writes, "The Chinese contract laborer occupied a liminal, ambiguous intermediary position throughout the nineteenth century, brought to the Americas to supplement, replace, and obscure the labor previously performed by slaves, yet to be differentially distinguished from them."[140] And although Agamben does not presuppose that the homo sacer is necessarily the racial other, Agamben's theoretical structure does allow space for enfleshment when he delineates the crisis in which the homo sacer refuses to die or survives even as he experiences a social death. This bodily challenge to the sovereign and the sovereign's inherent dependence on the death of the homo sacer is a form of enfleshment. But the structure of exception in Agamben's theory seems to fit more precisely with the racialization of Chinese Americans as exceptional model minorities and yellow peril than with the historical and problematic mundanity of anti-Black violence and death.

Despite their efforts to assert their humanity and free will, Chinese Americans were perceived by white Americans as reminiscent of African American slaves, despite different racializations and histories from African Americans, and thus ineligible for citizenship during the postbellum period. For example,

---

136. Chuh, *Difference Aesthetics Makes*, 2; and Rachel C. Lee, 26–27.
137. Hartman, 21.
138. Weheliye, 44–45.
139. Weheliye, 44–45.
140. Lowe, 27.

the Civil Rights Act of 1870 permitted African Americans the right to vote
and the Naturalization Act of 1875 permitted them naturalized citizenship
while, together with the Page Act of 1875, they prohibited Chinese Americans
from the same rights.[141] As I later discuss, the dominant discourse of Chinese
American inferiority spurred Toy, Tape, Wong Chin Foo, Yan Phou Lee, and
Yung Wing to enflesh themselves and strive for success and achievements, but
such efforts were misrecognized as evidence of their inherent exceptionalism
and thus absorbed by nineteenth-century US liberalism as superhuman and
"sacred." In this way, they both protested and perpetuated nineteenth-century
liberalism despite their efforts to dismantle and rebuild it.

NARRATIVES OF THE FLESH

Nevertheless, in their *infrastructures of activism* Toy, Tape, Wong Chin Foo,
Yan Phou Lee, and Yung Wing offered enfleshed[142] narratives of illiberalism,[143]
corporeality,[144] and affirmation and presence,[145] which critiqued the contradictions, specifically the social and legal exclusions, of nineteenth-century
US liberalism. Toy and Tape, as Chinese American women, were limited to
presenting their enfleshment through their publicized court cases. Wong
Chin Foo, Yan Phou Lee, and Yung Wing wrote autobiographies and autobiographical essays, which asserted their legally excluded Chinese American
selves during the driving-out era. Defending Agamben's theory of the homo
sacer and bios, Rachel Lee states, "Asian American literature's recourse to
the *bildungsromane* and autobiographical forms—the quintessential genres
of narrating (autonomous liberal) personhood—can be seen as a means of
establishing Asian immigrants and their children as just like other protected
citizens (bios), at least in the narratological form of their life course, if not in
the actuality of their legal status and civil treatment."[146] Although Rachel Lee
persuasively argues that, for the bodily fragmented Asian American subject,
"'Asian American' as a fictional (discursive) construct—only ambivalently,
incoherently, or 'problematically' linked to the biological body[,]"[147] Toy, Tape,
Wong Chin Foo, Yan Phou Lee, and Yung Wing did the work of asserting

---

141. Pfaelzer, 61; and Seligman, 86.

142. Weheliye, 19.

143. Chuh, *Difference Aesthetics Makes*, 2–3.

144. In *The Difference Aesthetics Makes*, Chuh writes, "This corporeal common sense leaves
the specificity of each sense intact, and understands each as equally but incommensurably con-
tributing to the ability of the body to apprehend the world it traverses" (22).

145. Lowe, 40.

146. Rachel C. Lee, 50.

147. Rachel C. Lee, 8.

the Chinese American body and self through their activist voices and auto-biographies. Their work was a form of "self-contained" divine violence that challenged the exclusions of nineteenth-century US liberalism.[148] Wynter has emphasized the power of mythmaking and "storytelling" in the construction of the liberal homo oeconomicus; conversely "storytelling," for her, is also the liberated human as praxis, which Toy, Tape, Wong Chin Foo, Yan Phou Lee, and Yung Wing arguably never achieved in using the tools of liberalism to dismantle liberalism.[149] However, through their storytellings, they defied but also deployed their exceptionalism as "bare life": Toy, Tape, Wong Chin Foo, Yan Phou Lee, and Yung evince still a narrative diversity among themselves, which points to what Weheliye calls the different "genres of the human"; theirs are what "illiberal humanisms [that divergently] bespeak an orientation that recognizes liberal humanism as but one version, one that has come to have the effect of truth through the powerful machinery of modernity."[150] Getting away from, but at times reaffirming, the "liberal subject as the ideal human,"[151] these five figures offer a politics of inclusion where liberalism had excluded during the driving-out era. In their work, Toy, Tape, Wong Chin Foo, Yan Phou Lee, and Yung do not simply reject the sovereignty of liberalism; rather, as homo sacer who align themselves with the driven-out Chinese Americans of the Gilded Age, they hold up asymmetrical mirrors of included exclusions to a liberalism that does not follow its own laws. But it is also through the altru-ism of liberalism that they were able to gain public traction with their voices and thus their efforts did not dismantle liberalism completely; instead, they helped to usher in the governmental and social reforms of the new liberal Progressive Era.

In my first chapter, "Ah Toy and Mary Tape: Legal Exceptionalism and Early Chinese American Women's Voices," I contextualize early women's voices in the Chinese community such as the famous prostitute Ah Toy and activist Mary Tape during a period in which Chinese women were discursively assumed to be indentured prostitutes, which culminated in the Page Act in 1875. Their court cases demonstrated what Benjamin argues is the coincidence of violence and law. In this chapter, the two women suggest the only two posi-tions that were available to Chinese American women—a spurned prostitute or an assimilated Victorian housewife. Moreover, both Toy and Tape reasserted the discourse of exceptionalism by allowing themselves to be put on display through court cases in order to critique laissez-faire liberalism but in differ-ent ways. While Ah Toy exercised her free will by choosing to be a prostitute

---

148. Girard, 21.
149. McKittrick, 72.
150. Weheliye, 2, 2–3; and Chuh, *Difference Aesthetics Makes*, 5.
151. Chuh, *Difference Aesthetics Makes*, 3.

and a madam, Mary Tape showcased her humanity by publicizing her anger at injustice. Both Ah Toy and Mary Tape resisted the exceptional minority rhetoric of the Page Act, which positioned Chinese American women as the model of hyperfemininity and hypersexuality and subjected them to fatal venereal diseases and police brutality, by insisting on their human rights.

In my second chapter, "Wong Chin Foo: The Excessive Making and Remaking of a Heathen Protofeminist," I argue that, like Ah Toy and Mary Tape, Wong was also proponent of early Chinese American women's rights. Throughout the book, I use the term *protofeminist* to recognize the anachronism of "feminism" in the nineteenth century and to designate first-wave feminism as reinforcing domesticizing gender norms even while protesting the social oppression of women. As he toured the country in the 1870s, giving talks about Chinese culture, he explained and adamantly opposed the crippling Chinese female custom of footbinding.[152] Wong was also a prolific writer and editor. His excessive remaking of the self demonstrated his struggle with enfleshment but also derailed what Bataille calls the excess of death during the driving-out era.

Chapter 3, "Trauma and Activism: Yan Phou Lee Writes Back," claims that, like Wong Chin Foo, Yan Phou Lee addressed gender differences in China but in more traditional, masculinist terms and in defense of Chinese culture. This chapter argues that what I call Yan Phou Lee's *exceptional minority activism* must be contextualized in the driving-out era in which he suffered from and responded to personal traumas as well as the era's collective, racial trauma. From the outset of his autoethnography,[153] or ethnographic autobiography, *When I Was a Boy in China*, Yan Phou Lee emphasizes his "boyhood" and acknowledges the gender inequality between men and women in China.[154] Yan Phou Lee likewise debunks myths surrounding the treatment of Chinese girls while desexualizing them as Lotus Blossom figures. He claims that although Chinese girls are treated differently from boys, he defends the Chinese culture against charges of female infanticide.[155]

In my fourth chapter, "Yung Wing: Exceptional Minority Discourse in the Plague Era," I contextualize Yung Wing's *plague writing*, which heralds Asian American modernism and promotes his masculinist, conservative activism in the driving-out and coincident and subsequent plague era. Of all the figures of my study, Yung practiced what Lowe calls "affirmation and presence" through his belatedly published autobiography. His founding of the Chinese Educational Mission went against liberal laissez-faire and called for more

---

152. Seligman, 23.
153. Cheung, 26.
154. Yan Phou Lee, *When I Was a Boy in China*, 29.
155. Yan Phou Lee, *When I Was a Boy in China*, 53.

government action in shaping society and culture, ushering in the reforms of the Progressive Era. In addition, editors Frank Chin, Jeffery Paul Chan, Lawson Fusao Inada, and Shawn Wong mention Yung Wing's *My Life in China and America* as assimilationist "Chinese" rather than Chinese American literature in their second anthology, *The Big Aiiieeeee!*, in 1991.[156] Yung's asserted masculinity is impossible to ignore in his autobiography;[157] however, it was important for him to demonstrate his healthy vigor during the plague period in which all Chinese Americans were assumed to be diseased. He also demonstrates sympathy toward the women in his life in his autobiography during the gendered exclusion period of the Page Act. As a strict autobiography rather than autoethnography, *My Life in China and America* allows Yung, more so than Yan Phou Lee, an enfleshment that reveals his bodily vulnerabilities during the early era of Asian exclusion.

These chapters tell a narrative of different kinds of Chinese American enfleshment that both challenged and contributed to sovereign liberalism in the nineteenth century. According to Agamben's conceptualization of sovereign power and violence, the pervasive discourse of liberalism during the nineteenth century objectified Chinese men as the exceptional, model minority and yellow peril by viewing them as diseased, cheap labor while also differently objectifying Chinese women as prostitutes. Against the discourse of the superhuman, "sacred" exceptional minority, Ah Toy, Mary Tape, Wong Chin Foo, Yan Phou Lee, and Yung Wing offered vulnerable voices of Chinese American humanity that are subject to trauma and loss during a period of violent Chinese American objectification. Moreover, they claimed different kinds of femininities and masculinities in order to contest the exceptional hypersexualization of Chinese women that culminated in the exceptionalizing rhetoric of the Page Act and the stereotype of the yellow peril during the plague period. That is, because Chinese Americans were discursively discriminated against as women, Toy, Tape, Wong Chin Foo, Yan Phou Lee, and Yung all supported Chinese American women in their disparate radical and liberal politics. However, liberals did not find Toy's, Tape's, and Wong's radical work legible during the conservative Gilded Age, and they could not detect Yan Phou Lee's and Yung Wing's activist exceptionalism during the reformist Progressive Era. Even though these five figures critiqued the exceptionalism of liberalism and helped to reform it, they could not escape the hegemony of its discourse.

---

156. Chin et al., *Big Aiiieeeee!*, xii.
157. Yung Wing, *My Life in China and America*, 23.

CHAPTER 1

Ah Toy and Mary Tape

Legal Exceptionalism and
Early Chinese American Women's Voices

UNDER THE VICTORIAN GAZE

The discourse of Chinese exceptionalism began before the driving-out era of the 1870s and 1880s with the hyperbolic sexualization of Chinese women in the mid-nineteenth century US. That is, the yellow peril discourse of Chinese American female hypersexualization and hyperfeminization was rampant during the mid- to late nineteenth century; it culminated in the first Chinese exclusion act, the 1875 Page Act, which barred the immigration of Chinese women on the basis of their sexual immorality and led to a social and often physical death for Chinese American women. Assumed to be prostitutes, all Chinese American women experienced a social death by being continually subject to police raids, and Chinese American sex workers suffered literal deaths by being left to publicly pass away on the streets from venereal diseases.[1] However, of the estimated three hundred prostitutes residing in San Francisco during the Gold Rush era, there were more white American prostitutes than Chinese American—ninety were white, seventy-five were Chinese, and the rest were other women of color.[2] And yet, it was the Chinese women who were exceptionalized as sexually immoral, hyperfeminine, and barred from

---

1. Hirata, 3–29.
2. Rutter, 5.

the United States. Passed during the era of Chinese American driving-out, the 1870s–80s, the Page Act spectacularly objectified Chinese American women as prostitutes and thus perpetuated the exceptionalizing discourse of the Chinese during this era. During the late nineteenth century, as Alfred Barstow attested, women were also unjustly lynched for killing in self-protection from men, even while expecting children.[3] Just as the Page Act placed all Chinese women under public scrutiny, both Ah Toy (1829–1928) and Mary Tape (1857–1928) were put under the public's microscope during their court cases. The Page Act legislated the discourse of Chinese women's homo sacer exceptionalism that circulated well before the law's passage; on the other hand, Ah Toy and Mary Tape reclaimed the discourse of the exceptional minority by allowing themselves to be put on display to radically challenge laissez-faire liberalism, which did little to protect the rights of people of color, in the antebellum and postbellum US.

The Page Act demonstrates what theorist Walter Benjamin argues—that violence structures law.[4] Benjamin goes on to state, "The meaning of the distinction between legitimate and illegitimate violence is not immediately obvious."[5] The exceptional violence against Chinese women for their purported hypersexuality culminated in the Page Act. As Toy and Tape respectively demonstrated, part of the violence of the discourse that culminated in the Page Act was categorizing Chinese American women as dissolute prostitutes or assimilated Victorian housewives. Moreover, the Page Act worked toward the extinction of the Chinese population in the US, which was predominantly a bachelor's society during a period in which miscegenation was illegal. As free (not chattel slaves) and unfree (mostly, nonconsensual prostitutes or so-called yellow slaves), Chinese and Chinese American women were the symmetrical homo sacer that mirrored the contradictions of proslavery and antislavery liberalism: as René Girard, in his precursor to Agamben's *Homo Sacer*, writes, "The common denominator is internal violence—all the dissensions, rivalries, jealousies, and quarrels within the community that the sacrifices are designed to suppress. The purpose of the sacrifice is to restore harmony to the community, to reinforce the social fabric"[6] of, in this case, liberalism. During this time, the Chinese were the largest Asian American demographic group in the US and thus what happened to them was representative of most Asian Americans. In harnessing their discursive exceptionalism as

---

3. Barstow, Alfred, California Biographical Mss. '49 Experiences: BANC MSS C-D 31-41 FILM, Bancroft Library, University of California, Berkeley.

4. Benjamin, 236.

5. Benjamin, 238.

6. Girard, 8.

Chinese American women, legislated by the Page Act, Ah Toy and Mary Tape enacted a "law-destroying" non-violence, or what Benjamin calls "divine violence," against the law by developing their enfleshed,[7] activist voices in court. Although Ah Toy's court cases predated the Page Act, Chinese American women were discursively viewed as prostitutes and the targets of Vigilance Committees—a form of liberal vigilantism—during her time, and Chinese exclusion, particularly aimed at Chinese miners, was rampant in the 1850s and 1860s when she was bringing her cases to court.[8] Toy and Tape radically fought against the liberal discourse and legislation, respectively, that determined that Chinese American women were exceptional in their hypersexuality, "not-quite-human" and "supplemental"[9] to men.

Legally active during different periods of liberalism and liberal reform—the antebellum period and the Gilded Age, respectively—Ah Toy and Mary Tape were radicals in their own right; that is, they were inspired by Radical Republicans but differed from their notions of white universalism. As Cohen writes, before the Civil War, "radicals, the virtual political representatives of the antislavery organizations, were a minority faction in the Republican Party but nonetheless influential nationally";[10] immediately after the war, "Radicals demanded the extension of the suffrage to African American men in accord with a principled democratic universalism."[11] Like Radical Republicans, Tape and Toy believed in universalism; however, the universalism that the Radical Republicans touted did not include them: Cohen writes, "While Radicals labored to be in the vanguard of a nonracial justice, they could not wholly escape the racialism through which the contradiction of slavery and freedom in American society became manifest."[12] Very much before their time, Toy and Tape imagined a universalism that was not based on the liberal white man.[13] Despite the sufferings inflicted on them by the press as a result of their court cases and their belief in American democracy, Toy and Tape were often considered the first Chinese American women[14] on account of their established and publicized voices in the nineteenth century.

---

7. Benjamin, 250; and Weheliye, 44.

8. Kanazawa, 783, 787.

9. Weheliye, 3; and Lowe, 34.

10. Cohen, 25.

11. Cohen, 28.

12. Cohen, 67.

13. Chuh, *Difference Aesthetics Makes*, 2.

14. Gamble, 12. In his article, Duane calls Ah Toy "the First Chinese Woman." Likewise, Gentry writes that she was the second Chinese woman to arrive in the United States and, whereas the first one was a servant, Ah Toy was a voluntary prostitute (51).

In the first year of Ah Toy's arrival, 1849, about twenty-five years before the Page Act, when the discourse of Chinese female hypersexuality was already circulating, she brought white American men to court for cheating her by paying for her peep show in brass filings instead of gold dust.[15] Her white clients believed in her exceptional minority economic efficiency and submission and thus reasoned that they did not have to pay her for her labor. She fought against this stereotyping but also harnessed the discourse of spectacular exceptionalism by appearing again in court in 1851 to accuse men of stealing a diamond brooch from her after sharing a drink with her at her home.[16] Historian Curt Gentry speculates that "apparently Ah Toy enjoyed her experience with the judiciary" because in 1852 she appeared in court twice—the first time to file a complaint against her lover, Committee of Vigilance brothel inspector John A. Clark, who had beaten her for telling another man that she was Clark's lover, and the second time to act as counsel to defend a Chinese woman who had attacked a man after he refused to pay his "debts of honor."[17] Exemplified by the peep show that she discontinued after she lost her 1849 court case, Ah Toy's famed exhibition as a prostitute who continually sought help from the US judiciary system was used against her in 1854 and again in 1859 when she was arrested and brought before a judge for keeping a "disorderly house."[18] In this way, Ah Toy critiqued and contributed to the discourse of the hypersexualizing gaze that led to the 1875 Page Act.

Tape, in turn, endured the public gaze when she and her husband, Joseph, challenged the San Francisco Board of Education in the California Supreme Court case *Tape v. Hurley* in 1885, after their daughter Mamie was denied the right to attend public school on account of her race.[19] Even though the court ruled in their favor, the San Francisco Board of Education managed to circumvent the ruling by establishing a segregated Chinese school to which Tape was forced to accede.[20] Seven years later, a journalist covered a story on Mary Tape that praised her for her accomplishments as a beautiful, self-taught photographer, telegrapher, and artist who had raised four musically accomplished children without mentioning the 1885 Supreme Court case that had involved her daughter Mamie.[21] Tired of being badgered by the press for her 1885 court

---

15. Peffer, 31; Stephens, 147; Duane; Pryor, *Bawdy House Girls*, 39; Gentry, 52; Pryor, *Bawdy House Girls*, 37; McLeod, 176–77; and Espiritu, 38–39.

16. Gentry, 56; and Stephens, 148.

17. Gentry, 52, 57, 57.

18. Gentry, 57, 58.

19. J. Yung, 48–49; McCunn, 42, 45; and Lee and Stefanowska, 205.

20. McCunn, 45.

21. Gamble.

case, Tape stated in her interview that she did not want any newspaper publicity.[22] Like Toy, Tape did not enjoy being disciplined by the exceptionalizing public gaze, and yet, they endured it to radically challenge the status quo of a sovereign and exclusionary liberalism.

Contemporaries of each other in San Francisco, Toy and Tape were the first well-known Chinese American women in the nineteenth century by virtue of their publicized use of the US judicial system. Although Toy lost each case she brought to the courts, her continued use of the jury-deliberated, democratic judiciary system suggests her belief in American democracy, even as a Chinese immigrant who would later be considered an "alien ineligible to citizenship" according to the 1882 Chinese Exclusion Act. Moreover, believing in her civil rights and not being deterred by Victorian mores that would have shamed her profession, she normalized sex work and was thus an unwelcome voice of modernity. Her lost cases of course also exemplified the failures of democracy. And even though Tape won her California Supreme Court case *Tape v. Hurley* (1885), which allowed her daughter Mamie to enter a white American school, the San Francisco Board of Education refused to comply and created a segregated Chinese school for Mamie and her brother Frank to attend. Both Toy and Tape respectively contributed to and endured the objectifying, Victorian "male gaze"[23] before the cinematic kinetoscope was created in 1891. In *Ornamentalism*, Anne Anlin Cheng argues that Asian and Asian American women are "thingly" but exceptional ornaments: "Encrusted by representations, abstracted and reified, the yellow woman is persistently sexualized yet barred from sexuality, simultaneously made and unmade by the aesthetic project."[24] Asian and Asian American women, or "the yellow woman,"[25] as Cheng puts it, are and have been perpetually hypersexualized and objectified throughout history. The hypersexualization and hyperfemininity of Asian American women exemplify their exceptional minoritization in terms of their hyperbolic figuration as the apotheosis of sexuality and femininity, respectively. In this way, Chinese American women in the nineteenth century were discursively figured as homo sacer.[26] Moreover, critic Lily Wong writes of the Chinese sex worker that she, "in particular, has served as a recurrent trope; this figure uniquely signifies both Asian American sexuality and Asian modernity."[27] The exceptionalism, that is, the collapsible yellow peril

22. Gamble, 12.
23. Mulvey, 25.
24. Anne Cheng, 18, 4–5.
25. Anne Cheng, 1.
26. Agamben, 17.
27. Lily Wong, 5–6.

hypersexuality and model minority hyperfemininity and submission, but also threatening modernity of Chinese American women, resulted in the passage of the 1875 Page Act, which spectacularly excluded Chinese women from the US by deeming them all hypersexualized prostitutes and subject to police raids and fatal diseases.[28] This chapter documents nineteenth-century Chinese American women whose activist voices responded to and contributed to their contemporary social and legal ornamentalism and exceptionalism legislated by the Page Act. The Victorian ideology of female moral reform, which disparately led to suffragism and the Protestant mission homes that rescued Chinese American prostitutes, invoked early Asian American activism: through their court cases and writings, Toy and Tape demonstrate that early feminism in the US is historically unfinished in its exclusion of the Chinese American women who contributed to it.[29] At the same time, the public attention paid to them dually traces the early beginnings of more inclusive, altruistic liberalism by personal allies such as Florence Eveleth Fontecilla and journalists such as Charles P. Duane and Leland Gamble; the public attention also evinces the hypersexualizing discourse of the Page Act.

Canonized in Lily Xiao Hong Lee and A. D. Stefanowska's *Biographical Dictionary of Chinese Women: The Qing Period, 1644–1911* (1998), Toy's and Tape's lives are particularly remarkable given the historical context in which most Chinese American women did not have a voice,[30] the contemporary driving-out of Chinese Americans during the late nineteenth century, and the exceptionalizing rhetoric of the 1875 Page Act. White Americans considered Chinese prostitution to be *outdated* and un-American "yellow slavery"[31] during the postbellum period after emancipation. Since all Chinese women were discursively considered prostitutes well before the legalization of the 1875 Page Act, Toy and Tape endured becoming exceptional, public spectacles as part of their subjection[32] to articulate themselves. The first Chinese American women who publicly established their voices contributed to and emerged out of the exceptionalizing rhetoric that surrounded the 1875 Page Act and the coincident contradictions of Victorian gender values. That is, Victorian gender values were informed by the liberal, female moral authority which dually propelled suffragism and Protestant rescue homes for Chinese prostitutes, but it also emphasized women's subordination to men in the home. The 1875 Page Act reflected Victorian gender values and rhetorically and literally drove out

---

28. Okihiro, 44; Barnhart, 48–50; Shah, 83; and Pfaelzer, 98.
29. I owe this conclusion to Shirley Lau Wong.
30. J. Yung, 8; and Lee and Stefanowska, 205–6.
31. Pryor, *Bawdy House Girls,* 43, 45; and Pryor, *Fascinating Women in California History,* 20.
32. Hartman, 4.

Chinese women by generalizing all Chinese women as social outcasts and prostitutes left to spectacularly die in the streets.

Authored by Republican California Congressman Horace F. Page, who later helped pass the 1882 Chinese Exclusion Law,[33] the 1875 Page Act stated,

> Be it enacted by the Senate and House of Representatives of the United States of America in Congress assembled, That in determining whether the immigration of any subject of China, Japan, or any Oriental country, to the United States, is free and voluntary [. . .] it shall be the duty of the consul-general or consul of the United States residing at the port from which it is proposed to convey such subjects [. . .] to ascertain whether such immigrant has entered into a contract or agreement for a term of service within the United States, for lewd and immoral purposes; and if there be such contract or agreement, the said consul-general or consul shall not deliver the required permit or certificate.[34]

The Page Act appeared to be against sex trafficking as much as it was against Chinese sex workers and all Chinese women. Despite its intent, this law alleged that all Chinese American women were prostitutes, regardless of their marital status, and were publicly persecuted as such.[35] In other words, Chinese American women were so hypersexualized that a law against sex trafficking was designed to keep Chinese women out of the US. Though Chinese prostitutes were often consensual sex workers, starting with Ah Toy, after 1870 most Chinese women were forced into prostitution against their will by kidnapping and luring.[36] The American public focus on Chinese prostitution was a particularly gendered form of "domestic American orientalism" that ushered in Chinese exclusion.[37] The Page Act was a product of the nineteenth-century Victorian era, which preached that sexual "morality, duty, and quality of life" was the responsibility of society rather than simply the individual.[38] And yet, while Victorian "moralists" advocated for sexual repression and asexual principles, "redlight districts flourished."[39] Victorian women exchanged social and economic rights for "moral influence."[40] However, the same gender roles that oppressed women in the name of morality empowered women to take on

---

33. Chang, 132.
34. Page Act of 1875.
35. Okihiro, 44.
36. Hirata, 8, 9.
37. Espiritu, 22.
38. Barnhart, 8.
39. Barnhart, 10.
40. Pascoe, 35–36.

female moral reform such as the Christian rescue and rehabilitation of prostitutes in the nineteenth century.[41] White Americans considered Chinese prostitutes to be the "most degraded" of sex workers, and they viewed Chinese men and sometimes women who sold them into prostitution, rather than their white clients, as the exploiters of Chinese women.[42] Conflating consensual Chinese sex workers and sex slaves, white Americans, particularly the white mission women who created mission homes to rescue them, used the term "yellow slavery" to describe the ways in which Chinese prostitutes were usually sold, tricked, or kidnapped in China and brought over to the US as slaves.[43] On the other hand, this liberal term inaccurately described all Chinese prostitution since, as Ah Toy exemplifies, some prostitution was consensual.

FEMALE MORAL REFORM: THE COMMON IDEOLOGY OF SUFFRAGISM AND PROTESTANT RESCUE HOMES

Since liberals considered slavery "anti-American" in the years following the Civil War,[44] pro-white labor suffragists like Mary Kenworthy viewed all Chinese labor, including prostitution, with disdain. As the vice president[45] of the Knights of Labor, Kenworthy

> likened the anti-Chinese movement to the recent fight to end slavery. In the 1860s, she had supported the Union over the "terrible slaver[s]" because she was "a loyal-hearted woman" who wanted her children "to live in a free country." As a woman and a mother, Kenworthy believed it was her duty to save her children from the curse of competing with slaves. Now, she believed she was face-to-face with the reincarnation of black slavery: Chinese coolieism.[46]

Here, Kenworthy invokes the Victorian discourse of female moral reform—"a loyal-hearted woman" who fought against "terrible slaver[s]" for her children "to live in a free country"—to fuel her anti-Chinese hatred.[47] A member of the Women's Suffrage Association, Kenworthy began a public speech by

---

41. Pascoe, xvi, 5.

42. Barth, 152–53.

43. Pryor, *Bawdy House Girls*, 43, 45; Pryor, *Fascinating Women in California History*, 20; Zesch, 59; and J. Yung, 30.

44. Lew-Williams, 132; and Sinn, 240–41.

45. "Anti-Chinese Demonstration"; and "Demonstration."

46. Lew-Williams, 132.

47. Lew-Williams, 132.

repudiating Chinese labor but concluded with a gendered, Victorian proto-feminist claim, "The women are the safeguard of the Nation. When everything else fails, come to the mothers for relief. Three cheers for women's suffrage!"[48] White suffragism also grew out of the Victorian discourse of female moral reform. However, the liberalism of white suffragists was ideologically contradictory—that is, they promoted social equality for white women but not necessarily for people of color. While the leading protofeminists of the nineteenth century, such as Elizabeth Cady Stanton and Susan B. Anthony, the primary leaders of the nineteenth-century suffragist movement, initially promoted abolitionism of slavery with the famous William Lloyd Garrison, they renounced their stance after the Fifteenth Amendment was ratified in 1870; they were also uneasy about promoting labor rights. That is to say, although they cooperated with the labor movement, the suffragist movement was primarily aimed toward middle-class white women: "rather than women wage-earners, the suffragists found that their demand for the vote and their vision of female independence attracted middle-class women."[49] Comparing hierarchical, non-companionate marriages to chattel slavery, specifically prostitution, white suffragists like Stanton and Anthony deemed "unconsenting sexual relations within marriage" "legalized prostitution."[50] Here, they dually critique mercenary marriages and sex work by conflating sex trafficking with consensual prostitution, which some Chinese prostitution was. Assuming sex work was nonconsensual, white suffragists, like the Protestant mission women, imposed their Victorian ideologies on prostitutes by sympathizing with and reforming them.[51] While working to reform prostitutes and rescue them from what they perceived as slavery and sex trafficking, suffragists also "reactivated themselves [in the 1860s and 1870s] into a militant and successful campaign to halt government regulation of prostitution. The system of regulation, already in existence in France and parts of England, forced women alleged to be prostitutes to submit to vaginal examinations and licensing; its purpose was to allow men to have sex with prostitutes without the risk of venereal disease."[52] At the same time, the women were also targeted by the social attack on prostitution, exemplified by "the campaign to raise the age of sexual consent."[53] While this campaign protected girls from abusive relationships with older men, it also restricted the sexuality of young women.

---

48. Lew-Williams, 133.

49. DuBois, *Woman Suffrage and Women's Rights*, 69, 74.

50. Pascoe, 53; DuBois, *Feminism & Suffrage*, 31–32; DuBois, *Suffrage*, 4; and DuBois, *Woman Suffrage and Women's Rights*, 77–78.

51. DuBois, *Woman Suffrage and Women's Rights*, 146.

52. DuBois, *Woman Suffrage and Women's Rights*, 146–47.

53. DuBois, *Woman Suffrage and Women's Rights*, 147.

While middle-class white suffragists worked to rescue mainly white prostitutes, the white Protestant mission women, who did not promote suffragism, attempted to reform Chinese women by proselytizing them to Christianity and assimilating them to Victorian values such as patriarchal marriages.[54] Some Chinese American women did subscribe to Victorian marriages: between 1888 and 1901, San Francisco mission homes took credit for arranging 160 marriages of Chinese women.[55] However, in keeping with the white American notion that Chinese men exploited women, some Chinese women took shelter in mission homes to "gain leverage in polygamous marriages."[56] Considering the mission-home women's disinterest in suffragism, Chinese American women were educated in Christianity and Victorian mores[57] but not endowed with the same ambition for equal rights as white women in the nineteenth century. Toy and Tape, whose only choices from the discourse of Chinese exceptionalism were to be a professional prostitute or a more traditional Victorian housewife, were inspired by the suffragists' discourse of equal gender rights, and gained their activist voices at a great cost—by putting themselves on public display as exceptions, either sexually or through the court system. The discourse of Chinese prostitution, culminating in and promulgated by the 1875 Page Act, affected the ways in which the earliest recorded Chinese American woman activists could promote themselves and their democratic rights. Even if it was not intended for Chinese Americans, the suffragist rhetoric of equal gender rights influenced Chinese American women, like Toy and Tape, who also contributed to the protofeminist rhetoric and used their voices for activism.

THE ANTINOMIES OF SUFFRAGISM

In 1848, just one year before Ah Toy arrived in the United States, one hundred women and men met together for the first woman's rights conference in Seneca Falls, New York. Modeling their aims after the Declaration of Independence, "they asserted that 'all men and women are created equal, that they are endowed by their Creator with certain inalienable rights, that among these are life, liberty, and the pursuit of happiness.'"[58] These early feminists or protofeminists, spearheaded by Stanton and Anthony, believed suffrage to be a part of their natural rights as US citizens, which would act "to transform woman's consciousness, to reanchor her self-image, not in the subordination of her

---

54. Pascoe, 47, 95.
55. Pascoe, 157.
56. Pascoe, 161.
57. Pascoe, 81.
58. Wellman, 10.

familial role but in the individuality and self-determination that they saw in citizenship."[59] From its inception during the antebellum reform years, suffragism emerged from the Victorian notion of the liberal, female moral authority but also "from women's growing awareness of their common conditions and grievances" and "the antislavery movement."[60] The reform movement continued to gain momentum after the Civil War during Reconstruction.[61] Many suffragists, including Stanton and Anthony, believed women's oppression, in Victorian society and institutions such as hierarchical marriage, to be akin to African American slavery. The majority of white suffragists aligned themselves with William Lloyd Garrison and his abolitionist movement. Furthermore, Garrison's Christian utopianism, to which he had converted in 1837, offered Stanton and other suffragists freedom from Christian orthodoxy.[62]

When the Fourteenth Amendment was passed in 1868, in part issuing citizenship and the rights of citizenship to African Americans, Stanton was quoted as saying, "Three cheers for God! [. . .] Out of this struggle we must come with higher ideas of liberty, the masses quickened with thought, and a rotten aristocracy crushed forever [. . .] I have no misgivings as to the result."[63] And yet, when she learned that the Fourteenth Amendment was to grant rights to African American men to the exclusion of white American women, "Stanton's worst fears were confirmed."[64] Ellen DuBois and Cándida Smith write of Stanton, "She readily shifted between expansive statements about equal rights for all citizens to brutal dramatizations of the plight of native-born white American women that belittled black and immigrant men."[65] Moreover, Stanton and Anthony were actively opposed to the passage of the Fifteenth Amendment, which granted African American men the right to vote and, they felt, punctuated sexual inequality.[66] The rhetoric they used in their opposition to the amendment was definitively racist.[67] Associating African American men with "lunatics," "idiots," and "fools," Stanton also declined to promote Black female suffrage.[68] Although Frances Ellen Watkins Harper, a free-born African American poet, was permitted to speak during the eleventh National Woman's Rights Convention in 1866, of which

---

59. DuBois, *Woman Suffrage and Women's Rights*, 36.
60. DuBois, *Feminism & Suffrage*, 22, 22.
61. DuBois, *Woman Suffrage and Women's Rights*, 69.
62. DuBois, *Feminism & Suffrage*, 33, 34.
63. DuBois, *Feminism & Suffrage*, 53.
64. DuBois, *Feminism & Suffrage*, 60.
65. DuBois and Cándida Smith, 4.
66. DuBois, *Feminism & Suffrage*, 174.
67. Ginzberg, 131.
68. Ginzberg, 85.

Stanton was chair,[69] Stanton refused to place Black women suffrage at the center of nineteenth-century feminism.[70] Whereas white women suffragists such as Charlotte Perkins Gilman could be publicly proclaimed "a woman of really original genius,"[71] African American women took a backseat in political visibility while Chinese American women were politically invisible. Universal rights, for Stanton, were white American women's rights even though Black suffragists, such as Ida B. Wells, were making great social strides in pairing antilynching campaigns with Black suffrage.[72] Although Stanton and Anthony did not include women of color in their campaign, their efforts were actively opposed by anti-Chinese labor activists such as Denis Kearney. In fact, at a Greenbacker convention in 1880 in which Republicans were gathering to nominate a presidential candidate, Denis Kearney attempted to prevent Anthony from addressing the convention about woman suffrage, citing that such an address should be limited to "daughters of Eve."[73] And yet, despite this opposition, Stanton and Anthony did not ally their efforts with early Chinese American activists.

Further solidifying their exclusionary and racial stand on suffragism in the 1860s, Elizabeth Cady Stanton and Susan B. Anthony accepted money from, traveled with, and associated themselves with George Francis Train, a renowned racist who was against the Fourteenth and Fifteenth Amendments.[74] Train was also a controversial activist in the suffragist movement who, according to DuBois, was "an intrepid world traveler, the prototype for Phileas Fogg, hero of Jules Verne's *Around the World in Eighty Days,* a major American proponent of Irish independence, financier of the Union Pacific Railroad, and later organizer of the notorious Crédit Mobilier financing scheme, and [. . .] a wacky political performer, an egomaniac, and a dandy with delusions of becoming president."[75] William Lloyd Garrison viewed Stanton and Anthony's association with Train as a massive betrayal of abolitionism: he wrote to Anthony, "'I cannot refrain from expressing my regret and astonishment that you and Mrs. Stanton should have taken such leave of good sense, [. . .] as to be traveling companions and associate lecturers with that crack-brained harlequin and semi-lunatic, George Francis Train! [. . .] The colored people and

---

69. DuBois, *Suffrage,* 59, 58.

70. Ginzberg, 127.

71. *San Francisco Examiner,* Sunday Morning, May 6, 1894, Sorbier Papers: box 7: Newspaper Clippings 1893–1928 Bulk: 18981921, *California Historical Society,* San Francisco, California.

72. Ginzberg, 127. In *Suffrage,* DuBois points out that in 1910 Wells-Barnett published an article, "How Enfranchisement Stops Lynching" (15).

73. Gyory, 192.

74. DuBois, *Feminism & Suffrage,* 94.

75. DuBois, *Suffrage,* 66–67.

their advocates have not a more abusive assailant.'"[76] Their association with Train "was not [. . .] Stanton and Anthony's finest moment."[77]

Despite the inherent racism of their actions and white American universalist rhetoric, Stanton and Anthony made suffragism a discourse that influenced people of all races and to which people of all races could contribute, including Toy and Tape. Stanton and Anthony spearheaded white American suffragism during the three quarters of a century between Seneca Falls in 1848 and the ratification of the Nineteenth Amendment, which granted women the right to vote, in 1920. Although suffragism emerged from the conservatism of Victorian female moral authority, suffragists such as Stanton and Anthony also challenged many of the sexist institutions such as hierarchical marriages and involuntary prostitution. Stanton also disagreed with the Victorian view of women's sexual purity. In a letter to her mentor Lucretia Mott, she wrote, "We have had women enough sacrificed to this sentimental, hypocritical prating about purity. [. . .] This is one of man's most effective engines for our division and subjugation."[78] However, she did not go as far as some of her fellow suffragists as to renounce marriage altogether and embrace "free love."[79] Victoria Woodhull, with whom Stanton and Anthony "cooperated," was a radical advocate of "free love," which emerged from the same suffragist notion that Victorian marriage was "legalized prostitution."[80] Free love was also evidence of the contradiction of Victorian free and repressed sexuality in the nineteenth century. Like Stanton and Anthony—who did not believe African Americans should have the right to vote—Woodhull never mentioned Chinese American women in her advocacy of free love; nevertheless, Ah Toy established herself as a consensual sex worker and free lover when she arrived in the United States in 1849. That is to say, despite their exclusion of people of color, white suffragists made public the vocabulary with which to establish gender independence.

AH TOY: A "FREE LOVER"

It is unclear whether Toy was familiar with early protofeminist rhetoric, but she abided by and contributed to it in her life. There are several myths about Toy's arrival in San Francisco in the United States. In 1998 author JoAnn Levy published a fictitious novel about Toy. During Toy's contemporary time,

---

76. DuBois, *Suffrage*, 69.
77. Ginzberg, 123.
78. DuBois, *Woman Suffrage and Women's Rights*, 103.
79. DuBois, *Suffrage*, 87.
80. DuBois, *Woman Suffrage and Women's Rights*, 69, 102, 77–78.

California State Senator Elisha Oscar Crosby wrote briefly of Toy in his 1878 *Statement of Events in California*: "The first Chinese courtesan who came to San Francisco was Ah Toy. She arrived, I think, in 1850, and was a very handsome China girl. She was quite select in her associates, was liberally patronized by the white men, and made a great amount of money."[81] The most common story is that Toy arrived in the United States in 1849 as a twenty-year-old consensual prostitute who had left behind her husband in Hong Kong to, as she put it, "better her condition."[82] Others, such as historian Alton Pryor, have claimed that Toy sailed from China with her husband, who died en route to the US, and, while still on board the China Clipper ship, became the captain's mistress. Upon landing in San Francisco, she had enough money from the captain to start her peep show, her first business as a prostitute.[83] Upon her death in 1928, journalist Charles P. Duane wrote,

> I have seen a line of men extending to the length of nearly a whole block, each man armed with a large pistol in his belt, waiting his turn to get a chance to gaze on the countenance of the charming Ah Toy. [. . .] When Ah Toy put herself on exhibition, it cost the miners one ounce of gold dust to satisfy their curiosity and she had her scales read to weigh the [gold] of each visitor, so that she could not be cheated.[84]

Duane was also the chief engineer of the volunteer fire department, also known in San Francisco for his womanizing behavior; some newspapers perhaps erroneously name him as former commander-in-chief of the Vigilance Committee, even though he had been outlawed and deported from San Francisco twice by the secret Committee of Vigilance.[85] Regardless of his affiliation with the Committee of Vigilance, he felt strongly enough about Toy upon her death that he wrote a biographical piece about her in which he lauded her English, which was "sufficient to make herself understood."[86] Despite her purported consent to her profession, another obituary in 1928 stated she had once considered herself a "slave."[87] This difference suggests that her feelings about her profession changed over time. Historians and travel writers who

---

81. *Statement of events in California as related by Elisha Oscar Crosby* (1878), 124, BANC MSS-C-D 52-62 FILM, Bancroft Library, University of California, Berkeley.

82. J. Yung, 33; Sinn, 219; Lee and Stefanowska, 3; Espiritu, 38–39; Okihiro, 99; and Gentry, 51.

83. Pryor, *Bawdy House Girls*, 38–39.

84. Duane, "First Chinawoman."

85. Boessenecker, 20; San Francisco Vigilance Committee, BANC FILM 2594: 04, Bancroft Library, University of California, Berkeley 39; and Boessenecker, 3, 4.

86. Boessenecker, 62.

87. "China Mary, Widely Known Clam Seller, Dies at Age of 99."

subjected her to the male gaze as they documented her life suggest that she was enslaved, regardless of whether she chose to be a prostitute. In his obituary of her, Duane objectifies and exceptionalizes her: "she was a tall, well-built woman. In fact, she was the finest-looking Chinese woman that I have ever seen."[88] Likewise, the historian Alexander McLeod writes, "the porcelain-faced flower from the Celestial Kingdom was not unaware of her attraction and its money-making possibilities." In describing her peep show, Pryor reveals his own sexual fascination with Toy:

> Ah Toy rented a two-room building and added a platform in one room. Small peep holes were drilled into a wall. She decided to open a "look but don't touch show." Her show was a great success.
>
> She hired a Chinese man to collect one ounce of gold from each man occupying a peep hole. When each peep hole was occupied, Ah Toy would appear on the small stage, wearing a form-fitting silk kimono. Underneath, she was totally nude.
>
> Her show lasted only a few moments. But as she seductively removed her kimono, the lusty miners at the peep holes stamped their feet and howled at the sight of the beautiful Chinese girl.[89]

Drawing attention to her "form-fitting kimono" "underneath" of which "she was totally nude," Pryor, as a liberal historian, sensationalizes Toy's sex work just as the "lusty miners" who had paid to watch her exhibition even as he seeks to represent her. Twenty-first-century historians such as Michael Rutter have likewise subjected her to the male gaze when discussing her seduction of the ship's captain en route to the United States: "she sasheyed in front of the love-starved captain and batted her eyes affectionately."[90] The term "sasheyed" suggests Rutter's view of Toy's sexual manipulation. Moreover, Rutter suggests that inasmuch as Toy was victimized by prostitution and her clients, she also became a victimizer in "enslaving" and trafficking young girls from China and subjecting them to be "broken in" or raped on the ship to the United States.[91] Toy exemplifies the cycle of abuse in which the victim victimizes others to gain agency over their original abuse.[92]

Since Toy elected to be a prostitute, she perhaps enjoyed being the object of the male gaze even as she was being subjected to it. And yet, when she

---

88. Duane.
89. Pryor, *Bawdy House Girls*, 38–39.
90. Rutter, 128.
91. Rutter, 46, 132.
92. See Clark, *Asian American Players*.

brought the men to court in 1849 for cheating her with brass filings instead of gold, she resented being a spectacle: still objectified by the early liberal press that was attempting to document her activism—"dressed in an apricot satin jacket and willow-green pantaloons, with a colorful pair of tabis on her small, tightly bound feet. [. . .] Her hair was arranged in the traditional chignon, her pencil thin black eyebrows contrasting exotically with her white, rice-powdered cheeks"—she was horrified by being "laughed" and "guffawed"[93] at; moreover, she lost her case even after presenting the evidence of a china basin of brass filings instead of gold. Declining to objectify her, Duane simply writes that, after she lost her case, "Ah Toy discarded her Chinese robes and adopted the dress of American females."[94] Before the Civil War when Toy argued her cases and immediately after, "liberal reformers variously touted laissez-faire, to restore the fundamental principle of individual liberty, or administrative reform, to restore pure and efficient government. [. . .] Laissez-faire deprived the state of effective power in the market; administrative governance insulated the policymaking institutions of the state from the influence of the people."[95] Toy was an enfleshed Chinese American who believed in her natural rights, made public her humanity even when it would later be legislatively denied by the Page Act, and defied a "do-nothing" government by attempting to seek out her own justice. Averse to being the "laughing-stock" object of the white male gaze in court, she closed her peep show, discarded her exoticizing kimono while donning only American clothing, and only accepted Chinese male clientele as a prostitute.[96]

Soon Toy rose to the ranks to being a madam and became quite wealthy in doing so.[97] Some historians applaud her for her "enterprising" nature, whereas others criticize her for "subjecting other young girls to the same life that she had endured upon arriving in the city."[98] While white suffragists attempted to raise the age of sexual consent among women to prevent prostitution,[99] consent for prostitutes was particularly difficult to establish in the severely patriarchal society in which single women had very few avenues of work in the Victorian-era US. Toy consented to the profession and was a voluntary prostitute. In this way, her consent contributed to the dominant discourse of

93. Gentry, 52; McLeod, 176–77; Duane; and Gentry, 52–53.

94. Duane.

95. Cohen, 221.

96. Gentry, 51, 53; and Pryor, *Fascinating Women in California History,* 37.

97. J. Yung, 34; Sinn, 219; Smith, 76; Pryor, *Bawdy House Girls,* 39; Gentry, 53–54; and Lee and Stefanowska, 3–4.

98. Sinn, 219; and Smith, 76.

99. DuBois, *Woman Suffrage and Women's Rights,* 147.

all Chinese women as prostitutes that led to the Page Act of 1875. That Toy turned to clamming as a career choice in the second part of her life suggests that her involvement in prostitution was eventually not suited to her.

As Toy demonstrates, the Chinese were discriminated against almost as soon as they arrived in the United States. Chinese Americans, upon their arrival in 1849, were "considered almost indispensable" as the economically efficient model minority; however, they were soon discriminated against by the 1850 Foreign Miners License tax law, which charged all non-native-born citizens twenty dollars per month to mine in California.[100] In 1858 California passed legislation "prohibiting Chinese immigration and calling for fines and possible imprisonment for anyone found guilty of transporting Chinese workers into the state."[101] However, as Kanazawa notes, the contradictions of sovereign liberalism did not allow for complete exclusion of the Chinese until the 1875 Page Act and the 1882 Chinese Exclusion Act.[102] As liberalism gradually became more dependent on the market and as the Chinese were seen as exceptional because of their economic efficiency and submission, Chinese exclusion did not proceed unabated. However, even before the Page Act, "under the Additional Powers Act given to the city by the state legislature, the board of supervisors in 1865 passed an 'Order to remove Chinese women of ill-fame from certain limits in the city.'"[103] Despite coming from a Chinese culture in which women were often perceived as slaves or as gender subordinates[104] and the discrimination that she faced as a Chinese American prostitute, particularly being cheated by white clients,[105] Toy contributed to the rhetoric of "free love" from white suffragists and freely established consensual relationships with men outside of her profession. In 1851, when the San Francisco Vigilance Committee sent brothel inspector John A. Clark to investigate Toy, they became lovers instead.[106] The San Francisco residents organized a "socially constructive," "sovereign" Anglo-American Vigilance Committee, which some scholars distinguish from a lynch mob while other conflate it with a lynch mob, in 1851 and 1856.[107] At the time, there were dissenters to the Vigilance Committee, such as Reverend Mr. W. A. Scott, who vociferously

---

100. Coolidge, 22, 29.

101. Kanazawa, 795.

102. Kanazawa, 802–3.

103. Barnhart, 48–49.

104. McLeod, 174.

105. Peffer, 31; Stephens, 147; Duane; Pryor, *Bawdy House Girls,* 39; Gentry, 52; Pryor, *Bawdy House Girls,* 37; McLeod, 176–77; and Espiritu, 38–39.

106. Gentry, 54, 55.

107. Waldrep, 54–55.

compared it to a lynch mob.[108] Toy's relationship with Clark nevertheless saved her from being arrested for keeping a brothel.[109] Before her relationship with Clark, the *Alta* reported, on May 22, 1850, that she had married a white man named Henry Conrad.[110] However, as Gentry writes, "Henry must have been no more dependable than Ah Toy's customers; there is no further mention of him and in a little over a year Ah Toy had taken a lover."[111] Her obituary mentions her unnamed Chinese husband who had died twenty years prior; after she was widowed, she lived with her brother-in-law, "Chinese Louis."[112] Although she enjoyed a life of free love despite the hazards of her profession, her relationships were sometimes abusive: in 1852 she appeared in court, "with hair disheveled, dress torn, and both eyes blackened. She had innocently told another man that she was Clark's mistress; Clark in turn had beaten her."[113] This case demonstrates Benjamin's argument that lawmaking and law-preserving violence are conflated and not penalized:

> Police violence is emancipated from both [lawmaking and law-preserving] conditions. It is lawmaking, because its characteristic function is not the promulgation of laws but the assertion of legal claims for any decree, and law-preserving, because it is at the disposal of these ends. The assertion that the ends of police violence are always identical or even connected to those of general law is entirely untrue.[114]

Although not exactly police, Clark was part of a similarly civic committee that regulated social conduct and was not exempt from law for his violence. As might be assumed, Judge Edward McGowan dismissed the case, stating that "he couldn't interfere in what was obviously a family quarrel."[115] Afterwards, he called Toy a "dirty dog," "this contemptible piece of humanity," and was in disbelief that Clark, whom he called a "poor ignorant creature," "had actually expended thousands of dollars upon" her.[116]

Especially given the racial and sexual biases of the judges, Toy always lost her court battles. And yet, she turned to the judicial system four times between the years 1849 and 1852 to seek justice for herself and other Chinese

---

108. San Francisco Vigilance Committee, 13, BANC FILM 2594: 04, Bancroft Library, University of California, Berkeley.
109. Gentry, 55; Lee and Stefanowska, 3–4; J. Yung, 34; and Sinn, 219–20.
110. Gentry, 53–54.
111. Gentry, 53–54.
112. "China Mary, Widely Known Clam Seller, Dies at Age of 99."
113. Gentry, 57.
114. Benjamin, 242–43.
115. Gentry, 57.
116. Gentry, 57.

Americans. The same judicial system in which she had placed her hopes for democracy and justice convicted her for keeping a "disorderly house" as a means of survival in 1854 and 1859, suggesting that the exceptionalizing discourse of Chinese prostitution circulated well before the Page Act of 1875. Often on display for white American men to fetishize or mock, whether it was in her peep show or in court, Toy paid a heavy price to establish her voice and rights as a Chinese American woman. Newspaper accounts fail to record her words, and, as a result, she only appears as the object of the gaze even though she clearly asserted herself in court. Moreover, none of her court cases were pursued to the federal level, and therefore no court local district or circuit court transcripts would have survived the earthquake of 1906.[117] Although the court transcripts failed to survive history, she did use her voice for activism: "She had mastered English and felt comfortable enough with it to argue her case before a judge. It was rare for a white woman to face the rigors of the legal system without a lawyer. For a Chinese woman, an immigrant from a culture looked down upon by the Anglos, it was almost unprecedented."[118] Despite her bravery, the lack of public attention paid to her court cases, insofar as they never progressed to the federal level, evince her struggle with her voice as a Chinese American prostitute. Her prostitution was also based on the exceptional minority discourse, which hyperbolized Chinese American women's femininity and sexuality: Toy's prostitutes purportedly disseminated the notion that Chinese women's vaginas were exotically horizontal rather than vertical.[119] Despite her losses, Toy clung to the notion of democracy and social justice even during an era in which democratic citizenship did not apply to her as a Chinese American and a woman. Her free choice in those she loved was the closest she came in taking part in American democracy. Although white suffragists did not include Chinese American women in their platform, she added her own definition to the vocabulary of "free love."

PROTESTANT MISSION HOMES: FEMALE MORAL AUTHORITY

While the white suffragists did not consider Chinese American women in their campaign for women's rights, white mission women made them their primary focus of rescue or the "white woman's burden" in the nineteenth century.[120]

---

117. Miller, Archives Specialist, National Archive at San Francisco; Carey, Librarian/Archivist, San Francisco History Center.

118. Rutter, 131.

119. Okihiro, 99.

120. Hirata, 28.

Protestant mission homes were established in the 1870s and emerged from the contradictory Victorian rhetoric of sexual purity and liberal, female moral authority. In her famous historiography of the women's rescue-mission homes, Pascoe writes that Victorian Protestant women worked against "male abuse."[121] Such efforts came out of the antebellum reforms of the 1830s and 1840s.[122] Although the Protestant missionary women aimed to help all "female victims of male abuse," their focus was primarily on Chinese prostitutes. The Chinese Mission Home in San Francisco was started in 1874 after Mrs. John Gulick, a missionary to China, spoke to a group of white Christian women about impoverished orphanages in Shanghai, China; this talk spurred these women to establish the "California Branch of the (Philadelphia) Woman's Foreign Missionary Society."[123]

Informed that Chinese women were often "enticed, others purchased, and many kidnapped," the Protestant mission women made every effort to eradicate the "yellow slavery" that they considered "a slavery worse than death."[124] Moreover, they had also been informed that Chinese wives were also enslaved by their patriarchal marriages, "hemmed in by cultural prescriptions and by their own bound feet that 'very few of them are allowed to go on the streets, and the vast majority never leave their rooms.'"[125] The establishment of Chinese mission homes for Chinese women, including wives and prostitutes, in the 1870s was controversial, as groups such as the Workingmen's Party targeted Chinese prostitutes along with other Chinese workers as "scapegoats for economic problems."[126] Ironically, Chinese mission women used the same antislavery rhetoric that labor suffragists such as Mary Kenworthy used to rally against the Chinese on the West Coast to rescue Chinese women from patriarchal oppression. The "rescue" of Chinese women from involuntary prostitution was not without its Western ideologies, however. Although the female moral authority that the mission women espoused "was sharply critical of male privilege" and "attempt[ed] to control male sexual behavior and limit the vulnerability of women to sexual abuse"[127] the Protestant missionaries reformed the Chinese women to be "upstanding" Victorian housewives.[128]

---

121. Pascoe, xvi.

122. Pascoe, 5.

123. Pascoe, 13, 13.

124. Pascoe, 14; Pryor, *Fascinating Women in California History,* 20; Pryor, *Bawdy House Girls,* 43, 45; and Pascoe, 13.

125. Pascoe, 52.

126. Pascoe, 15.

127. Pascoe, 50, 42.

128. Pascoe, 42, 95.

Moreover, Victorian ideology assumed a racial hierarchy in which the Chinese were seen as racially inferior to Caucasians.[129]

Despite the ideological drawbacks of the Protestant mission homes, they succeeded in educating Chinese women as they proselytized them.[130] Chinese American women were educated and enfranchised to, like Toy, choose to be with those they loved. On the other hand, their lives were strictly structured and forcefully delineated to assimilate as Victorian women as the Page Act would violently dictate. The mission homes' aims were to marry off the Chinese women or to turn them into "native helpers."[131] Native helpers helped "liberate" nonconsensual and consensual Chinese prostitutes, alike, from their purported enslavement and faced many threats from brothel owners and other agents of prostitution.[132]

One of the most famous Protestant mission women in the nineteenth century was Donaldina Cameron. Although Cameron had intended only to serve the San Francisco Chinese Mission for one year in the capacity of teaching Chinese women and girls to sew, she ended up taking over the directorship of the San Francisco Chinese Mission Home in 1897 upon the death of the previous director, Margaret Culbertson, who had directed the home since the 1870s.[133] Cameron "is credited with saving more than three thousand women and children during her forty-seven years at the mission."[134] Vehemently opposed to "the yellow slave trade," Cameron raided brothels to "free" both voluntary and involuntary Chinese prostitutes throughout California and was famously photographed with "policemen, hatchets in hand, standing outside a Chinese brothel, about to raid the premises in search of a particular prostitute."[135] Cameron "often sent twenty or thirty Chinese women from the home to work from four to eight weeks in the fields. It is not difficult to see why a number of women had been 'rescued' by the missionaries later escaped from their saviors."[136] Pictured in 1934 wearing a Chinese dress, Cameron, who was forced to retire by national mission officials from the Chinese Mission Home in the 1920s, proclaimed that through her work in the Chinese

129. Pascoe, 198.

130. Pascoe, 81.

131. Pascoe writes of the term "native helper" that it was "a term that suggests the mixture of fascination and condescension with which mission women regarded them" (113).

132. Pascoe, 113.

133. Pryor, *Fascinating Women in California History,* 21; Pryor, *Bawdy House Girls,* 40; and Pryor, *Fascinating Women in California History,* 22.

134. Pryor, *Bawdy House Girls,* 40.

135. Pryor, *Fascinating Women in California History,* 20; and Pascoe, 95–96.

136. Hirata, 28.

Mission Home, China became a "nation I love."[137] Through their dedication to rescuing Chinese American women from prostitution—whether involuntary or consensual—and abusive, patriarchal marriages, Protestant mission women such as Cameron empowered Chinese American women by educating them and positioning them to be in companionate marriages of their choice but also disempowered them by forcing them to assimilate as Victorian-era American women.

Their rescue efforts also proselytized the Chinese American women and were elemental of Victorian reform and the contradictory ideology of female moral authority and women's subordination to men in the home. Despite their efforts to enfranchise women, particularly Chinese American women, Protestant mission women overall did not take up suffragism—although there were some who did;[138] nevertheless, suffragism also emerged from the reform discourse of female moral authority. Even though "suffrage was so far from the grasp of home mission women,"[139] Mary Tape was one Chinese American woman whose feminism was influenced by and contributed to both mission women and suffragists in the nineteenth century. The ideology of female moral authority differently spurred on suffragism, to which Toy's belief in social justice, democracy, and free love contributed; female moral authority also influenced Protestant mission rescue homes, which were intricately tied with Tape's position as a Victorian housewife—the only other possible social position for a Chinese American woman, as violently regulated by the Page Act—and activist whose Chinese American radicalism was not legible to a liberal US society.

MARY TAPE: THE "ANDALUSIAN BEAUTY"

Tape was an English-speaking Chinese American woman who was raised in an orphanage in Shanghai, China, and, accompanied by missionaries, immigrated to the US at the age of eleven.[140] Historian Mae Ngai speculates that Tape had been sold by her mother as *mui tsai,* an indentured Chinese servant-girl who is destined to involuntary prostitution.[141] After she arrived in the United States in 1868, she was abandoned, if she had been accompanied by missionaries as many historiographies posit, and a Reverend Loomis found her and brought

---

137. Pascoe, 118.
138. Clark, *Asian American Avant-Garde,* 29.
139. Pascoe, 47.
140. J. Yung, 48.
141. Ngai, 15.

her to the non-sectarian Ladies' Relief Society outside of Chinatown, where she was raised and educated for five years.[142] The Ladies' Relief Society was a rescue home for Chinese prostitutes where a woman named Miss McGladery raised and gave Mary her surname.[143] It was at the Ladies' Relief Society where she met the Methodist missionary Reverend Otis Gibson, again, one of the Protestant rescue missionaries with whom Wong Chin Foo worked. The Ladies' Relief Society was on Joseph Tape's, whose Chinese name was Jeu Dip, milk delivery route, and that is how Joseph and Mary met.[144] Upon marrying Joseph, who later worked as an interpreter for the Chinese consulate, Tape raised "four musically accomplished children."[145] Avoiding Chinatown where Mary had memories of recovering as a *mui tsai*, the Tapes lived in a primarily white neighborhood in San Francisco.[146] In many ways, they fulfilled the nineteenth-century model minority stereotype of efficient and hyperbolically accomplished workers and white assimilation, which automatically reverted to the yellow peril stereotype of "swarming" overpopulation and the forced automation of a modern futurity.[147] They were soon faced with their exclusion from US society: when their eight-year-old daughter Mamie was prevented from entering the neighborhood Spring Valley School, the Tapes challenged the board of education in a California Supreme Court case known as *Tape v. Hurley* in 1884, just thirty years after *People v. Hall*. Encouraged to file the lawsuit by their white neighbor Florence Eveleth, who had tutored the Tape children, the Tapes fought valiantly during a period in which the Chinese in the United States were considered "aliens ineligible to citizenship" by the Chinese Exclusion Act and in which all Chinese women and girls over the age of twelve were considered libidinous prostitutes by the Page Act.[148] In her testimony as an adult, Mamie did not recall Florence's involvement in the case but did state that Florence Eveleth, later Fontecilla, did tutor her privately.[149] On the other hand, Fontecilla stated,

> They were the finest people in the world—They have always been my life long [*sic*] friends.—I was the one that made the test case of entering a Chinese child into the Public Schools of San Francisco, and that was Mamie.

142. J. Yung, 48.

143. Ngai, 19–20.

144. Ngai, 14.

145. J. Yung, 49; and Gamble.

146. Ngai, 49, 59.

147. Thompson, 3; and Hayot, 103, 104, 122.

148. Ngai, 43, 44; Takaki, 14; and Shah, 83.

149. Gertrude Chan, Immigration Papers, San Francisco National Archives.

She was 6 years old, and I took her to the Public School to enter her, and she was not received until that test case, and they made a test case of it, and that was what created the Chinese School in San Francisco. When at first she could not get in, that broke her mother's and her father's hearts, because they were fine people and did not associate with the Chinese people.—I took the children to my house and taught them myself—started them on their education.[150]

Fontecilla demonstrates the contradictions of liberalism: on the one hand, she problematically qualifies the "fineness" of the Tapes with their refusal to "associate with the Chinese people"; on the other hand, she also initiated the trial and test case and, as a result of the board's refusal to comply with the law, "started [the Tape children] on their education."[151]

The Tapes were encouraged by the 1884 ruling by the US Circuit Court for the Ninth Judicial District that allowed a Chinese American boy named Look Tin Sing who had been born in Mendocino County, California, to return to the United States after a five-year visit to China, despite the 1882 Chinese Exclusion Act: "Since Mamie was 'a natural-born citizen,' it stood to reason that she should be entitled to the free education that was every American's birthright."[152] On behalf of the Tapes, the Chinese Consul, F. A. Bee, wrote the San Francisco School Superintendent Andrew Jackson Moulder: "The reasons given by you, if correctly reported through the press. Are so inconsistent with the treaties, Constitution, and laws of the United States, especially so in this case as the child is native born, that I consider it my duty to renew the request to admit the child, and all other Chinese children resident here who desire to enter the public schools under your charge."[153] Moulder and the San Francisco Board of Education responded by voting in favor of a resolution to dismiss any principal or teacher who would admit "a Mongolian child" in their school.[154] The San Francisco Board of Education's decision to ban Asians from their public schools evidenced the liberal "conservatism" of the Gilded Age, which some historians state began after the Civil War in 1865, while others argue it began after Reconstruction in 1877 and which ended at the Progressive Era of the 1890s.[155]

---

150. Gertrude Chan, Immigration Papers, San Francisco National Archives.
151. Gertrude Chan, Immigration Papers, San Francisco National Archives.
152. McCunn, 42.
153. McCunn, 41.
154. McCunn, 41.
155. Hofstadter, 3, 8–9.

Despite historian Richard Hofstadter's longstanding argument about the conservatism of the Gilded Age, Cohen has argued that liberal reform actually began earlier in the Gilded Age rather than the Progressive Era as Hofstadter has claimed.[156] The Tapes' victory at both the circuit court and Supreme Court levels evinces the liberal reforms that were occurring during the Gilded Age. The US Circuit Court judge, Judge Maguire, to whom the Tapes initially brought their case, ruled in favor of the Tapes on January 9, 1885.[157] While the board of education appealed this decision, the California Supreme Court backed Maguire's ruling on March 3, 1885. In defiance of the law, the San Francisco Board of Education established a segregated Chinese school for Chinese American students to attend and even "dragged their feet" in doing so.[158] The Chinese school, with Mamie at the top of her class, however, was not expected to succeed due to low enrollment by local San Francisco Chinese.[159] The board's refusal to abide by the Supreme Court legal decision showcases the gradual conservatism of the era in which radicals eventually converted to liberalism.[160]

Tape demonstrated her radicalism in challenging the liberal-supporting laissez-faire government in the conservative Gilded Age. Despite her achievements and bravery in taking the board to court, and although the California Supreme Court "ruled that all children, regardless of race, had the right to a public school education," the school district still refused to desegregate its schools and instead created a separate school for Chinese students in Chinatown.[161] Tape continued to assert herself in a public letter to the board:[162]

To the Board of Education—DEAR SIRS: I see that you are going to make all sorts of excuses to keep my child out of the Public schools. Dear sirs, Will you please to tell me: Is it a disgrace to be Born a Chinese: Didn't God make us all!!! What right! have you to bar my children out of the school because she is a chinese [sic] Descend. They is no other worldly reason that you could keep her out, except that I suppose, you all goes to churches on Sundays! Do you call that a Christian act to compel my little children to go so far to a school that is made in purpose for them. My children don't dress like other Chinese. They look just as phunny amongst them as Chinese dress

---

156. Cohen, 137.
157. McCunn, 42.
158. McCunn, 42.
159. "Chinese School."
160. Cohen, 68.
161. J. Yung, 49, 49; and McCunn, 42, 45.
162. J. Yung, 49.

in Chinese look amongst you Caucasians. Besides, if I had any wish to send them to a chinese [sic] school I could have sent them two years ago without going to all this trouble. You have expended a lot of the Public money foolishly, all because of a one poor little Child. Her playmates is all Caucasians ever since she could toddle around. If she is good enough to play with them! Then is she not good enough to be in the same room and studie with them? You had better come and see for yourselves. See if the Tape's is not same as other Caucasians, except in features. It seems no matter how a Chinese may live and dress so long as you know they Chinese. Then they are hated as one. There is not any right or justice for them.

You have seen my husband and child. You told him it wasn't Mamie Tape you object to. If it was not Mamie Tape you object to, then why didn't you let her attend the school nearest her house! Instead of first making one pretense. Then another pretense of some kind to keep her out! It seems to me Mr. Moulder has a grudge against this Eight-year-old Mamie Tape. I know they is no other child I mean Chinese child! care to go to your public Chinese school. May you Mr. Moulder, never be persecuted like the way you have persecuted little Mamie Tape. Mamie Tape will never attend any of the Chinese schools of your making! Never!!! I will let the world see sir What justice there is When it is govern by the Race prejudice men! Just because she is of the Chinese descend, not because she don't dress like you because she does. Just because she is descended of Chinese parents I guess she is more of a American then a good many of you that is going to prewent her being Educated.[163]

Here, Tape's claim that Mamie acts and dresses like her Caucasian friend substantiates the exceptional minority stereotype of assimilation even as she attempts to fight against Chinese exclusion. Specifically, here she problematically frames her rights in white supremacist rhetoric to appeal to liberals as Ozawa, Thind, and Lum did in *Ozawa v. US* (1922), *Thind v. U.S.* (1923), and *Gong Lum v. Rice* (1927). Critic Ian F. Haney López writes that the Ozawa and Thind cases "established the significance of physical features on two levels. On the most obvious one, they established in stark terms the denotation and connotation of being non-White versus that of being White. To be the former meant one was unfit for naturalization, while to be the latter defined one as suited for citizenship."[164] Recognizing this liberal dichotomy, Tape plays on the language of white supremacy in order to win her case. She also appeals

---

163. Tape. Mistakes in original.
164. Haney López, 15–16.

to the nineteenth-century model minority stereotype to contradict the yellow peril racism of Superintendent Andrew Jackson Moulder, who "was a die-
hard racist who long vowed 'to resist, to defeat, and to prohibit' the admission
of 'African, Chinese, and Diggers [Miwok Indians] into our schools,'" while
the principal Jennie Hurley was a Canadian immigrant.[165] This letter to the
San Francisco Board of Education establishes Tape's voice as one of the earliest Chinese American activists in the nineteenth century. Although she was
likely disparaged for it at the time, her dialect, as recorded in this letter, demonstrates her insistence on her Americanness and citizenship in spite of her
"Chineseness" or nation of origin. In her letter, acknowledging her historical
moment of widespread anti-Chinese violence and driving-out, Tape states the
Chinese "are hated as one."[166] Her righteous rage against "Race prejudice men"
in this letter and her claim to humanity, especially as a woman advocating for
her daughter's education—"May you Mr. Moulder, never be persecuted the
way you have persecuted little Mamie Tape"—qualify her as a protofeminist.[167]
Yung makes the proviso that "as an outspoken woman able to stand up for her
rights, Mary Tape was a rarity among Chinese women in nineteenth-century
San Francisco."[168] And yet, her letter was not acknowledged by the board,
which never responded to her.[169] Although Tape initially refused to send
Mamie to the segregated Chinese school, she eventually had no other choice
but to send Mamie and her son Frank there.[170] In addition to "foretelling the
'separate-but-equal' doctrine of 1896's *Plessy v. Ferguson*," the January 1885
Tape v. Hurley ruling catalyzed the rise in hate crimes against Chinese Americans in the weeks that followed.[171] Like Ah Toy, Tape effectively lost her court
case, but her appeal to the US judiciary system demonstrated her belief in
democracy even if it did not legally apply to Chinese Americans. Tape's feats in
activism were dimmed by violence: the contemporary anti-Chinese violence of
the driving-out era "threatened Joseph's business in the immigration trade and
the Tapes' hope that they could assimilate into white, middle-class society."[172]
Moreover, the lack of historical attention paid to her case, as opposed to *Plessy
v. Ferguson*, suggests that it was dismissed by the exceptional minority discourse. Although she deployed it for political ends, the exceptional minority

---

165. Ngai, 49–50.
166. Tape.
167. Tape.
168. Tape.
169. Low, 71.
170. McCunn, 45.
171. Pfaelzer, 76, 133.
172. Ngai, 49.

discourse, which suggests that Chinese Americans assimilate to and hyperbolically thrive in the white status quo, dismisses the activism that established US citizenship and cultural integration for Asian Americans.

That Tape remains largely unknown in American history implies her erasure by the exceptional minority discourse even though ironically she deployed it for activism. Raised by missionary women who were no doubt influenced by the Victorian discourse of female moral authority, Tape appeared to be an assimilated Victorian woman, which perpetuated her appearance as the exceptional minority rather than an activist. One journalist wrote of her assimilated children: "All attend American schools, and take a keen interest in the arts and sciences as their parents. The girls are expert bird stuffers, embroiderers and photograph colorers, and the boys all have taste for higher mechanics, construction and practical sciences."[173] In 1892, when journalist Leland Gamble visited the Tapes to find out more about a mysterious self-taught Chinese woman photographer, he remarked of their Victorian home: "I then had a chance to look around me, and found that everything in the room bore the unmistakable signs of refinement that had nothing to make any one believe it the home of a Chinese family."[174] By the Progressive Era, Tape had clearly fallen prey to the culture of diluting her radical politics in favor of "consumerism" and liberal reform.[175] Even though he enfranchised Tape through representation, as a liberal Gamble declined to mention anything about the California Supreme Court case that involved the family just seven years earlier and placed her under the male gaze, under which all Victorian women arguably fell, in his depiction of her:

> Mrs. Tape whom I took to be about 35 years old, was dressed in a gown of soft clinging silk or some Indian stuff which set off her figure to good effect. Her hair was arranged in the latest American fashion and was as black and glossy as ever graced the head of Andalusian beauty. [. . .] Her face was comely, one might even say pretty, because it had so much intelligence and was set off by a fine mouth, behind which were a set of pearly teeth that showed whenever she laughed.[176]

He comments on her exceptional femininity—"her figure to good effect"—and notably westernizes her as an "Andalusian beauty" in order to justify his

---

173. "Our Chinese Edison."
174. Gamble, 12.
175. Cohen writes, "Historians seem to have accepted that the death of politics by consumption was a progressive era phenomenon and that consumerism inevitably generates political apathy" (256).
176. Gamble, 12.

perception of her "comely, one might even say pretty" appearance. However, he also comments on her "intelligence," which he reinforces by recording that her English, in which she was "well-versed," was spoken in "a refined accent."[177] One may speculate that like Toy, who was a voluntary prostitute, Tape enjoyed the negotiated power of looking back at her viewers while being under the gaze. However, without referring to the court case, Gamble distinctly writes that she did not enjoy being under the public's microscope during the trial, for she did "not wish to get any newspaper fame" and only accepted the interview to "be of interest to your readers to hear about my studies in photography I shall only be to [sic] happy to tell about it, and also about myself and how I came to take it up."[178] Rejected by the public school system, Tape made every effort to demonstrate that she was deserving of participating in the US democratic system. She was accommodating—"happy to tell about [her photography]" to Gamble's readers—and also a skilled musician, artist, and telegrapher who was versed in the Morse system.[179] In fact, she was such an accomplished photographer that her work was shown in the Mechanics Institute in San Francisco.[180]

Although her accomplishments smack of the exceptional minority stereotype, she concluded the interview insisting on her Americanness when asked by Gamble whether she and her family would return to China:

> We may some day if we feel that we can afford the trip, but it will only be as tourists visiting a foreign country. California is our home. All of our best and happiest moments have been passed here, and here we shall live and die.[181]

Gamble undermined Tape by staging her according to the exceptional minority stereotype in his interview, but as a liberal he nevertheless documents Tape's rejection of her "forever foreignness" as an Asian in the US; that is, she insisted on her Chinese American activism and cultural nationalism a century before the Civil Rights era. Mary Tape died on October 9, 1934, in Berkeley, California.[182] Later, Mamie Tape Lowe, when testifying on behalf of her sister Gertrude Tape Chan's status as a US citizen so she could return after traveling abroad, revealed that her mother had so assimilated that she never revealed to Mamie her Chinese name; moreover, neither Mamie nor her siblings knew

---

177. Gamble, 12.

178. Gamble, 12.

179. Gamble, 12.

180. Palma You, Gallery Coordinator, Chinese Historical Society of America, San Francisco, California.

181. Gamble, 12.

182. Gertrude Chan, Immigration Papers, San Francisco National Archives.

Chinese.[183] Mamie followed in Mary's footsteps in feminist activism on behalf of involuntary Chinese prostitutes: she befriended and became involved with the efforts of Wu Teen Fook, the assistant and interpreter of the famous Protestant rescue missionary Donaldina Cameron.[184]

CHINESE AMERICAN WOMEN'S VOICES FOR DISPLAY

As liberals, Gamble and Duane represented Tape and Toy, respectively, and delivered them from a subaltern existence even though they, in many ways, reinforced the exceptionalizing discourse of ornamentalism, which culminated in and was promulgated by the Page Act. This discourse also violently forced Chinese women into Manichean social positions as *whores* or *Madonnas*—that is, as prostitutes or Victorian housewives. Although Toy and her spectacularizing court cases preceded the Page Act, the exceptional discourse of the threatening hypersexuality and hyperfemininity of Chinese American prostitutes and the discourse of "yellow slavery" circulated in US society since the arrival of Chinese women and led to the 1875 law. The rhetoric and consequent treatment of all Chinese women as prostitutes resulted in social deaths of police brutality and isolated but spectacularized and stigmatized deaths from venereal disease. In this way the Page Act reproduced, for Chinese women, the same exceptionalizing discourse of the 1870s and 1880s that drove out Chinese men in West Coast cities. The exceptional, yellow peril / model minority stereotype contributed to the hyper-exoticization, sexual fetishism, and hyperfemininity of Chinese American women, which Toy endured even publicly in court. In considering all Chinese American women to be prostitutes, the Page Act placed their sexuality on public display and perpetuated the exceptionalizing rhetoric of Chinese Americans during the 1870s and 1880s. In a period in which Chinese American women did not have a public voice or presence in early feminism or suffragism, Toy and Tape were forced to abide by the discourse of Chinese American exceptional hypersexuality and prostitution, which existed before but was promulgated by the Page Act, and put themselves on display in order to establish a public voice for Chinese American women. In this way, the liberal discourse of exceptionalism aided them in promoting their radical politics of inclusion but undermined their work as simply part and parcel of liberalism. For example, as Myers argues, Emerson's notion of self-reliance, to which both Toy and Tape devoted themselves, was a cornerstone of nineteenth-century US liberalism.[185]

183. Gertrude Chan, Immigration Papers, San Francisco National Archives.
184. Ngai, 85–87.
185. Myers, 147.

Toy and Tape reclaimed the discourse of Chinese exceptionalism and put themselves in the public eye to gain traction for their activism and to mirror and expose the symmetrical exceptionalism of sovereign liberalism, which often found itself exempt from its own laws of freedom and equality. And yet, their efforts were often simply absorbed by the contradictions and ubiquity of nineteenth-century US liberalism. However, their court activism did succeed in critiquing the liberal tenet of laissez-faire, which shifted across the nineteenth century, from conservatism to liberal reform:[186] Skowronek writes, "consider the idea of laissez faire: at the start of the 19th century, it implied the liberation of individual entrepreneurship; by the end, it had become a defense of overweening corporate power."[187] While some Progressives pronounced "the death of laissez faire" in the 1890s,[188] Toy and Tape critiqued the lack of centralized government power and regulation of equal rights of all people that laissez-faire espoused before the Progressive Era and thus predicted its demise.

Although radicals at various points in their lives, Toy and Tape were also inspired by and emerged from the contradictory liberal, Victorian rhetoric of female moral authority; however, their influence by this movement also limited them to be either a sex worker or a housewife, and also challenged and reaffirmed patriarchy and white supremacy: this ideology disparately led to suffragism and the Protestant mission homes for Chinese prostitutes. Although the two Victorian reform movements seemed to be mutually exclusive, both empowered and were discursively shored up by Tape's Chinese American activism and advocacy of her daughter Mamie's education and racial integration. However, Tape's activism has often been subsumed by her embodiment as the exceptional minority—an assimilated Victorian woman, as Leland Gamble depicted her. As a consensual Chinese American sex worker, Toy was radically empowered by and contributed to the democracy of suffragism and its platform of free love. The hypersexual and hyperfeminine exceptional minority promoted Toy's business as a prostitute and madam, whereas the yellow peril stereotype ended it when she was arrested several times for running brothels. Although both Toy and Tape ultimately lost their court cases, their establishment of Chinese American woman voices was a feat in the nineteenth century and the closest they came to partaking in a democracy that was not meant for them.

---

186. Hofstadter, 141–42.
187. Skowronek, 388.
188. Cohen, 176.

CHAPTER 2

Wong Chin Foo

The Excessive Making and
Remaking of a Heathen Protofeminist

RECOVERING WONG CHIN FOO

Like Toy and Tape, Wong Chin Foo enfleshed himself and other Chinese Americans by writing and speaking autobiographically during the exceptionalizing driving-out era of the 1870s and 1880s. His 1885 letter to President Grover Cleveland, thanking him for intervening in the lynchings and driving-out of Chinese Americans, demonstrates that he was well aware of and motivated in his writing by what was happening to his fellow Chinese Americans.[1] However, Wong Chin Foo's prolific but ultimately unrecognized writing career suggests that the exceptional minority stereotype, particularly in the nineteenth century, so objectified Chinese Americans that even when Wong Chin Foo's deployment of the stereotype attempted to mirror and expose the sovereign liberal contradictions of racial (in)equality, liberals did not receive it as such. Like Toy and Tape, his radical efforts both reflected and were, in the end, absorbed by Gilded Age and Progressive Era liberalism. In this chapter, I specifically argue that the enfleshed "excess" of Wong Chin Foo's prolific output as a writer and editor diametrically reflects what theorist Georges Bataille claims

---

1. Letter from Yuet Sing, Wo Kee, Kwong Hing Lung, Tom Lee, Li Kwong Jin, Wong Chin Foo, Dock Hai, Quong Chin Cean and thirty others to President Grover Cleveland, November 10, 1885, Grover Cleveland Papers, Library of Congress, Washington, DC.

is the excess of death[2] in general but also the excessive deaths of the Chinese American driving-out era. In summing up Bataille's work on the excess of death, theorist Jean Baudrillard writes, "Death as excess, always already there, proves that life is only defective when death has taken it hostage, that life only exists in bursts and in exchanges with death, if it is not condemned to the discontinuity of value and therefore to absolute deficit."[3] Instead of letting death, specifically the mass deaths of the driving-out era, take his life hostage, Wong Chin Foo enfleshes his life by initiating excessive "bursts" of productivity that "exist[ ] [. . .] in exchange(s) with [excessive] death." Baudrillard goes on to state, "In Bataille, then, there is a vision of death as a principle of excess and anti-economy. Hence the metaphor of luxury and the luxurious character of death. Only sumptuous and useless expenditure has meaning; the economy has no meaning, it is only a residue that has been made into the law of life, whereas wealth lies in the luxurious exchange of death."[4] In mirroring and fighting against death, Wong Chin Foo's enfleshed, autobiographical, and activist work is so prolific that it is "luxurious" and anti-economical in more ways than one; that is, he found himself exhausted by his efforts and often lost money on his investment in newspapers. Elaborating on Bataille's work, Mbembe claims that Bataille establishes a correlation between the "excess" or the "*absolute expenditure*" of death and sovereignty: "Bataille firmly anchors death in the realm of *absolute expenditure* (the other characteristic of sovereignty)."[5] By opposing through enfleshed reflection the excess or absolute expenditure of death, Wong Chin Foo critiques and correlates death with unfree or racially unequal liberalism, the sovereignty he experiences in his life. On the other hand, he associates life and his own excessive enfleshment with liberals like William Lloyd Garrison Jr. who espouse freedom and racial equality. Bataille's editor Allan Stoekl writes that it is possible that "*absolute expenditure*" could be associated with both life and death: "Bataille here confronts as a kind of 'impasse' the 'last question of man.' Is the community a means to the end of free expenditure, or is this expenditure a means to the end of a stable community?"[6] Likewise, Bataille underscores two principle "human impulses": appropriation (eating or taking in) and excretion (of bodily fluids), which is tied to and foretells the "*absolute expenditure*" of death: "production can be seen as the excretory phase of a process of appropriation."[7] Mirroring

---

2. Bataille, 94.
3. Baudrillard, 140.
4. Baudrillard, 140–41.
5. Mbembe, 15, 15.
6. Bataille, xxii.
7. Bataille, 94, 95.

and refusing *absolute expenditure* or death as a homo sacer,[8] Wong's radically enfleshed productivity protested the driving-out era, memorialized the victims, and attested to but was ultimately absorbed by the pervasiveness of a contradictory liberalism in the Gilded Age and the Progressive Era.

We see the conundrum of his efforts over and against his reception in his constant, performative enfleshment of autobiographically writing himself during the pervasive driving-out era which perpetually objectified and exceptionalized Chinese Americans; we also see it in the ways in which newspapers continually reintroduce him as a yellow peril heathen and his later reclamation of heathenism in his 1887 essay, "Why Am I a Heathen?" and in the *New York Times* article, "Wong Chin Foo's Troubles," in which he is quoted as saying "I paid [. . .] more than 50 cents per pound of this heathen flesh, so that it is valuable" when he is forced to pay a tax to enter Canada from the United States.[9] At other times, he, like Toy and Tape, deploys and performs the exceptional minority stereotype to advance his career. His constant enfleshment, or autobiographical writing and activism, although an attempt to get away from the assimilationist exceptional minority stereotype, is nevertheless absorbed by and substantiates the stereotype. The seeming assimilation of the exceptional minority erases the memory of his enfleshed autobiographical history and hard work, and thus, as Wong demonstrates in his work, his critique of death-bound and life-giving, unfree and free, and racially unequal and equal liberalism was overtaken by liberalism's contradictions.

Despite the minimizing reception of his prolific work, Wong Chin Foo was a nineteenth-century civil rights activist who is credited with founding the term "Chinese American"; in 1883 he published New York's first Chinese newspaper bearing the same name,[10] during a period in which Chinese Americans were legally excluded in the United States. During the driving-out era, Wong Chin Foo published the one essay by which he is known today: "Why Am I a Heathen?" It was published by the *North American Review* and was not recovered until Judy Yung, Him Mark Lai, and Gordon Chang republished it in *Chinese American Voices* in 2003 and Southgate Books republished it in 2019 as *A Heathen in New York: Why Americans Should Embrace Confucius,* just seven years after Ying Xu devoted a chapter to Wong Chin Foo in her dissertation, six years after Scott Seligman revitalized scholarly interest in him with his biography, *The First Chinese American: The Remarkable Life of Wong Chin Foo,* and one year after Beth Lew-Williams wrote her historiography of the driving-out period, *The Chinese Must Go.* In his civil rights activism, Wong

---

8. Agamben, 99.
9. "Wong Chin Foo's Troubles."
10. Seligman, xxiii.

Chin Foo published over fifty ethnographic essays and five major magazine and newspaper articles, and he founded and edited three Chinese American newspapers. Despite his prolific output, fewer Asian American literary critics have paid attention to Wong Chin Foo as a Chinese American writer and activist than they have to Yan Phou Lee and Yung Wing, whom I discuss in the chapters to follow. Critic Ying Xu has suggested that it is because the latter wrote monographs whereas Wong did not.[11] During his life, however, he was well known at various points: he lectured in the United States in such circuits that included known liberal writers and activists as William Lloyd Garrison Jr., Mark Twain, Booker T. Washington, Frederick Douglass, Ralph Waldo Emerson, and Arthur Conan Doyle; he also crossed paths with prominent figures such as China's first provisional president, Dr. Sun Yat-sen, in 1896.[12] In his claim to literary fame, he was also represented by Major James B. Pond, a manager who also worked with many of the aforementioned African American civil rights activists and other literary figures, including Doyle.[13] Given that Wong Chin Foo was, at times, a known figure in the United States, why is it that the names of these others have endured in history and Wong Chin Foo's has not? In addition to liberalism's absorption of his radicalism, I argue that the poor endurance of his reception was because Wong Chin Foo was a difficult figure to place: assimilating to American culture by cutting off his long, braided queue and wearing American clothes, he nevertheless insisted on his unconventional heathenism in the US and demonstrated his protofeminism by defending women's rights in the United States and China. He was a radical in a liberal reformist era. But at other times, he embraced the exceptional minority stereotype to advance his career. Moreover, the archive of his writing is scattered and difficult to recover.[14] Civil rights–era activists such as Frank Chin and Elaine Kim[15] went to pains to dismiss early Chinese American literary figures such as Yung Wing and Yan Phou Lee as assimilationist, Christian autobiographers. Wong Chin Foo did not fit that description and was not even mentioned by these first Asian American literary anthologists. His diminished reception by literary critics during his lifetime and since demonstrates that he was either difficult to place or otherwise relegated to being an exceptional minority figure. The diminishment of his achievements, *naturalized* by his race, works in concert with the exceptional minority stereotype. Racialized as an exceptional

---

11. Xu, 34.

12. Seligman, xxv, 244, 254, 259.

13. Seligman, 153.

14. For example, only two editions of his first newspaper, the *Chinese American,* have been recovered (Seligman, 95).

15. Chin et al., *Aiiieeeee!,* xxvii; Chin et al., *Big Aiiieeeee!,* xii, 8; and E. Kim, 25.

minority competitive producer or "machine,"[16] Wong Chin Foo's career demonstrates that his radical, prolific efforts to enflesh or autobiographically represent himself and other Chinese Americans were undermined by the ubiquity of liberal reform in the late nineteenth-century US; and although some liberals helped him in his political efforts during the driving-out era, others constantly threatened to render him a spectacular, exceptional object.

PLAYING THE PART OF THE YELLOW PERIL

Although Wong Chin Foo constantly enfleshed himself through autobiographical writing and activism and embraced his American citizenship in cutting off his queue and wearing American clothes, he rejected the assimilationism of the exceptional minority stereotype by embracing heathenism. His activism also countered the submissive silence of the exceptional minority stereotype: fueled by his anger at the 1892 Geary Act, a federal injunction whereby Chinese were forced to register with the possibility of imprisonment and deportation for being undocumented immigrants, he began the Chinese Equal Rights League; the league mainly aimed to get the Geary Act repealed. Seligman speculates that he probably authored the *Appeal of the Chinese Equal Rights League to the People of the United States for Equality of Manhood,* published by the Chinese Equal Rights League in 1892.[17] Despite all his activism and achievements, Wong Chin Foo died in relative obscurity at the age of fifty-one in 1898 when he returned to China for a family reunion with his son.[18] As if he could predict the obscurity of his death, he continually worked to enflesh and remake himself as an activist, author, and editor—the excess of which diametrically reflected and confronted the excess of death during the driving-out era. He later published the *New York Chinese Weekly News* in 1888 and the *Illustrated Chinese Weekly News* in 1893. The *Illustrated Chinese Weekly News* was also known as the *Chinese American,* the same name as the first newspaper he began in 1883. Like Wong Chin Foo himself, his newspapers were constantly remaking themselves. He writes of his venture in starting the *Chinese American:* "it brought in three hundred dollars cash, and one thousand dollars in notes, bills receivable, and promises."[19] Moreover, the first issue received many criticisms from Americans and Chinese, alike; Wong writes:

---

16. Hayot, 103, 104, 122.
17. Seligman, xxiv.
18. Seligman, 286.
19. Wong Chin Foo, "Wail of Wong Chin Foo."

The American E.C.s were contradictory in substance, but unanimous in their drift. [. . .] The editor, they said, was a Chinese gentleman with more money than brains. He was also a myth and a joke. He was also a Jesuit, a Buddhist missionary, and an Imperial emissary in disguise. Then came the Chinese E.C.s. My native tongue, as I wrote it, was uncouth, illiterate, unintelligent, vapid, hollow, fantastic, bombastic and idiotic. I was a wretch who was endeavoring to ruin the Flowery Kingdom in the eyes of Christendom; I was a renegade, an apostle, and the victim of American gold.[20]

Wong's humor and sarcasm are of note as he internalizes his criticisms—"I was . . ." And yet, his humor also suggests that he was accustomed to criticism and the continual process of having to remake himself to pass muster in American society. Confronting the exceptional minority stereotype and the cultural amnesia toward Chinese American history and labor that it assumes, Wong had to constantly layer one of achievement on top of the other to enflesh himself in his career. In 1883 he published the *Chinese American,* the first Chinese newspaper in New York.[21] Although the paper did not last a year,[22] he started another Chinese newspaper, the *New York Chinese Weekly News* five years later. Seligman writes that the "final publication date" of the *Chinese Weekly News* "is not clear, but it does not seem to have lasted very long."[23] Five years after, in 1893, Wong started yet another newspaper, the *Illustrated Chinese Weekly News,* which was also known as the *Chinese American,* but this time in Chicago, "with the goal of 'Americanizing' local Chinese."[24] His use of the name *Chinese American* twice also suggests that, to some extent, he was aware of his repetitive efforts to remake himself and the Chinese American community. Although each of his newspaper ventures were short-lived and did not earn him much of a salary, he was still able to enflesh, and raise awareness of, the victimized Chinese American community and sought to "Americanize" the Chinese in the US through these publications during the driving-out era.[25]

In addition to his publications, Wong Chin Foo's reputation as a public figure ebbed and flowed in the thirty years he lived in the States. For instance, in 1873 the *San Francisco Chronicle* wrote a profile on Wong Chin Foo titled "A Remarkable Chinaman," which was republished by the *Buffalo Daily Courier*

---

20. Wong Chin Foo, "Wail of Wong Chin Foo."
21. Seligman, xxiii.
22. Seligman, 99.
23. Seligman, 175.
24. Seligman, xxv.
25. Seligman, 125, xxv.

and the *Hartford Courant* the same year.[26] However, several months later the *Courant* ran another article on Wong which "restyled" him as a "'swindling' Chinaman."[27] Even though he was becoming known by the press as a popular Chinese American figure, he also faced racial discrimination on a regular basis: he got into a violent fight over donning his queue in Reading, Pennsylvania, for which he was arrested in 1875; later that year, a landlord in Wilkes-Barre refused to rent to him because he was a "coolie."[28] Perpetuating the social amnesia that the homo sacer, exceptional minority stereotype entails, the press continually reintroduced him as a stranger without a preceding reputation. For example, the *New York Times* covered the attempts made on Wong's life three times in 1883, 1884, and 1885 with the same, uninventive title, "Wong Chin Foo Assaulted." In 1883 he was introduced professionally as "Wong Chin Foo, the editor of the *Chinese-American,* who is better known in literary circles as Ah Wong."[29] In 1884 the journalist introduced him as an unknown: "A little Chinaman, with a bright, intelligent face, bustled into the Tombs yesterday afternoon, and, with a perfect English accent, told Justice Smith that he had been assaulted and asked for a warrant."[30] Finally, in 1885 the journalist acknowledged him professionally again: "Wong Chin Foo, the editor, had quite an exciting adventure here last evening."[31] As exemplified here in tone, the journalists dehumanized him by making light of the attempts on his life in each story. By 1888, however, Wong Chin Foo seemed to need no more introduction in the *New York Times*: in a story entitled "Wong Chin Foo in Danger," the journalist simply writes: "Wong Chin Foo, in the Essex Market Police Court yesterday, asked Justice Patterson for a warrant for the arrest of Lee Sing, another Chinaman, whom he charges with assaulting him."[32] The *New York Times,* in 1893, described him as an important "representative" of "the Chinese Government."[33] In 1895 Wong again needed no introduction in a *New York Times* article, "Wong Chin Foo Wants a Job." Even as he established his reputation, he was perpetually associated with his ancient Chinese culture rather than with being a Chinese American: papers often referred to him as "a Chinese aristocrat" and "a Mandarin of bluest Celestial blood."[34] At the same time, he contributed to his association with an ethnographic past when

---

26. Seligman, 309, 49.
27. Seligman, 50.
28. Seligman, 66.
29. "Wong Chin Foo Assaulted," June 10, 1883.
30. "Wong Chin Foo Assaulted," July 15, 1884.
31. "Wong Chin Foo Assaulted," May 21, 1885.
32. "Wong Chin Foo in Danger," May 7, 1888.
33. "Plea for the Chinese."
34. Xu, 135.

he reported his plans to the *New York Times* in 1884 to produce two tragedies that would be "a picture of the Oriental civilization of 3,000 years ago." The same article also caricatures him as an over-the-top figure: "Mr. Wong Chin Foo, ex-lecturer on Confucius and ex-editor for the *Chinese American,* sat tilted back in his chair against his writing-table, in his apartments on the first floor—from the roof—at No. 443 Pearl-street, yesterday afternoon, and discoursed upon his latest project."[35] Again, the journalist describes him as an objectified fixture—"sat tilted back in his chair against his writing-table" and a caricature as he "discoursed upon his latest project." Another example in which he is associated with a non-coeval past is in 1877, when the *New York Times* ran an article entitled "The Buddhist Religion," which described him as a representative of Buddhism and dubbed him the spectacular, ethnographic "attraction of the evening." The journalist nevertheless denigrates him as the yellow peril and forever foreigner—"not unlike that of the ordinary Chinaman" with "some difficulty in conveying certain ideas in clear and unambiguous language."[36] Conversely, other stories praised Wong Chin Foo for his exceptional minority "perfect English."[37] Thus, the exceptional minority stereotype worked for and against him—the model minority stereotype that initially brought him to fame ultimately denounced him as the yellow peril, or at least the forever foreigner. That is to say, even though China's minister to the US, Zheng Zaoru, relied on the submissive, model minority stereotype to further Chinese diplomacy, citing that "only eight [Chinese in New York] had been convicted of crimes during the previous decade [in the 1870s], and that not one had been guilty of intoxication, disorderly conduct, burglary, or highway robbery,"[38] Wong Chin Foo exposed the stereotype as a myth that did not, in fact, aid Chinese Americans during the age of legal exclusion.

AMBIVALENT APPEALS TO THE EXCEPTIONAL MINORITY

As a self-proclaimed "heathen" in favor of performing the model minority's binary, the yellow peril, Wong Chin Foo revealed but also perpetuated the exceptional minority myth in his first English-language article, "The Chinese in Cuba," in the *New York Times* in 1874. Liberal reformers welcomed Wong Chin Foo's narrative, in "The Chinese in Cuba," of the US as a refuge for Chinese coolies that countered the stark racism in being stereotyped as the yellow

---

35. Wong Chin Foo, "Plans of a Chinese Manager."
36. "Buddhist Religion."
37. "Plea for the Chinese."
38. Seligman, 120.

peril in Cuba. He used this *New York Times* article to speak out against "the continual instances brought under my notice of the helpless condition of my own countrymen in foreign lands[, which] fill my heart with grief."[39] Describing his fellow countrymen as "helpless" also perpetuates the stereotype of the hyperbolically submissive exceptional minority. Although such foreign lands include the United States, his editorial criticized the unjust Tartar rulers of China. This focus undoubtedly supported the US and the liberal reformers who published him. It is not a coincidence that Wong Chin Foo published the article just three years after the Los Angeles Massacre of 1871. As I mentioned in this book's introduction, the Los Angeles Massacre in which eighteen Chinese men and women were lynched occurred after Chinese Americans put on an assimilative American wedding, which offended the white Americans in Los Angeles by threatening white supremacy through mimicry.[40] While liberals viewed them as the diseased yellow peril, a misperception which was fueled by discourse in the aftermath of the 1868 smallpox epidemic in San Francisco, they also persecuted the Chinese for their model minority industriousness as cheap labor and submission in nonretaliation. In short, as homo sacer, Chinese Americans were driven out for being the exceptional minority—both the hyperbolically submissive, economically efficient model minority and the diseased and competitive yellow peril. While Chinese Americans distinguished themselves as "free" labor, some African Americans in Los Angeles made specious distinctions between the "pagan foreigners" and themselves based on their own American citizenship, military service, and Christian faith.[41] The Chinese in California, and in the United States more broadly, were discursively labeled as a diseased, "heathen" menace to a society that threatened the American working class by providing cheap labor.[42] The mass lynching of the seventeen Chinese men and one Chinese woman suggests that their discursive subjectification as the exceptional minority—model minority "cheap labor" and yellow peril invasions—reduced them to disposable objects.

In line with Zesch's claim about white Los Angeles residents fearing association with the lynch mob, I argue that the liberal reformers of the *New York Times* published Wong Chin Foo in order to distinguish themselves from disgraceful liberal, white supremacists such as those who made the news in the Massacre of 1871 and others who participated in the anti-Chinese hate crimes of the driving-out era. After the massacre, the County Coroner Joseph Kurtz

---

39. Wong Chin Foo, "Chinese in Cuba."
40. J. Yung, 22.
41. Zesch, 99.
42. Zesch, 143.

ordered an investigation of the murders.[43] Two weeks after Kurtz's inquest, the county court judge, Ygnacio Sepúlveda, organized a special grand jury to investigate and try the members of the lynch mob.[44] Of the twenty-seven people who had warrants out for their arrest,[45] only ten men were tried, and none were sentenced for the crime of murder.[46] Seven of the ten men tried were given sentences of three to six years at San Quentin State Prison.[47] Sam Yuen, the Chinese organization Nin Yung's leader, was tried for the death of a white man, Robert Thompson, during the massacre but was later discharged.[48] When L. F. "Curly" Crenshaw was tried for the manslaughter of Gene Tong, he was found guilty but only as an accessory to murder, which resulted in a three-year sentence at San Quentin.[49] Zesch states that the verdict of Crenshaw's guilt "was also a huge relief to nearly everyone but Curly Crenshaw, for it meant that Los Angeles would be spared from further denigration in the national press the next day."[50] While the lynching of eighteen Chinese people suggested their discursive objectification as disposable bodies would secure white supremacy, the racial superlative of whiteness embodied by the lynch mob needed to be quickly renounced by liberals; for, it exposed, too, the objectification of white supremacy ("the lynch mob"), when, in fact, the white Americans of the lynch mob and the lynched Chinese Americans were equally human. In other words, liberals had to disavow the lateral objectification of whiteness by the lynch mob. In his discussion of the sacrifice of the sacred, Agamben writes of sovereign violence, which preserves social sovereignty such as liberal, white supremacy: "The violence exercised in the state of exception clearly neither preserves nor simply posits law, but rather conserves it in suspending it and posits it in excepting itself from it."[51] That is, liberal reform in the US needed to "except itself" from the lynch mob of the Massacre of 1871 in order to conserve its nevertheless sovereign violence and preserve the state. According to Wynter, such is the origin "storytelling" that shapes and gives birth to the liberal homo oeconomicus:[52] the "Word" of the storytelling "charters" the liberal homo oeconomicus "*referent-we*" and thus the pervasive discourse of liberalism, which encompassed both liberal reform and white

---

43. Zesch, 166.
44. Zesch, 178.
45. Zesch, 184.
46. Zesch, 200.
47. Zesch, 200–201.
48. Zesch, 206.
49. Zesch, 196, 201.
50. Zesch, 195.
51. Agamben, 64.
52. McKittrick, 68.

supremacy during the nineteenth century exceptionalized Chinese men as diseased, cheap labor while also differently exceptionalizing Chinese women as prostitutes as discussed in the previous chapter.[53] Perpetuating the exceptional minority discourse, Wong Chin Foo's article detailed the violent enslaved sufferings of a Cuban coolie, Chun Young Hing, who escaped to the United States as a place of refuge. Thus, in a paradoxical turn of fate, the Massacre of 1871 made possible Wong Chin Foo's publication in the *New York Times*.

Wong Chin Foo's biographer likewise alludes to the connection between his opportunities for publication and the driving-out era. Seligman contextualizes his career amid the driving-out era, which included the Rock Springs Massacre in which President Cleveland had to defend the Chinese.[54] Wong Chin Foo was also well aware of the anti-Asian violence of the driving-out era: when Cleveland sent troops to quell the continued anti-Chinese riots in Seattle and Tacoma on November 7, 1885, Wong Chin Foo and other Chinese American merchants wrote Cleveland, by Wong Chin Foo's dictation, a letter of gratitude:

> To His Excellency
> The Honourable
> Grover Cleveland
> President of the United States of America
>
> At a meeting of the Chinese merchants of the City of New York held November 10, 1885 the following resolutions were unanimously adopted:
> After many outrages have been committed upon our fellow countrymen in lawless districts by desperate, ignorant and wicked men, it gives us, the Chinese merchants of New York, great and unspeakable pleasure to learn that the President of the United States and the American people has [*sic*] issued an official proclamation to protect our people, address the wrongs done to the injured, punish the malefactors and prevent by his great power a repetition of the actions which have caused so much suffering and death.
> We desire to express our gratitude and to thank the President for his righteous course, his courage, and love of justice.
> We assure him that he has increased our admiration and veneration for his fearlessness and wisdom and our respect and obedience to all of his laws.
> We also assure him respectfully that our countrymen in the United States endeavor to be good, peaceful, honest and law-abiding citizens and that they are always anxious and eager to obey and enforce his laws and so

---

53. McKittrick, 72.
54. Seligman, 170.

promote that prosperity and peace which are as dear to them as to the great offices and writers of his land.

We instruct our scribes to interpret this into English and to send it with all expressions of our esteem and veneration to his Excellency the President.

Given at our hall in New York the fifth day of the Ninth Moon of the Eleventh Year of the Reign of Zuang Suuey.

Signed   Yuet Sing
          Wo Kee
          Kwong Hing Lung
          Tom Lee
          Li Kwong Jin
          Wong Chin Foo
          Dock Hai
          Quong Chin Cean
          and thirty others

Wong Chin Foo
Secretary[55]

Wong et al. acknowledge and refer to the driving-out era as the "many outrages [that] have been committed upon our fellow countrymen in lawless districts by desperate, ignorant and wicked men" as they express their appreciation and respect for the actions taken by the "venerable" President Cleveland. In their letter, they side with the binary exceptional stereotype of the model minority to prevent the Chinese from being viewed as the yellow peril, citing the Chinese as "good, peaceful, honest and law-abiding citizens [. . .] always anxious and eager to obey and enforce his laws and so promote [. . .] prosperity and peace." While it must be admitted here, such insistence perpetuates the yellow peril stereotype—the potential to be lawless criminals—in his other writings, Wong Chin Foo strove to enflesh or humanize Chinese Americans apart from the stereotype of exceptionalism even as he deployed it to publicize his activism. His awareness of and response to the driving-out era was also demonstrated by one of his fiercest critics, who went by the initials WMF, and who wrote to the *New York Times Tribune,* denying his claim in "Why Am I a Heathen?" that American Christians had been involved in the Rock Springs Massacre.[56]

---

55. Letter from Yuet Sing et al. to President Grover Cleveland.
56. Seligman, 141.

Wong Chin Foo's Chinese American activism, which both deploys and opposes the exceptional minority stereotype, is recorded many times in the newspapers. In the *New York Times* article "The Chinamen Organizing," Wong is quoted as railing against the 1882 Exclusion Act:

> FELLOW COUNTRYMEN: I congratulate you heartily on this sudden movement on your part to obtain representation and recognition in American politics. We are a small drop in the mighty ocean of American politics, but small and insignificant as we are, I feel certain that had we only attended to this duty as citizens of this country we might have prevented the passage of the shameful Anti-Chinese bill by the Republican Congress led by that arch-Republican politician, Mr. Blaine. [Applause and hisses.] For you must remember that the politician who lords it over you to-day is an arrant coward, and trims his sails to every breeze that blows. When you don't vote and don't wish to vote he denounces you as a reptile: the moment you appear at the ballot box you are a man and a brother and are treated (if you consort with such people) to cigars, whiskies, and beers. Why can't we make our marks in politics as well as any of our brother races? Why can't we become good and substantial citizens like those from England, Ireland, Germany, and other European and Asiatic and even African countries? We had our diplomats, nay, philosophers and sages, when those about us were half-naked savages, and they are yet but in their infancy in point of true civilization compared with the peaceful, industrious, and conscientious sons of the Middle Kingdom.[57]

Here he questions why Chinese Americans cannot assimilate like white Europeans, other Asiatics, and Africans and participate in politics. The cultural amnesia, or the belief that Chinese Americans are exceptional objects without history, particularly with respect to their hard work and the historical establishment of Chinese Americans in the US, which the exceptional minority stereotype assumes, was and continues to be, in part, to blame for the historical lack of representation of Chinese American people in US politics. Moreover, he answers his own question by pointing out the politicians like Blaine dehumanize Chinese Americans by considering them "reptiles." In a statement of pride, he reverses the association of China with the past by calling American politicians or "those about us" "half-naked savages" compared with the progress of "the peaceful, industrious, and conscientious sons of the Middle Kingdom." And yet, his positive, passive language in describing Chinese Americans only substantiates the exceptional minority stereotype.

---

57. "Chinamen Organizing."

He uses the exceptional minority rhetoric in his protest of the 1892 Geary Act in his 1897 *Chicago Daily Tribune* piece, "Wong Chin Foo Protests against Class Legislation." In this article, although he associates Chinese with the submissive, model minority—"an obedient race"—he distinguishes between the Chinese and the "Americanized Chinese" who are "cosmopolitan in nature." By cosmopolitan, he means activist since they acknowledge the driving-out of Chinese Americans on "the Pacific slope, and they have dared to rise up against it." He goes on to say of the Geary Act that it is "unconstitutional, cruel, oppressive, unmanly, and unjust." Wong Chin Foo clarifies that he does not advocate for undocumented, mass immigration of Chinese; instead, "We only appeal for those of our countrymen who by long years of residence and by birth become Americans in fact. Their families, their property, their social and financial interests are all here, and by reason of their practices as Americans it has made their residence in China impossible. Therefore, they have no other place they can legally call their home."[58] Even though he exposed and protested against the exceptional minority stereotype, he also deploys the stereotype for his own political ends in keeping his radical demands centrist, modest, and demure by appealing only for the Chinese Americans who have established themselves in the States.

On the other hand, Wong Chin Foo resented the Democratic Party for perpetuating the exceptional minority stereotype in generally not acknowledging the need to support Chinese Americans during legal exclusion. By the 1890s, shortly before his death, the *Chicago Daily Tribune* published an article entitled "Chinese in a New Role: Wong Chin Foo Intends to Found a New Political Party," which covered his efforts to found a new political party amid the failures of the Democratic Party. The article states, "He came to Chicago last week hoping for an opportunity to address the Democratic convention. Disappointment in both cases drove him to the conclusion that a new party was an absolute necessity." In this article, it is clear that he blames the Republicans for Chinese exclusion and the Democrats for their fiscal irresponsibility.[59] Although very different movements, both Democratic Populism and Progressivism in the 1890s demonstrated their contradictory liberalism by promoting women's suffrage and supporting democratic reform of "a monopoly-controlled society by rallying for anti-immigration laws directed specifically at Chinese immigrant laborers."[60] Even as Wong Chin Foo criticizes all three parties—the Republicans, the Democrats, and the Greenbackers—for neglecting Chinese American rights, he nevertheless discriminates against "even the blackest people under the sun" for being "granted" the

58. "Wong Chin Foo Protests against Class Legislation."
59. "Chinamen Organizing."
60. Clark, *Asian American Avant-Garde*, 39.

"privilege" of "citizenship" while the Chinese are not.[61] His offensive discrimination responds to the ways in which white Americans perceived African Americans as socially superior to Chinese Americans, but only during the Gilded Age when African American men were given the right to vote in 1870 while the Chinese were barred (1875) and excluded from citizenship (1882). Hofstadter writes of the Gilded Age that "the most serious of abuses" was that the Gilded Age liberal "resolutely ignored or accepted complacency as an inevitable result of the struggle for existence or the improvidence and laziness of the masses."[62] Exasperated by the Democratic Party for not advocating for the Chinese in the age of legal exclusion, Wong Chin Foo also promoted assimilation and willingness to "speak[ ] only for the Chinese who have cut off their queues, adopted the national dress and language, and have made America their home for good, for themselves and their children."[63] Wong Chin Foo, who cut off his queue in 1881, knew well that cutting off one's queue was considered treason against the Qing Chinese government and was punishable by death.[64] And yet, he so identified himself with being a "Chinese American" that he defied the laws of his nation of origin with great risk to his person. His exceptional assimilation in appearance and ideologies—apart from continuing to identify as a heathen—often perpetuated the exceptional minority stereotype, which in part explains the rise and fall of his reputation and his obscurity at his death and thereafter.

His exceptionalism and popularity also led to numerous threats on his life by Chinese who resented both his popularity and his deployment of Chinese American exceptionalism—a stereotype that was equally damning during the driving-out era and useful for political activism. Just a few days after the *MacGregor* affair, in which he was credited for rescuing Chinese sex slaves,[65] "Wong was visiting Wolfe's Shoe Factory on Market Street, ostensibly to help secure a foreman's position for a friend. But as soon as the Chinese shoemakers learned who he was, the *San Francisco Bulletin* reported, 'they set upon him in a mob, throwing shoes, bottles and everything they could lay their hands upon at him.' He was hurled halfway down a staircase, and he ultimately pressed assault and battery charges against three of his assailants."[66] Wong's American liberal beliefs in sexual freedom caused him to become the target of unassimilated Chinese Americans who perhaps resented the exceptionalism

61. Clark, *Asian American Avant-Garde*, 39.
62. Hofstadter, 142.
63. "Chinese in a New Role."
64. Seligman, xxiii, 272.
65. "Heathen Missionary."
66. Seligman, 41–42.

of Chinese hypersexuality that had led to the Page Act. Another attempt on his life was made in 1880 by Chinese who severely injured his head when they attacked him with hatchets and razors. Another man named Chan Pond Tipp attempted to murder Wong Chin Foo in 1883 after Wong defended another man named Lee by testifying that the latter had not extorted money from gambling houses. After going to the police seeking a warrant for Chan's arrest, Wong Chin Foo used the *Chinese American* to document his charges against him, a retributive act, which resulted in Chan suing Wong for libel.[67] Tragically, for his efforts to assimilate, which were hardly reciprocated by his new society, he continued to face threats on his life by other Chinese Americans who disagreed with his exceptional attempts at Americanization.

Despite his own tribulations in assimilating as a Chinese American, Wong Chin Foo, like Toy, continued to seek social justice by going to the police for protection and relying on the court system. The court system was one of the few ways in which democracy—being heard as a minority—was palpable, particularly during the period of reform in both the Gilded Age and the Progressive Era.[68] In 1885 he served as an interpreter and associate counsel for a man named Chuen Yin, a Montreal laundryman who was denied payment by three brothers by the last name Fong.[69] Wong Chin Foo, who also studied law during this time, was prepared for this case. After Chuen won his suit, another unsuccessful attempt was made on Wong Chin Foo's life—this time by the Fong brothers.[70] Chuen's witness Sing Lee was murdered in New York during the trial, and Wong Chin Foo also helped the police find the killer.[71] In the same year, he again served as an interpreter in St. Louis for another murder trial in which six Chinese gangsters were accused of murdering another Chinese police informant. The court convicted the defendant and Wong Chin Foo's efforts prevailed. Despite the Chinese homo sacer, bare-life enforcing ruling of *People v. Hall* (1854), Wong Chin Foo's efforts in exercising enfleshed faculties of speech and argumentation during these two murder trials in 1885 serve as a sharp rebuke to such bare-life rulings. In 1893 he came to Chicago to serve as a secondary lawyer for Wong Aloy, a Chinese student who was beaten by Moy clan members.[72] Wong Chin Foo once again faced attempts on his life for doing so.[73] He later wrote, "My journalistic career culminated recently

---

67. Seligman, 84, 104, 107.
68. Cohen, 227.
69. Seligman, 129.
70. Seligman, 129.
71. Seligman, 130.
72. Seligman 224.
73. Seligman, 225.

in the Supreme Court. I had, with the best intentions in the world, allowed an article to appear in my sheet which 'showed up' a certain individual in a moderately sensational way."[74] His biographer speculates that his involvement in these trials were forms of "publicity" or "good vehicle[s] for furthering his legal education."[75] His constant attempts to enflesh and remake himself in the face of the cultural amnesia, or the politics of forgetting racial others, which were fostered by the exceptionalizing minority stereotype, were unfortunately chalked up to the same stereotype and the liberalism that relied on it.

In addition to his three newspapers and four major articles, his publication of fifty ethnographic articles between 1883 and 1886 perpetuated the economic efficiency of the exceptional minority: such articles included "Fashions in China," "The Chinese Stage," "Infant Burial in China," "Chinese Monasteries," and "Silk Making in China."[76] In his 1883 article "Fashions in China," for *Harper's Bazaar*, he writes,

> The Chinese have also their fashionable societies, their belles, and their dudes, almost as civilized as you Americans are, only their fashions, their belles, and their duties last longer than on this side of the mighty water. Their fashions of dressing, especially among the ladies, are well known not only to the narratives, but to nearly every civilized nation in the world, owing to their longevity.

He argues that Chinese fashions, though "almost as civilized as you Americans are," are superior insofar as they "last longer than on this side of the mighty water" and are "known [. . .] to nearly every civilized nation in the world." The "longevity" of Chinese fashion that is "antiquated in their style," however, perpetuates the association of China with the non-coeval past. For example, he begins his short story "Po Yuin Ko, the Serpent Princess" with ethnography: "Then the Middle Kingdom, released from all hideous and avenging divinities, whose watchful jealousy determines human fate, enjoys a vacation from the reign of the gods. Festivities continue for a month. Pastries, lined with nuts and sweetmeats, are the common diet."[77] Wong's career flourished through these articles and pieces of fiction because he was accepted as a representative of an ancient culture. He also published articles in the same popular magazines and journals in which some of the first Asian American fiction writers in the twentieth century such as Sui Sin Far and Carlos Bulosan would later

74. Wong Chin Foo, "Wail of Wong Chin Foo."
75. Seligman, 131.
76. Seligman, 131.
77. Wong Chin Foo, "Poh Yuin Ko, the Serpent Princess," 181.

publish: *Youth's Companion, Harper's, The Independent,* the *Atlantic Monthly, Frank Leslie's,* and *Puck.*[78]

Another one of Wong Chin Foo's claims to fame was his debate with the California labor leader and "sand-lot orator" Denis Kearney, publicized by the *Boston Globe* and the *New York World* and documented by several papers, including the *Chicago Tribune.* On July 12, 1896, the *Chicago Tribune* described Kearney and Wong Chin Foo in the following ways:

> As they faced each other the contrast was striking. Denis is about 5 feet 9 inches high, broad-shouldered, deep-chested, and muscular, with a broad, round head set solidly on a thick, brawny neck. His little ears bulge out over wads of thick cervical muscles and his grayish-blue eyes peep out above his chubby cheeks the color of ripe cherries. His hands are broad and thick and his fingers stubby. His short-cut brown hair and bristly little red mustache highten [sic] the pugnacious aspect created by his broad, low forehead, slightly turned-up nose, wide mouth, and square chin.
>
> Wong is about five feet two inches high, slender and agile as a greyhound. His features are distinctively Mongolian and his hands long and slender. He seemed what a sporting man would call a little fine; that is, there wasn't an ounce of superfluous flesh on his slender frame, and his black eyes were snappy and sparkling. He wears his hair cut short in the American fashion, and his little figure was covered with a black suit whose leading feature was a modish frock-coat.[79]

Painting Kearney as "bristly and pugnacious," and Wong Chin Foo as "agile as a greyhound," the liberal journalist of the *Chicago Tribune* clearly favored Wong in the debate. Seligman writes, "The *Chicago Tribune* used the word 'broad' four times in its depiction of Kearney and 'slender' three times in describing Wong. At five feet nine inches, Kearney was not a tall man, but he had more than half a foot on Wong. The *Tribune* made him sound positively Neanderthal." Although Wong "bested" Kearney in the debate, the discourse of white hegemonic masculinity—"he had more than half a foot on Wong"— favored Kearney.[80] Moreover, as Kearney was losing the debate, he resorted to calling Wong Chin Foo the yellow peril: "Then he launched out into a torrid description of the big Chinese procession he saw in San Francisco, where thousands of men marched behind a 'fat greasy Joss,' to whom they offered

---

78. Seligman, 97, 132, 135, 160, 228, 132–33.
79. "Wong Chin Foo and Denis."
80. Seligman, 150, 151.

'baked snails, roast rats, cats, dogs, and diseased pork.'"[81] As I mentioned ear-lier, even though Wong Chin Foo perpetuated the exceptional minority ste-reotype by Americanizing his dress, cutting off his queue, which he deemed a "'badge of submission' imposed by the Manchus,"[82] and donning Western clothing, he was still scapegoated as the heathen yellow peril since he was not willing to assimilate by converting to Christianity; nor did he, as a protofemi-nist, make it a point to prove his masculinity in his writing.

WONG'S PROTOFEMINISM

Like Toy and Tape, Wong Chin Foo was a radical protofeminist during a period in which Chinese American women were legally hypersexualized by the Page Act and excluded from suffragism. Fighting the excess of death, particularly during the driving-out era, with the excess of life in his writing, he was also the most prolific writer and editor of the five Chinese American figures whom I discuss in this book. As he toured the country in the 1870s, giving talks about Chinese culture, he explained and adamantly opposed the crippling Chinese female custom of footbinding.[83] Moreover, he helped to res-cue eight enslaved Chinese prostitutes who came to San Francisco on the SS *MacGregor* in 1873. In a letter to the chief of police, he wrote, "the girls say they will brave it out this time, and tell the truth before the Court and before their mistresses that they were brought here against their wish."[84] Although Reverend Dr. Otis Gibson, whom Tape had met at the Ladies' Relief Society, provided a mission in which the eight Chinese women could find refuge, the *San Francisco Chronicle* "credited Wong with the rescue of the eight girls."[85] He also later helped rescue an unconsenting sex slave named Suen Yee, in 1890.[86] After his rescue of the *MacGregor* women and before he helped Suen Yee, Wong also had a brief affair with a white American prostitute named Irene Martin.[87] The *Democrat* documented his affair with her in a hotel in Rochester, New York, and reported that Irene stated, "Chinee or not Chinee, Wong Chin Foo was a gentleman and she loved him."[88] The *Democrat* further

---

81. "Wong Chin Foo and Denis," 26.
82. Seligman, 87, 272.
83. Seligman, 23.
84. Seligman, 40.
85. Seligman, 41.
86. Seligman, xxiv.
87. Seligman, 46.
88. Seligman, 47.

predicted that "cavorting with a prostitute—still more a married mother of two—would seriously handicap Wong Chin Foo's career as a lecturer 'of great piety' if it became widely known,"[89] but his biographer concludes that "it never did."[90] His relationship with Irene Martin also suggests his modernity, similar to Ah Toy, in normalizing sex work. Although he had a wife in China whom he assumed to be dead,[91] he, like Toy, believed in free love: he later pursued a relationship with Ida May, a Circassian woman, who was unhappily married to an Irishman named Tommy Holahan.[92]

In his writing, he envisioned gender and sexual equality. In his article "The Family in China and America," he writes that in China, men and women divide child-rearing equally: "In China, whether the head of the house follow Confucius, Buddha, or Lao-Tze, the family training is every-where the same. Father and mother are tied to their children in every way. It is their duty to clothe, nourish, and educate them, as it is here. [. . .] Father and mother co-operate in attending to their child. They feed and dress it, carry and nurse, eat, and drink, sleep, and play with it."[93] Rather than claiming that only women are subject to child-rearing, he uses plural pronouns "they" and "their." However, he does make a proviso about gender politics in China:

> Woman in China does not enjoy the privileges accorded her sex in this land. She is carefully educated and trained, but only for one object—to be a good house-wife, mother, and companion. Woman's Rights, as such, are unknown in the Celestial Kingdom. At ten or twelve years of age she is engaged by her parents, and shortly after is married and delivered over to her husband. Nor must it be supposed that this education converts a woman into a mere beast of burden. [. . .] One third of the silk and similar products of China come from the hands of wives and mothers. So a large part of the fruits, fine vegetables, dried foods, clothing, and art work are the outcomes of their industry. In literatures woman has produced poems, tales, essays, dramas, and scientific writings that are still classic. In medicine she discovered burned bamboo-shoots (corresponding to the *carbo vegetalis* of American drugstores) and the phosphoric lizard (corresponding to the American phosphites and hypophosphites).[94]

---

89. Seligman, 48.
90. Seligman, 48.
91. Seligman, 261.
92. Seligman, 161.
93. Wong Chin Foo, "Family in China and America."
94. Wong Chin Foo, "Family in China and America."

He acknowledges the social limits to the domestic sphere placed on women in China and suggests that "larger liberty and a wider education would be of benefit" to them.[95] However, his enumeration of all the work women have done suggests that they should be given equal rights and social standing to men. His protofeminism, as a male ally, supports my argument from the previous chapter that the narrative of early US feminism is unfinished in its exclusion of early Chinese American feminists.

Wong Chin Foo also demonstrates his protofeminism in his articles and fiction. For example, in his 1884 article "A Celestial Belle" in *Harper's Bazaar*, he writes:

> A celestial belle's most striking marks, however, are not moral. Her movements, restive yet restrained, must give evidence of a great deal of suppressed animation. As speech with the male sex is of course forbidden her, her features, eyes, cheeks, and silent lips must all be eloquent. Her skin must have great firmness of texture to endure the continual coats of white paste and vermilion paint which the laws of her being enjoin. Her feet must not exceed three inches in length, or one inch in breadth. The finger-nails of her last three fingers must be as long as their fingers.[96]

Comparing the Celestial belle to a "novelist,"[97] Wong Chin Foo implies that gender is a social construction, or at least a fiction. He begins his description of the celestial belle as "not moral," seeming to give in to the stereotype of Chinese female hypersexuality during the driving-out era. And yet, in the next turn of the phrase, he describes her movements as "restrained" and her "speech with the male sex" as "forbidden." Xu writes, "Wong revises the myth of the Chinese woman, making her unattainable rather than 'sexually available,' a stereotype of the Asian women perpetuated in nineteenth-century American society."[98] In her analysis of the short story "Poh Yuin Ko, the Serpent Princess," which Xu attributes to Wong Chin Foo,[99] published in *Cosmopolitan* in 1888, she argues that the story in which a serpent spirit deceives her husband, "the good Whey Goon,"[100] by pretending to be a woman and having sons with him, "represents the Chinese Other, that is, the stereotypical 'contaminating' Chinese woman, whose seduction of American men and

---

95. Wong Chin Foo, "Family in China and America."
96. Wong Chin Foo, "Celestial Belle," 475.
97. Wong Chin Foo, "Celestial Belle," 475.
98. Xu, 153.
99. Xu, 154.
100. Wong Chin Foo, "Poh Yuin Ko, the Serpent Princess," 190.

disturbance of the American family structure are already illustrated in popular racist cartoons and exclusionist narratives."[101] While I certainly agree with Xu, the argument is nuanced by the sympathetic portrait of Poh Yuin Ko, on the discovery of her true essence: she is blamed for her husband's death from fright and her own son, who does not recognize her as a serpent, cuts off her tail. The short story concludes, "And ever since, when the memory of her lost tail torments her, she thrashes about in the mountain, and her tortures cause the waters of the Great Yellow River rising there to overflow and drown the people of Soo Chow."[102] Her own torment and torture is what inadvertently causes harm to others. Wong Chin Foo's sympathy for women's social oppression appears in other fiction. In 1889 he translated *Wu Chih Tien, the Celestial Empress: A Chinese Historical Novel* in *Cosmopolitan,* in which the Chinese emperor Tung Ko Sung chooses a fifth wife, the priestess Wu Chih Tien, to bear him an heir. Although Wu Chih Tien eventually becomes a villain who poisons her own son to frame Tung Ko Sung's first wife, Wong's translation notes her very human transition from virtue to villainy: "Wu Chih Tien was the mildest and most beautiful of all; but when she found her vows annulled, and that she was the favorite of the emperor, then ambition entered her heart and all her nature became changed."[103] Moreover, although Wu Chih Tien is vilified, the heroine of the story is Tung Ko Sung's first wife, Wong Tai Ho: when Wu Chih Tien gives birth to Tung's son, "the empress, Wong Tai Ho, was very fond of children, and she rejoiced to think that even though this little one were not her own, now she could bear the title of 'Tai Ho,' or royal mother, which she so much desired."[104] When she is framed for the murder of Wu Chih Tien's son, Wong Tai Ho gives birth to a son in prison whom she wisely marks with a stamp so that he could be identified as the emperor's son as he escaped from Wu Chih Tien's assassination attempt. Wong Chin Foo describes the wisdom of another mother in his "The Story of San Tzon," about a Buddha figure whose parents are taken captive on a boat by a murderer when his mother gives birth to him: "She rose up with the child and, having first wounded his left foot that she might identify him in coming years, wrapped him in warm robes and launched him in a little boat on the great waters of the Yang-Tsz."[105] Although she painfully marks him, like Wong Tai Ho does her son, it is to mark him with a privileged identity. Wong Chin Foo's sympathetic portrayal of women and his tribute to their wisdom demonstrate his

---

101. Xu, 156.
102. Wong Chin Foo, "Poh Yuin Ko, the Serpent Princess" 190.
103. Wong Chin Foo, "Poh Yuin Ko, the Serpent Princess" 330.
104. Wong Chin Foo, "Poh Yuin Ko, the Serpent Princess" 330.
105. Wong Chin Foo, "Story of San Tzon," 258.

dedication to protofeminism. His protofeminism and insistence on his heathenism countered the stereotype of the assimilative and submissive exceptional minority.

THE DAMAGE OF THE EXCEPTIONAL MINORITY

Raised by Christian missionaries who brought him to the United States, Wong
Chin Foo was baptized when he was twenty years old but excommunicated
from the Shanghai Baptist Church;[106] by 1873 he began to lecture in the US and
"declare[d] himself China's first Confucian missionary to the United States."[107]
He grew to resent American Christianity and turned to heathenism later in his
adult years. In "Why Am I a Heathen?" he writes of the hypocrisy of Christianity and the forthrightness of heathenism: "Do unto others as you wish they
would do unto you' or 'Love your neighbor as yourself,' is the great Divine law
which Christians and heathen alike hold, but which the Christians ignore."
He goes on to give examples of Christian hypocrisy: "If we do anything chari-
table, we do not advertise it like the Christian, nor do we suppress knowledge
of the meritorious acts of others, to humor our vanity or gratify our spleen."
"On the whole, the Christian way strikes us as decidedly an unnatural one; it
is every one for himself—parents and children even."[108] Two years earlier, he
wrote, "What is lacking, then, in an American family? First, obedience to its
head; second, affection toward both father and mother; third, love among its
members."[109] Here, love, he concludes, is what is surprisingly missing from the
American Christian family even though love is a central tenet of Christianity.

Also in contrast to popular thought, he holds in "Why Am I a Heathen?"
that "we heathen are a God-fearing race." As a heathen, however, he cannot
understand the Christian forgiveness of the worst of sins: "It was not just, and
God is Justice." He gives an example of such an antinomian injustice by imagining that he will see the Christian Denis Kearney, "the California sand-lotter,"
in heaven, where he "should slip in and meet me there, would he not be likely
to forget his heavenly songs, and howl once more: 'The Chinese must go!' and
organize a heavenly crusade to have me out and others immediately cast out
into the other place?" Moreover, he criticized domestic abuse against women
among Christians: "We do not embrace our wives before our neighbor's eyes,
and abuse them in the privacy of home. If we wish to fool our neighbors at all

---

106. Lum, 172.
107. Wong Chin Foo, "Why Am I a Heathen?," 51.
108. Wong Chin Foo, "Why Am I a Heathen?," 12, 6, 11.
109. "Wong Chin Foo Protests against Class Legislation."

about our domestic affairs we would rather reverse the exhibition—let them think we disliked our wife, while love at home would be the warmer."[110] For Wong Chin Foo, Christianity condoned racism and sexism.

As was the case for his other protofeminist compatriots, Toy and Tape, Wong Chin Foo arrived in the United States after the Gold Rush of 1849: he arrived in 1867, a year before Tape arrived, and thirty years after Toy immigrated. He accompanied Sallie Holmes, the widow of Southern Baptist Reverend J. Landrum Holmes, with her sick son from China to the US and thereafter began to study at Columbian College Preparatory School, the forerunner of George Washington University in Washington, DC.[111] Two years after his arrival, he continued his studies at Lewisburg Academy, the predecessor of Bucknell University in Lewisburg, Pennsylvania.[112] He returned to China in 1870 and thereafter married a woman named Liu Yushan, who was also a former pupil in the Baptist school in Dengzhou. Their son Wong Foo Sheng was born in 1873. The same year, he returned to the United States to rescue the *MacGregor* girls and continued on to a cross-country lecture tour during which he was given US citizenship in Grand Rapids, Michigan. Despite his citizenship, he was denied a US passport in 1891.[113] His denial of a US passport evidences his own social death of sorts and the enduring xenophobia of the liberal reformist Progressive Era.[114]

During the Gilded Age, in 1887, five years after the Chinese Exclusion Act was passed, four years after the Rock Springs Massacre, and just a few years after the Chinese were also driven out of Tacoma, Seattle, Eureka, Arcata, and San Jose,[115] Wong Chin Foo published "Why Am I a Heathen?" Published in response to the driving-out era of Chinese Americans, his essay is an eloquent defense of Chinese Confucianism and "yellow-peril" heathenism, which differs from atheism and agnosticism. Dispelling common myths about heathenism, he points out that heathens actually believe in God:

> We heathen are a God-fearing race. Aye, we believe the whole Universe-creation—whatever exists and has existed—is of God and in God; that, figuratively, the thunder of His voice and the lightning His mighty hands; that everything we do and contemplate doing is seen and known by him; that He has created this and other worlds to effectuate beneficent, not merciless,

110. Wong Chin Foo, "Why Am I a Heathen?," 11, 3–4, 4, 8.
111. Seligman, 17.
112. Seligman, 20.
113. Seligman, xxiv.
114. Clark, *Asian American Avant-Garde*, 39; Cohen, 73–74; and Hofstadter, 8–9.
115. Lew-Williams, 1; Pfaelzer, 219; Lew-Williams, 103, 105, 106, 113, 114; and Pfaelzer, 192.

designs, and that all that He has done is for the steady, progressive benefit of the creatures whom He endowed with life and sensibility, and to whom as a consequence He owes and gives paternal care, and will give paternal compensation and justice; yet His voice will threaten and His mighty hand chastise those who deliberately disobey His sacred laws and their duty to their fellow man.[116]

Wong demonstrates his reverence for God by capitalizing "His" pronouns throughout the essay. Moreover, his argument that God "has created this and other worlds to effectuate beneficent . . . progressive benefit of the creatures whom he endowed with life and sensibility" refers to the driven-out Chinese Americans from the "other worlds" in the US. He thus opens up the possibility for radical otherness in American liberalism. The consequences of white Christian Americans for "disobey[ing] His sacred laws" and enacting such violence against "their fellow man" are, according to Wong Chin Foo, imminent, if not in life then in the afterlife. He questions their legitimacy as Christians and their election to heaven. Most distressed by the Christians who murdered and drove out Chinese Americans along the West Coast in the 1870s and 1880s, he writes,

> The more I read the Bible the more afraid I was to become a Christian. The idea of coming into a daily or hourly contact with cold-blooded murderers, cut-throats, and other human scourges, who had had but a few moments of repentance before roaming around heaven, was abhorrent.[117]

He references specifically the "cold-blooded murderers, cut-throats, and other human scourges" responsible for the violence against Chinese Americans. Chiding the Final Dispensation for allowing for last-minute repentance, he chooses to not let go of these seemingly unforgiveable sins. And yet, Wong constantly dilutes his language, attempting to win the favor of the liberals who were publishing him: for instance, instead of calling out Christian hypocrisy, he describes Christianity as "eccentric." Wong uses the public platform of his essay to acknowledge those who were driven out, without whom he would not have been published.

Facing the cultural amnesia that the exceptional minority stereotype effected in the nineteenth-century US, which catalyzed Wong's constant efforts to remake himself, he aligns himself with the ancient Chinese history

---

116. Wong Chin Foo, "Why Am I a Heathen?," 11–12.
117. Wong Chin Foo, "Why Am I a Heathen?," 4.

of heathenism, proclaiming that it existed centuries before Christianity: "The main element of all religion is the moral code controlling and regulating the relations and acts of individuals towards 'God, neighbor, and self;' and this intelligent 'heathenism' was taught thousands of years before Christianity existed or Jewry borrowed it. Heathenism has not lost or lessened it since."[118] Again, he counters the view that heathens are without God or religion. And yet, his self-legitimization through the ancient religion of heathenism only perpetuates his otherness:

> Born and raised a heathen, I learned and practiced its moral and religious code; and acting thereunder I was useful to myself and many others. My conscience was clear, and my hopes as to future life were undimmed by distracting doubt. But, when about seventeen, I was transferred to the midst of our showy Christian civilization, and at this impressible period of life Christianity presented itself to me at first under its most alluring aspects; kind Christian friends became particularly solicitous for my material and religious welfare, and I was only too willing to know the truth.[119]

Rejecting the hypocritical "showiness" of Christianity, Wong is "born and raised a heathen," and seems fine until Christianity intervenes. He also demonstrates that he cannot assimilate into American culture despite cutting off his queue and donning Western dress: he "was only too willing to know the truth." The truth of Christianity, he later discovered, was hypocrisy:

> Nor do we heathen believe in a machine way of doing good. If we find a man starving in the streets we do not wait until we find the Overseer of the Poor, nor for the unwinding of other civilized red tape before relieving the man's hunger. If a heathen sees a man fall from a tree-top, and seriously injure himself, he does not first run to a hospital for an ambulance, nor does the ambulance-man first want to know what precinct the injured man belongs to; but forthwith he is cared for and taken to the nearest shelter for other needed treatment, and when the danger is over then red tape may come in—the Christian machinery. [. . .] If we do anything charitable, we do not advertise it like the Christian, nor do we suppress knowledge of the meritorious acts of others, to humor our vanity or gratify our spleen. An instance of this was conspicuous during the Memphis yellow-fever epidemic a few years ago, and when the Chinese were virulently persecuted all over the

118. Wong Chin Foo, "Why Am I a Heathen?," 1.
119. Wong Chin Foo, "Why Am I a Heathen?," 1.

United States. Chinese merchants in China donated $40,000 at that time to the relief of plague-stricken Memphis, but the Christians quietly swallowed the sweet morsel without even a "thank you." But they did advertise it, heavily and strongly, all over the world, when they paid $137,000 to the Chinese Government as petty compensation for the massacre of 23 Chinamen by civilized American Christians, and for robbing these and other poor heathen of their earthly possessions.[120]

His phrase "Christian machinery" reverses the exceptional minority stereotype of the Chinese as "machines." Heathens, on the other hand, do not "believe in a machine way of doing good." Instead, they move more naturally, without "red tape," to aid others with compassion and without "advertising" their charity. It is the Chinese, not Christians, who help other Chinese Americans. Conversely, the Christians took the credit or the "sweet morsel" of benefit for work that the heathens did. Moreover, here, he references the Rock Spring Massacre after which US Congress paid China $137,000 "to cover indemnities."[121] Wong Chin Foo rejects this "petty compensation" as well as Christian showiness, which masks the hypocrisy of the violence they do to their neighbors.

Despite its high cost, he refuses assimilation into "unnatural"[122] American Christianity since it inevitably involves such cultural "exhibition": he chooses to sincerely and "warmly" "love at home" rather than put on a show in public. Moreover, he points out his observations of Christian idolatry of money: "We heathen believe in the happiness of a common humanity, while the Christian's only practical belief appears to be moneymaking (golden-calf worshipping); and there is more money to be made by being 'in the swim' as a Christian than by being a heathen. Even a Christian preacher makes more money in one year than a heathen banker in two. I do not blame them for their moneymaking, but for their way of making it."[123] He applies Old Testament idolatry of "golden-calf worshipping" in describing contemporary Christian moneymaking. He faults Christians for their hypocritical emphasis on money rather than preaching and worshipping God. He refuses to distinguish between hypocritical Christians who took part in the driving-out era and other benevolent white Christians who supported Chinese Americans in the States. This refusal feeds his insistence on being a heathen—a subject position that would ultimately deny his assimilation and contribute to his obscurity as an early

120. Wong Chin Foo, "Why Am I a Heathen?," 6.
121. Yung, Lai, and Chang, 75.
122. Wong Chin Foo, "Why Am I a Heathen?," 11.
123. Wong Chin Foo, "Why Am I a Heathen?," 5.

Chinese American literary figure. Nevertheless, Wong insists on rejecting Christianity. As historian Kathryn Gin Lum points out, Wong "adopt[ed] the label of 'heathen' as a moniker of resistance against White Christianity"; moreover, "Wong used the notion of heathenism to promote rather than denigrate Confucianism."[124] From the beginning of the Gold Rush in 1849, American missionaries eagerly worked to convert the Chinese to Christianity. By the driving-out era of the 1870s, Chinese American Christianity bloomed because many Chinese Americans were inspired by the "egalitarianism of an abolitionist-inspired evangelicalism."[125] On the other hand, heathenism was linked to the stereotype of the yellow peril. Wong Chin Foo was one of the first to publicly reclaim "heathenism," which was unpopular during the nineteenth century, as a form of social egalitarianism. He deployed his discursive exceptionalism and the public platform of his essay "Why Am I a Heathen?" to acknowledge those who were driven out of West Coast cities without whom he might not have been published.

As a self-proclaimed heathen, he viewed himself as a heathen or "Confucian missionary":[126] "He offered a primer on his version of the five cardinal principles held by followers of Confucius—gravity, propriety, sincerity, virtue, and filial piety—speaking at length on each."[127] For this reason, he was spurned by Christian Evangelicals as being "heathen to the core."[128] Christian Evangelicals go on to state, "Mr. Wong Chin Foo is nobody's fool. He undertook to bluster and threaten with the law some of our editors for their exposure of his lying pretensions and heathen practices, but he wisely concluded to fly to a region where impostors do not seem to be at a discount."[129] Despite his rejection by the church, on numerous occasions, he compared Confucius to Christ insofar as their perspectives converge in Christ's second greatest commandment, to "Love your neighbor as yourself":[130] in his 1874 Boston speech, he stated, "the whole religion of Confucius was summed up in his Golden Rule, spoken more than 2,300 years ago: 'Do not unto others what you would not have others do unto you.'"[131] Also, as a Confucian missionary, he railed against white Christian persecution of Chinese Americans and African Americans alike. In his campaign against the Geary Act (1892), which forced

---

124. Lum, 197, 211.
125. Tseng, 5.
126. Wong Chin Foo, "Why Am I a Heathen?," 51.
127. Seligman, 58.
128. "Wong Chin Foo."
129. "Wong Chin Foo."
130. Matt. 22:39, New International Version.
131. Seligman, 59.

Chinese to register themselves to prove that they were legal aliens, Wong also received help from his close friend William Lloyd Garrison Jr., son of the famous abolitionist who had worked with Frederick Douglass for a period.[132] That Wong was against slavery of any kind is evident in his efforts to rescue the *MacGregor* women and Suen Yee earlier in his life. Inasmuch as he was against any type of slavery, Wong was also for the abolition of liberalism from its proslavery roots. The kind of universalism to which he subscribed was a counteruniversalism to liberal humanism—a universalism that was racially inclusive. In his 1892 *Appeal of the Chinese Equal Rights League to the People of the United States for Equality of Manhood,* he references the emancipation of slaves and the heroes of the Civil War in support against the Geary Act, which required documentation of Chinese Americans:

> We appeal to the human, liberty-loving sentiment of the American people, who are lovers of equal rights and even-handed justice, a people from whom sprung such illustrious characters as Washington, Jefferson, Clay, Sumner, lastly Lincoln, the citizen of the world, the friend of humanity, and the champion of freedom: such illustrious warriors as Sherman, Sheridan, Logan and Grant, whose deeds of valor in the cause of freedom are to be seen in the grand march of American development—a development which merits the emulation of the nations of the earth.[133]

Against the universal objectification of the lynched Chinese and the white lynch mobs during the driving-out era, Wong appeals to the "humanity" of the white American people and reminds them of the freedom they have just granted African Americans even as they restrict Asian American freedoms. And yet, of course, his efforts were in vain. Moreover, the 1875 congressional amendment to the 1790 Naturalization Act, which added "aliens of African nativity and to persons of African descent" to the exclusion of Asian Americans, drove him to lead the Chinese American activists Moy Yee, Moy Sam, and Moy Hong Kee to seek naturalization in 1881.[134]

Publishing "Why Am I a Heathen?" six years later, Wong Chin Foo was writing during a postbellum period in which African Americans were increasingly lynched and still discriminated against but also given de jure US

132. Seligman, 205.

133. Wong Chin Foo (attributed), *Appeal of the Chinese Equal Rights League to the People of the United States for Equality of Manhood,* New York: Chinese Equal Rights League, Garrison Family Papers, Sophia Smith Collection, Smith College, Northampton, MA, series VI, box 181, folder 11.

134. Seligman, 45, 86.

citizenship. By contrast, Chinese Americans, who were not subject to chattel slavery but considered to be "coolies" and thus too close to slaves in an emancipated nation,[135] were denied citizenship by liberals. Liberals considered Chinese Americans to be the exceptional minority and—unaware to them—their homo sacer in the nineteenth century. Chinese Americans were concurrently viewed as a yellow peril threat to white American labor.[136] For example, in his debate with Kearney, Kearney stated that naturalization "applies only to the Black man. It doesn't apply to the brown man at all."[137] In response to such a worldview, Wong appeals to liberals in 1897: "We do not believe that the American people at large desire to create a caste in this republic by making their fellowmen cringe and crawl before them; we do not believe any right-minded citizen will say that our demands are unfair, and we do not believe there is a man in this entire republic who will say that this cruel and outrageous law of the Pacific coast should not be repealed, or at least modified so as to vie the members of the Chinese Equal Rights League of America and all patriotic American residents the rights of franchise in the same way as it has been granted to the colored race."[138] Once again, he demonstrates that white Americans viewed Chinese Americans as socially inferior to African Americans, who were no longer enslaved and were permitted citizenship, even though both racial groups were continually lynched and driven out during this era. Here, he also trusts that while liberals want to create a casteless society and trusts them, as "patriotic Americans," to revoke Chinese exclusion.

THE PROBLEMS AND POSSIBILITIES OF LIBERALISM

Liberals aided in Wong Chin Foo's career, but not without their biases. As I mentioned, during the 1874–75 season, he worked with Boston's Redpath Lyceum Bureau. Shortly after and before he took on Pond as an agent, he changed agents and worked with Rev. William Henry Benade from Philadelphia. During this time, some of Benade's Swedenborgian New Church funds were under the auspices of Rev. J. P. Stuart. Benade asked Stuart's son, Lyman, to travel with Wong Chin Foo as he did his lecture tour in the Midwest in October of 1875. Wong Chin Foo conducted his first lecture on the Chinese and Chinese American life in Wyoming, Ohio: Lyman hoped to build up Wong Chin Foo's reputation slowly, but Wong was disappointed in the small

---

135. Lew-Williams, 132.

136. Lew-Williams, 119–20.

137. "Wong Chin Foo and Denis," 26.

138. "Wong Chin Foo Protests against Class Legislation."

crowds and demanded that he lecture in a larger city.[139] When Lyman followed through on Wong Chin Foo's "imperious" request and booked him a lecture at Indianapolis later on October 17, only fifty people showed up, and Wong Chin Foo, insulted by the small number, cancelled the lecture, and lost $75.[140] Lyman Stuart and Wong Chin Foo attempted to recover their losses in Richmond but did not make much headway, and thus Wong Chin Foo blamed Lyman for mishandling his lecture circuit. In a letter to Frank Ballou and others, on October 21, 1875, Wong writes, complaining of Lyman and Benade: "This is the last time I will ever have agents in America and am *satisfied.*"[141] Although the syntax does not clarify if he is satisfied with never having American agents again or if it is the last time he will be satisfied with having American agents, the context suggests the former.

The exchanges between Lyman Stuart, Benade, J. P. Stuart, and Frank Ballou, however, are revelatory of how poorly these liberals thought of Wong Chin Foo. From their letters, it is clear that Lyman Stuart, J. P. Stuart, and Benade blamed the Indianapolis debacle entirely on Wong Chin Foo's "imperiousness" and "pluckiness."[142] The Stuarts and Benade racialize him as a Chinese in associating him with imperial China. Although Rev. J. Nelson Smith, who called Wong "plucky," also exonerated him from blame—"The enterprise here has certainly turned disastrous, but by no fault of Wong"[143]—Lyman and J. P. Stuart hold him solely responsible in their letters. In his letter, Lyman first kindly introduces Wong Chin Foo and his distinct, "delightful" culture:

> We have, served up to us, at the hands of a "Genuine Chinese Mandarin," a most delightful dish of Chow Chow; or in boarding house parlance "Mystery" otherwise Hash. The difference however between the Chinese and the American dish is this: in the latter we know what we are getting, in the former we do not. Hence a plain statement of facts from me seems to be necessary.[144]

---

139. Seligman, 64.

140. Seligman, 64.

141. Letter from Wong Chin Foo and Rev. J. Nelson Smith to William Henry Benade, October 21, 1875, J. P. Stuart Papers, Academy of the New Church Archives, Bryn Athyn College, Bryn Athyn, PA.

142. Letter from J. Nelson Smith to W. H. Benade, October 21, 1875, J. P. Stuart Papers, Academy of the New Church Archives, Bryn Athyn College, Bryn Athyn, PA.

143. Letter from Wong Chin Foo and Rev. J. Nelson Smith to William Henry Benade, October 21, 1875.

144. Letter from Lyman Stuart to William Henry Benade, October 22, 1875, J. P. Stuart Papers, Academy of the New Church Archives, Bryn Athyn College, Bryn Athyn, PA.

Likening Chinese Chow and American Hash, Lyman seems to normalize cultural difference but nevertheless makes the proviso that "in the latter we know
we are getting, in the former we do not." For him, American culture is consistent and reliable, whereas Chinese culture, although a delight, is unreliable
and possibly a threat. Once again, the model minority stereotype devolves into
the yellow peril stereotype. Lyman writes:

> Mr. Wong failed in a few points:
> First, in his refusal to lecture to so small a house on Tuesday.
> Second—Failing to proceed to Richmond at the appointed time, as by
> this he would be able to advertise by his presence his lecture. Here I was at
> fault in losing my grip on him personally, Thursday night.
> *Third* in not returning to Indianapolis early Saturday—instead of late
> Saturday night.
> Fourth—in not doing as I requested him, as to his movements after his
> Sunday Lecture—but giving me entirely the slip—and undoing by his bun-
> gling, all that I had done towards the adjustment of our financial troubles.[145]

His father, J. P. Stuart, likewise blamed the "bungling" on Wong Chin Foo and
wrote to Ballou that the "financial defeat of the Wong Expedition at Indianapolis—is vexatious. [...] Wong half-way rebelled against the advice & an arrange-
ment of Lyman after the first Dial" and that he "bolted" from Lyman. Wong
Chin Foo's "rebellion" smacks of the yellow peril. However, Stuart concedes to
his talent, stating that "the failure was only financial—and with Indianapolis
full of spreeing soldiers was to be expected. The notices of Wong's Lecture
were every way favorable as you see from the inclosed [sic] slip."[146] However,
several days pass and in a letter dated a week after his initial one to Benade
and his father's to Ballou, Lyman's personal criticisms of Wong Chin Foo turn
into racial attacks: "I am very much disappointed at the result of the under-
taking, as well as mortified at being so thoroughly beaten by one so 'childlike and bland.'" Liberals often assigned the aforementioned depiction to the
exceptional minority stereotype of John Chinaman.[147] Lyman goes on to assign
Wong Chin Foo with yellow peril traits of criminality:

> He showed his want of principle as well as his heartless ingratitude by lend-
> ing himself to his new agents in *Villifying* [sic] me, and seeking thus W [sic]

---

145. Letter from Lyman Stuart to William Henry Benade, October 22, 1875.

146. Letter from J. P. Stuart to Frank Ballou, October 21, 1875, J. P. Stuart Papers, Academy
of the New Church Archives, Bryn Athyn College, Bryn Athyn, PA.

147. "Childlike and Bland."

glorifying himself, and also by deserting me at the very time that he should have taken hold with me . . . If so I have a pretty clear criminal case Against him—both for forgery & fraud.[148]

He continues to blame "Wong and the brace of unprincipled *dead beats* to whom he has attached himself" for the Indianapolis failure.[149] Both Lyman and J. P. Stuart refer to Wong Chin Foo as "the heathen"[150] and the infantilized "boy"[151] ten years before Wong reclaimed being a "heathen." Wong Chin Foo, later, makes an indirect retort to these insults in a letter to H. L. Slayton, the director of lectures and lyceums: "I have not given my consent to give by business to any Bureau as yet except to two or three private monopolists who will try this luck on the Heathen in Feb. / March which you see is more than Enough to demoralize any 'Heathen' to the so long traveling & living among the Savages—The Christians—for longer time than that I wont [*sic*] do it."[152] Here, he gets even with the white Christians who call him "heathen" by referring to them as "the Savages." The exchanges about Wong Chin Foo between Benade, Lyman Stuart, J. P. Stuart, and Frank Ballou reveal that although these liberals aided Wong in establishing his reputation, their personal criticisms of him slowly devolved into racial attacks when failures personally affected and cost them. Benade's, the Stuarts', and Ballou's attitudes toward Wong exemplify and expose the conservatism of the Gilded Age despite its initiation of reform.[153]

On the other hand, Wong Chin Foo's gracious and pleasant undated correspondence with Walter Hines Page, a journalist and the editor of the *Atlantic Monthly*, emphasizes the particularity of Benade's, the Stuarts', and Ballou's biases toward Wong. In his letter to Page, in which he thanks him for inviting him to lecture, he writes:

Dear Sir

I have just got back to town from a three week trip West. And found your esteemed favor of the 19th Just waiting [for] me[.] In reply I would say that I

---

148. Letter from Lyman Stuart to Frank Ballou, October 28, 1875.

149. Letter from Lyman Stuart to Frank Ballou, October 28, 1875.

150. Letter from Lyman Stuart to William Henry Benade, October 22, 1875; letter from J. P. Stuart to Frank Ballou, October 21, 1875.

151. Letter from J. P. Stuart to Frank Ballou, October 21, 1875.

152. Letter from Wong Chin Foo to H. L. Slayton, August 23, 1883, special collections, Magill Library, Haverford College, Haverford, PA.

153. Hofstadter, 3; and Cohen, 111, 137.

will be most happy to accept the great honor of speaking before the Distinguished Members of the 19th Club on March the 2nd.

Sorry I was not here to answer yours soon.

Humbly your obedient Servant
Wong Chin Foo
430 Pearl[154]

Self-deprecatingly referring to himself as "Humbly your obedient Servant," although a social and literary convention, nevertheless contrasts his personality with the "pluckiness" with which he was described in the Indianapolis incident. This contrast demonstrates both the racial biases of some Gilded Age liberals and the benevolence of others but also Wong Chin Foo's enfleshed humanity in his ability to be indignant, at times, and subdued, at others.

Wong Chin Foo was well aware of the concessions he would have to make to the racial biases of liberalism. The Geary Act was a product of the Progressive Era, which was "tinctured by conservatism" even though it is commonly known as the age of liberal reform.[155] In his *Appeal of the Chinese Equal Rights League to the People of the United States for Equality of Manhood,* he includes the speeches of Senator Sherman and Representative Hitt, who also opposed the Geary Act. In their speeches that decry the blatant legislated discrimination against the Chinese, however, Sherman states that the Chinese "must find the witnesses in different places where he may have worked or resided, and one witness must be a white man. Even colored men are not admitted as credible witnesses."[156] Likewise, Hitt reproduces the yellow peril rhetoric of Asian invasion when he states, "By a new and effective treaty we can stop all Chinese laborers coming, but we will not succeed in making treaties by breaking treaties." And yet, in their support of the Chinese, Sherman likens the Geary Act to recently outlawed African American slavery:

It is proposed to have 100,000 or, as some gentlemen assert, 200,000 men in our country ticketed, tagged, almost branded,—the old slavery days returned.

[. . .]

Never before was it applied by a free people to a human being with the exception (which we can never refer to with pride) of the sad days of slavery

154. Letter from Wong Chin Foo to Walter Hines Page, no date, call number bMS Am 1090 (788), Walter Hines Page Papers, Houghton Library, Harvard University, Cambridge, MA.

155. Hofstadter, 14.

156. Wong Chin Foo, *Appeal,* 7.

and the ticket-of-leave, and carry it around with them in a free country! Is that the treatment due to a great body of men to whom we have solemnly promised, in the treaty pledge of our national faith, that they shall have all the rights, immunities, and privileges of citizens and subjects of the most favored nation? The treaty by which we are bound says, in Art. 2, "Chinese laborers who are now in the United States shall be allowed to go and come of their own free will and accord, and shall be accorded all the rights, privileges, immunities, and exemptions which are accorded to the citizens and subjects of the most favored nation."

Here, Sherman likens Chinese exclusion to African American slavery: "tagging a man like a dog [. . .] the old slavery days returned [. . .] sad days of slavery and the ticket-of-leave." And yet, such a comparison becomes a slippery slope when Asian exclusionists use the parallel to their favor, arguing that Chinese coolies are un-American. Nevertheless, Wong finds agreement with Sherman and Hitt: in the main portion of his *Appeal,* he parrots Sherman's language:

We feel keenly the disgrace unjustly and maliciously heaped upon us by a cruel Congress. That for the purpose of prohibited Chinese immigration more than one hundred thousand honest and respectable Chinese residents should be made to wear the badge of disgrace as ticket-of-leave men in your penitentiaries; that they should be tagged and branded as a whole lot of cattle for the slaughter; that they should be seen upon your streets with tearful eyes and heavy hearts, objects of scorn and public ridicule. No! We do not believe it, that so great a people as the Americans would consent to so small a principle toward a mere handful of defenceless men.

Wong Chin Foo recalls that not so recently African Americans were "branded" as "cattle for the slaughter," begging the government "we love and admire" to not subject Chinese Americans to the same fate.[157] However, the invocation of postbellum ideologies of antislavery also worked in favor of Chinese exclusion since the Chinese were viewed as "coolie" slave labor.[158] For example, in Wong's debate with Kearney, Kearney argued for Chinese exclusion because he assumed the Chinese were slaves and did not belong in a postbellum US society: "It isn't the Chinese as a race I oppose, but their slavery system. I'm against them because they're brought here on contract"[159]—a widespread

---

157. Wong Chin Foo, *Appeal,* 8, 7, 7, 3, 3.
158. Lew-Williams, 132.
159. "Wong Chin Foo and Denis," 26.

misunderstanding of most Chinese laborers at the time. In the same main section of the *Appeal*, Wong Chin Foo calls the Geary Act "monstrous" and "inhuman," resonating with the driving-out era of the previous two decades. He clearly attempts to enflesh or humanize the long-objectified and exceptionalized Chinese Americans: "As residents of the United States we claim a common manhood with all other nationalities, and believe we should have that manhood recognized according to the principles of common humanity and American freedom. This monstrous and inhuman measure is a blot upon the civilization of the Western World, and is destined to retard the progress already made by the good people of this country in the East in art, science, commerce and religion."[160] A protofeminist who believed in women's rights but also perpetuated domesticating gender norms, he genders "common humanity" as "common manhood" to convince his liberal conservative and reformist audiences. Expressing his devotion to a country that rejects his countrymen and also gendering common humanity as male, he recognizes that he must maintain a moderate tone, much like the liberals, to gain any traction with the American public. And yet, it is precisely his radicalism as a heathen and protofeminist that has obscured his work in literary history.

In part because of his radicalism, he had the unwavering support of William Lloyd Garrison Jr.—the son of William Lloyd Garrison, the leader of the Garrisonian abolitionists. In a letter to Garrison Jr. dated January 4, 1893, he writes,

> I was glad to hear from you today. [. . .] We are preparing to hold a Mass Meeting in Washington some time [*sic*] this month. I have already secured influential letters of introduction to prominent people in Washington & I will get today letters from several newspapers & papers there. I will want all the assistance I can get from you by letters or otherwise.[161]

The familiarity with which Wong Chin Foo writes to Garrison suggests a relative intimacy in their relationship and a commonality of vision. Moreover, he recognizes his reliance on Garrison's influence in civil rights advocacy: "I will want all the assistance I can get from you by letters or otherwise." As an African American civil rights activist, Garrison's involvement in protesting the Geary Act demonstrates that Black liberation has always been linked to Asian American civil rights. Unlike Sherman and Hitt, Garrison

---

160. Wong Chin Foo, *Appeal*, 2, 2.

161. Letter from Wong Chin Foo to William Lloyd Garrison Jr., January 4, 1893, series VI, box 181, folder 11, Garrison Family Papers, Sophia Smith Collection, Smith College, Northampton, MA.

radically, unequivocally aided the Chinese without, at least openly, discriminating against Wong Chin Foo or other Chinese Americans. In his "General Appeal" to the US government, on behalf of the Chinese against the Geary Act, Garrison compares the law to the 1850 Fugitive Slave Act, which ordered the return of runaway slaves to the South: "Since the Fugitive Slave Law no such infamous enactment has disgraced the statute books of the nation. It violates all humane instincts, and disregards our plain treaty obligations with China, as Senator Sherman declared in his opposing speech."[162] As a liberal, Garrison does support Hitt's ambivalent speech: "The noble protest of Representative Hitt, of Ohio, against the passage of the bill is enclosed for your earnest consideration. It is specific in its description, and its indictment is not exaggerated."[163] Nevertheless, he does not perpetuate the yellow peril stereotypes; instead, he humanizes the Chinese Americans living in the US by nevertheless using the exceptional minority stereotype in referring to them as "innocent," "law-abiding" citizens who are also civil rights activists:[164]

> The innocent and law-abiding victims who are designated for this persecution await the sober second thought of the American Congress. [. . .] It cannot be possible that a people professing to be Christian can justify such legislation. [. . .] The Chinese Equal Rights League ask for your assistance to lift this heavy burden from the necks of their countrymen. [. . .] A meeting will be held at Tremont Temple in [sic] Friday evening, November 18, under the auspices of the League, to be addressed by Wong Chin Foo, a journalist of New York and a naturalized American voter, and by well-known citizens.[165]

Resonating with Wong Chin Foo's criticism of Christian hypocrisy in "Why Am I a Heathen?," Garrison is incredulous that white Christians could pass such a law, as he states that "it cannot be possible that a people professing to be Christian can justify such legislation." Moreover, he enfleshes Wong by crediting his activism, without any snide provisos, in mentioning him by name in his "General Appeal." For Wong Chin Foo, Garrison demonstrated, was a living example of the abolition of liberalism from racial inequality. Continuing to fight for Chinese American civil rights, Wong Chin Foo, on the

162. General Appeal from William Lloyd Garrison Jr., November 12, 1892, series VI, box 181, folder 11, Garrison Family Papers, Sophia Smith Collection, Smith College, Northampton, MA.

163. General Appeal from William Lloyd Garrison Jr., November 12, 1892.

164. General Appeal from William Lloyd Garrison Jr., November 12, 1892.

165. General Appeal from William Lloyd Garrison Jr., November 12, 1892.

other hand, maintained his radicalism during the Progressive Era when most radicals simply turned to liberal reform.[166]

Another liberal who conspicuously helped Wong Chin Foo was the renowned editor of the *North American Review,* Allen Thorndike Rice. Undoubtedly, Wong Chin Foo was made most famous by his 1887 *North American Review* essay, "Why Am I a Heathen?" At the time, the *North American Review,* which began in 1815, published a series of "Why Am I . . ." essays, including Zitkála-Šá's "Why I Am a Pagan" (1902) and, of course, Yan Phou Lee's rebuttal "Why I Am Not Heathen" a month after Wong's essay,[167] which I discuss in the next chapter. When Wong and Lee published in the *Review,* the magazine was under the editorship of Rice who, after 1876, "lift[ed] [the magazine] to a new life with boldness and originality" and transformed the magazine into a "modern" one.[168] The *Review* published both conservative and progressive perspectives: "For the *National Era,* the Washington magazine in which *Uncle Tom's Cabin* first appeared as a serial, Whittier wrote his 'Ichabod,' a blistering attack on Daniel Webster for his part in the passage of the Compromise. Webster was later defended by the *North American Review.*"[169] But the *Review* was most noted for its progressive publications such as Mark Twain's essay critiquing imperialism and Chinese exclusion, "To the Person Sitting in Darkness" (1901), and essays on the woman question: "Equal suffrage was discussed in nearly all the general magazines, but the *North American Review* outdid the others in 1879–80 with an article by the historian Francis Parkman on 'The Woman Question' and subsequent replies, in which he prayed God to deliver America from 'the most reckless of experiments' (meaning suffrage) propelled by 'a few agitators.'"[170] Howe writes, "Founded in 1815, [the *North American Review*] became the most influential intellectual periodical in the United States for most of the nineteenth century."[171] Thus, Wong Chin Foo's work would have been widely received in this high-impact magazine. His protofeminist criticism of domestic violence in "Why Am I A Heathen?" was consistent with such pieces published by the *Review.* At the helm of the *North American Review,* Rice was a liberal who made possible Wong Chin Foo's ascendency into the literary world. Again, though, other liberals whom Rice published, like Stowe, Howe, and Phillips, endured in literary history, whereas Wong Chin Foo, who was an out-of-place radical in

---

166. Cohen, 68.
167. Lum, 214; and Seligman, 144.
168. Garraty and Carnes, 405; and Tebbel and Zuckerman, 62, 405.
169. Tebbel and Zuckerman, 16.
170. Tebbel and Zuckerman, 90.
171. Howe, 629.

the Gilded Age and Progressive Era, had to be recovered in the twenty-first century. The pervasiveness of a contradictory liberalism—racially equal and unequal, conservative and reformist—reflected in his treatment by liberals, throughout both periods also deflated Wong Chin Foo's radicalism as his minimal reception has shown.

Throughout his career, to launch his literary counterattacks against white supremacy, Wong Chin Foo relied on liberals and endured their racial biases which also reared their heads during the driving-out era. Of all the figures of my study, Wong Chin Foo's interactions with different kinds of liberals—including reformers such as William Lloyd Garrison Jr. and Allen Thorndike Rice—and his radical insistence on Chinese American civil rights, expose and emphasize the ideological contradictions of nineteenth-century US liberalism the most clearly. His interactions with liberals also track the increasing reform of liberalism across the Gilded Age and the Progressive Era. Moreover, early Chinese American voices and writing by figures such as Toy, Tape, and Wong Chin Foo would not have been published without the driving-out era. Liberals helped Chinese Americans like Wong Chin Foo, in part, to distinguish themselves from the white supremacists who were also part of liberalism but engaged in anti-Chinese hate crimes. At the same time, he endured explicit and implicit racial discrimination by white supremacists and liberal reformers, alike, while living in the United States, even after becoming an American citizen. Even so, there were liberal reformers like Garrison and Rice who unequivocally supported him and other Chinese living in the US. Wong Chin Foo endeavored to rail against the driving-out era and to establish himself as a Chinese American through his writing. A protofeminist man who worked to free women sex slaves, he also radically embraced his exceptional, "yellow peril" stereotype by proclaiming himself to be a "heathen" against Christian hypocrisy. At times, Wong deployed the exceptional, model minority stereotype to defend the virtue of Chinese Americans against its binary, the yellow peril. On the other hand, the driving-out era, and the exceptional minority stereotype that stoked it, objectified Chinese American public figures to such a degree that he became someone whose work was not memorable and was easily forgotten. For this reason and to combat the excess of death during the driving-out era with that of life, Wong Chin Foo worked slavishly to enflesh and repeatedly remake himself in his writing and editing. Whereas the exceptional minority stereotype hypersexualized but also drove the feminism of Toy and Tape, the cultural amnesia that the exceptional minority stereotype entails put Wong Chin Foo at a disadvantage of never being able to rest on the laurels of his career: continually working in responding to the excess of death in the driving-out period, striving for acceptance as a citizen, he died of heart failure—possibly due in part to the stresses he endured in America—in China at the premature age of fifty-one. As the next two chapters demonstrate, the exceptional minority stereotype also drove Yan Phou Lee and Yung Wing to overachieve—the former the second Chinese American to graduate from Yale and the latter the first to do so—only to gain the quotidian privilege of being American citizens.

CHAPTER 3

Trauma and Activism

Yan Phou Lee Writes Back

THE COLLECTIVE TRAUMA OF TOKENISM

Asian American studies critics consider Yan Phou Lee's ethnographic auto-
biography *When I Was a Boy in China* (1887) to be the first piece of English-
language Asian American literature to be published in the US.[1] Unlike Wong
Chin Foo, who was omitted from mention during the founding of Asian
American studies in the 1960s and 1970s, Yan Phou Lee and his mentor Yung
Wing were also included in the earliest Civil Rights–era anthologies of Asian
American literature, but as Christian assimilationist writers; this reinforced
the twentieth-century model minority stereotype.[2] Yung was his mentor and
largely responsible for Yan Phou Lee's education at Yale where Yung had also
gone before, and began the Chinese Educational Commission (CEC, 1872–81)
on which Yan Phou Lee came to the United States; however, Yung was disciplined for his early Chinese American activism by the lack of public interest
in his work. Hence, Yan Phou Lee published his ethnographic autobiography
twenty-two years before Yung published his autobiography and only publication, *My Life in China and America* (1909). In addition to experiencing the
collective trauma of living through the driving-out era after he arrived in the

---

1. Xu, 89.
2. E. Kim, 25; Chin et al., *Aiiieeeee!*, xxvii; and Chin et al., *Big Aiiieeeee!*, xii, 8.

US in 1873, Yan Phou Lee was also tokenized, not only as the blanket exceptional minority who was hardworking, high-achieving, and seemingly able to assimilate into the white middle class but also for being what Madeline Hsu calls the "good immigrant"[3]—the docile, assimilationist Christian Chinese American that is compared with the bad, activist immigrant; by giving him fame as a "good immigrant," the American public pitted him against both his mentor Yung, who was a pioneer Chinese American activist and writer in the United States, and Wong Chin Foo who, despite his many successes, had an ambivalent reputation and died in obscurity as a "heathen."

As his work shows, Yan Phou Lee certainly experienced the collective trauma of the driving-out era. Collective trauma occurs because, as Dr. Judith Herman writes, "trauma is contagious."[4] In *Unclaimed Experience*, critic Cathy Caruth also writes about collective trauma that people can "step into" another person's "story."[5] Even though Yan Phou Lee was not himself subject to lynching or other forms of being spectacularly driven out, he witnessed it on a national scale and survived the national driving-out during this era. Caruth writes that to experience trauma, which in Greek translates to a psychic *wound,* one experiences the death twice—often watching others die and surviving it:[6] "Trauma consists not only in having confronted death but in *having survived, precisely, without knowing it.* What one returns to in the flashback is not the incomprehensibility of one's near death, but the very incomprehensibility of one's own survival."[7] As we will see, in asking himself "Why them (the driven-out victims) and not me?," Yan Phou Lee slowly distanced himself from his working-class Chinese American compatriots by joining the middle class through his education. Nevertheless, he was still haunted by posttraumatic stress disorder (PTSD). Caruth defines posttraumatic stress disorder as "the direct imposition on the mind of the unavoidable reality of horrific events, the taking over of the mind, psychically and neurobiologically, by an event that it cannot control. As such, PTSD seems to provide the most direct link between the psyche and external violence and to be the most destructive psychic disorder."[8] According to Babette Rothschild, MSW, LCSW, when one experiences a traumatic event or PTSD, one can have difficulty in making one's memory cohere.[9] Both Herman and Caruth concur that trauma creates

---

3. Hsu.
4. Herman, 140.
5. Caruth, 40.
6. Caruth, 3, 7, 8.
7. Caruth, 64.
8. Caruth, 58.
9. Rothschild, 29.

psychic fragments in memory.[10] Thus, to heal from trauma, or "a wound that cries out," one must create cohesive self-narratives.[11] This chapter examines Yan Phou Lee's essays and autoethnography—which worked to enflesh himself during the driving-out era as Wong's did—as cohesive narratives to heal from collective trauma, or collective memory, but also to exhibit his liberal activism as a Chinese American.

Yan Phou Lee's self-enfleshment in his autobiographical work during the driving-out era exposed the sovereignty of white supremacy: as Agamben writes, "The sovereign exception is thus the figure in which singularity is represented as such, which is to say, insofar as it is unrepresentable."[12] That is to say, Yan Phou Lee performed the exceptional minority stereotype par excellence to incessantly represent and expose the sovereign exceptionalism and the abuse of power of nineteenth-century US liberalism. His performance of the exceptional minority stereotype was both a political strategy to appeal to and critique conservative Gilded Age liberalism but also evidence of his trauma by the very stereotype that discursively led to the driving-out of other Chinese Americans during this era. Caruth writes, "In trauma, that is, the outside [of the exceptional minority stereotype which led to the lynchings and other forms of driving-out, in this instance,] has gone inside without any mediation."[13] That is, even though the exceptional minority stereotype was a *repetitive*[14] performance for Lee, he began to absorb and essentially live it. More so than Wong Chin Foo, Yan Phou Lee played on his exceptional minority stereotyping to advance his career, his Chinese American activism, and his liberal views on gender. Critics often decontextualize Yan Phou Lee from the driving-out era, which pervasively made Chinese Americans feel unsafe, and the hardship he experienced from witnessing his mentor's discipline; contemporary critics thus mistake his exceptional minority activism which he was forced to use as a symptom of these hardships for mere status quo–perpetuating assimilationism.

Twentieth- and twenty-first-century critics have generally not viewed the Christian-mission-educated writer Yan Phou Lee as an activist. For example, Floyd Cheung has argued that both Yan Phou Lee's and Yung's autobiographies are moderate, masculinist narratives in response to the yellow peril feminization of Chinese American men and the pervasive discourse of "manliness"

---

10. Herman, 2; and Caruth, 41, 61.
11. Caruth, 4; and van der Kolk, 234. See also Shay.
12. Agamben, 24.
13. Caruth, 59.
14. Caruth, 59.

that Theodore Roosevelt promoted during this era.[15] Nevertheless, Cheung nuances his claim by pointing out that Yan Phou Lee was "tactical" in performing the "docile" model minority in his writings.[16] At the same time, Yan Phou Lee's tempered masculinity comes through in his writing. Other critics have declined to see Yan Phou Lee's exceptional minority discourse as strategic: Elaine Kim's *Asian American Literature* and Xiao-huang Yin's *Chinese American Literature since the 1850s* only gloss Yan Phou Lee's *When I Was a Boy in China* as a corrective ethnography,[17] and Yin terms Yan Phou Lee a "Cultivated Chinese."[18] Although critic Amy Ling refers to Yan Phou Lee as a "Frontiersman" in Asian American literature, she nevertheless claims that Yan Phou Lee played the part of the ethnographic "tourist guide" who had and capitalized on his privilege as a man.[19] However, Yan Phou Lee was an activist insofar as he did not condone and actually protested the status quo of Chinese exclusion and anti-Chinese racism in his writing. In his famous 1889 *North American Review* essay, "The Chinese Must Stay," he sarcastically responds to the stereotyping charge of all Chinese women being prostitutes, which was legislated by the Page Act in 1875:

> Californians are pure, moral, and religious, in all that they do. As for having disreputable houses, or women with loose morals about them, I tell you they are as innocent as lambs. [. . .] If the virtuous community of San Francisco permitted their morals to be corrupted, it is their own fault.[20]

Yan Phou Lee's sarcasm about Californians' purity, morality, and religiosity through the "special policemen" of the vigilance committee is made clear when he places the onus of the sex industry on them: "it is their own fault."[21] Although it is unclear whether he knew Toy personally, his reference to "transmuting brass into pure gold" harks back to her famous court case. His use of the term "model" to discuss white Californians prophesizes the twentieth-century mythical Asian American model minority, which as I argue had already come into play as exceptionalism in US society, although the term was not yet circulating qua "model minority" until the 1960s. As this chapter demonstrates, Yan Phou Lee's Chinese ethnography, in making what is foreign

---

15. Cheung, 25, 32.
16. Cheung, 28.
17. E. Kim, 25; and Yin, 56, 59.
18. Yin, 55.
19. Ling, "Yan Phou Lee"; and Ling, "Reading Her/stories," 80–81, 83–84.
20. Yan Phou Lee, "Chinese Must Stay," 6.
21. Yan Phou Lee, "Chinese Must Stay," 6.

familiar and native, was part of his exceptional minority activism. That is to say, Yan Phou Lee appealed to the submissive, hyperbolically hardworking, exceptional minority stereotype by overachieving and attending Yale University and being, like Wong Chin Foo, prolific in his labor and writing; on the other hand, he performed the stereotype as an assimilated minority to appeal to the conservative, Gilded Age liberal public for Chinese American rights. His appeal to Gilded Age liberals was, in part, political but also relational as he healed from the trauma of the driving-out era. Herman writes, "Recovery [from trauma] can take place only within the context of relationships; it cannot occur in isolation."[22] At the same time, even as he protested the stereotype of Chinese economic efficiency which, in part, led to the driving-out era, in a way that was palatable to the Gilded Age liberals, he distanced himself from the community of working-class Chinese Americans by entering the middle class through education and vocation as a writer and public figure.

To both heal from the driving-out era and make his name, Yan Phou Lee wrote his 1887 *North American Review* article, "Why I Am Not a Heathen: A Rejoinder to Wong Chin Foo," on Wong's back, as it were. But as Ying Xu points out, there are very few political differences in defense of Chinese Americans between Wong's "Why Am I a Heathen?" and Yan Phou Lee's rejoinder besides Yan Phou Lee's promotion of Christianity.[23] Instead of calling on liberals to fulfill the promise of American democracy as Wong Chin Foo did, Yan Phou Lee instead called on liberal, white Christians to be true to their creed and accept all people within the US nation. Moreover, since scholars have historically charged ethnography with catering to a white mainstream audience,[24] critics have viewed Yan Phou Lee's ethnographic autobiography and articles as assimilationist.[25] In addition to framing Yan Phou Lee's narratives as attempts to heal from collective trauma, this chapter recuperates Yan Phou Lee as an activist from his literary reception as an exceptional minority, ethnographic assimilationist; it does so by re-examining and making conceptual links between his activist and autoethnographic work, including *When I Was a Boy in China,* and contextualizing him within the driving-out era and within the literary history of others like Toy, Tape, Wong Chin Foo, and Yung Wing. These contexts help us understand how, in his activism, he was

---

22. Herman, 133.

23. Xu writes, "Despite a title opposite to Wong's sensational article that confronts the hypocrisy of Christianity, Lee's defense of Christianity could be read, in fact, as a defense of Chinese immigrants from American exclusionist propaganda that proclaimed the Chinese immigrants to be unassimilable" (87).

24. See Fabian.

25. Ling, "Reading Her/stories," 83–84.

ultimately absorbed and labeled by the exceptional, model minority discourse he used to fight the yellow peril discourse, which was running rampant during the driving-out era. An example of his exceptional minority activism, Yan Phou Lee's liberal and masculinist gender politics that defended women but not to the extent of positing equal gender rights is inconsistent insofar as it seems dogmatic in certain ways but not in others; in this way, it both hid some of his traditionalist leanings and appealed to a conservative white, Gilded Age American audience. Even more moderate in his politics than Toy, Tape, and Wong Chin Foo, his liberal gender politics was part of his activist strategy to appease the conservative masses in order to convince them to be inclusive of Chinese Americans during this period. In this way, Yan Phou Lee's enfleshment through his writing emphasizes the complexities of Gilded Age conservatism and reform in his defense of Christianity, reflected in his political activism and his interracial marriages to two white women, respectively. His assimilation into the middle class also tracks the gradual shift of liberalism from the more conservative Gilded Age to the reformist, middle-class-driven Progressive Era.

EXCEPTIONAL MINORITY ACTIVISM

Besides Cheung and Xu, who argues that Yan Phou Lee displays a double-consciousness, "across lands" strategy in his writing,[26] few critics have focused on Yan Phou Lee's Chinese American activism. This neglect is due, in part, to Yan Phou Lee's "rejoinder" to Wong Chin Foo's essay "Why Am I a Heathen?" in his 1887 essay, just a few months after Wong's—"Why I Am Not a Heathen"—which appears assimilationist in its promotion of Christianity and retrograde in its politics at face value. However, a deeper investigation into the essay reveals Yan Phou Lee's stark critique of racism against Chinese Americans during the driving-out era. Like Wong Chin Foo, Yan Phou Lee criticizes Christian hypocrisy in the essay: "I not only discriminate between Christianity and its professors, but I also discriminate between true Christians and hypocrites."[27] Here, he attributes the recent lynchings and driving-out of Chinese Americans in the West to the Christian hypocrites. He goes on to discuss the Christian hypocrisy of other parts of the Western world: "If England were a truly Christian country, as she claims to be, the Opium War would have never taken place."[28] And yet, despite rampant Christian hypocrisy in

26. Xing, 87.
27. Yan Phou Lee, "Why I Am Not a Heathen," 309.
28. Yan Phou Lee, "Why I Am Not a Heathen," 311.

the West, Yan Phou Lee continues to place his dialectical faith in Christianity by following up his statement with "Christianity is nowhere so explicit as where it warns people against the sin of consciousness."[29] Despite the failures of Christian hypocrites, he holds that "the true Christian does good for the love he has toward all God's creatures."[30] Believing in the renewal of the "true Christian" despite the existence of Christian hypocrisy, Yan Phou Lee owes his entire career in the US to his Christian friends.[31] For Yan Phou Lee, social and political "equality" rests on the tenet of universal love in Christianity. The Christian friends Yan Phou Lee made even became politicized in supporting his denunciation of the Chinese Exclusion Law. In contrast with Wong Chin Foo, who calls on "true" liberals—like William Lloyd Garrison Jr., who was also Christian, or, like Allen Thorndike Rice, who entertained Christian beliefs in his publications—Yan Phou Lee specifically calls on white Christians, such as the ones who aided him and his career, to help the Chinese. For example, in "Why I Am Not a Heathen," Yan Phou Lee states, "The Christian men are the last hope of the Republic. The final appeal is to be made to the Christian sentiment of the nation. [. . .] I have some confidence left yet that Christianity will survive this last and most terrible of attacks."[32] Here, he actively makes an appeal to Christians to help Chinese Americans as Christianity has endured and "survived" the recent "attacks" on Chinese Americans by Christian hypocrites. His call for a *true* Christianity, rather than heathenism in Wong Chin Foo's case, demonstrates the conservatism of the Gilded Age despite the beginnings of liberal reform during this period.

In Yan Phou Lee's belief in the redemption of Christian hypocrisy, he does straightforwardly challenge many of Wong's claims in "Why Am I a Heathen?" For example, Yan Phou Lee harshly denounces heathenism, a word he would have identified with and to which he once prescribed as a child: "Heathenism teaches nothing if it does not teach fatalism and the control of Destiny. It does not go so far as predestination, it is because its notions of a future life are a confused heap of nonsense."[33] As an adult, he realizes the cynicism and "nonsense" of heathenism, which does not allow for grace. He also disagrees with Wong's stance on the differences between the Chinese and American families: Wong writes that what is lacking in an American family, compared with a Chinese family, are "first, obedience to its head; second, affection toward

29. Yan Phou Lee, "Why I Am Not a Heathen," 311.
30. Yan Phou Lee, "Why I Am Not a Heathen," 310–11.
31. Yan Phou Lee, "Why I Am Not a Heathen," 310–11.
32. Yan Phou Lee, "Why I Am Not a Heathen," 311, 312.
33. Yan Phou Lee, "Why I Am Not a Heathen," 306–7, 308.

both father and mother; third, love among its members."[34] On the other hand, Yan Phou Lee tries to find a more moderate recommendation by returning to Christianity: Yan Phou Lee holds that whereas American parents spoil their children and Chinese parents too strictly discipline their children, both have fallen short of Christian "harmony."[35] Rather than lionizing the white audience, Yan Phou Lee assigns "imperfect training" to "foolish [Chinese] parents" and the more serious flaw of the two, "natural depravity," to the "undutiful [American] children." In keeping with the merits of Christianity, Yan Phou Lee directly responds to Wong's plaints about the Final Dispensation, particularly with respect to the white labor leader Denis Kearney, who, at the time, was spearheading Chinese exclusion in his "sand-lot orations": "Applying this dogma, I began to think of my own prospects on the other side of Jordan. Suppose Dennis [sic] Kearney, the California sand-lotter, should slip in and meet me there, would he not be likely to forget his heavenly songs, and howl once more: 'The Chinese must go!' and organize a heavenly crusade to have me out and others immediately cast out into the other place?"[36] Believing that Kearney's hypocrisy could be redeemed, Yan Phou Lee states,

> If others believe that a man can enter heaven by repenting at the eleventh hour, what is that to me? How should that destroy my faith in the saving grace of Christianity? Such, indeed, is its power to change the heart of man, that even if Dennis [sic] Kearney should slip into the Heavenly Jerusalem, he would be lamb-like and would be heard to say: "The Chinese must stay! Heaven is incomplete without them."[37]

Yan Phou Lee flagrantly disagrees with Wong Chin Foo's self-righteousness in denying hypocrites forgiveness ("what is that to me?"). He believes true Christianity could change the heart of such a violent wolf to become "lamb-like." It is compelling, however, that both Wong Chin Foo and Yan Phou Lee believe that the Chinese, whether heathen or Christian, belong in heaven even though they approach Kearney differently.

Yan Phou Lee seems to have had a change of heart about Kearney's redemption two years later, when he directly contradicted Kearney's famous slogan "The Chinese Must Go!" in another *North American Review* essay, "The Chinese Must Stay." Like Wong Chin Foo, in his 1892 *Appeal of the Chinese Equal Rights League to the People of the United States for Equality of Manhood,*

---

34. Wong Chin Foo, "Family in China and America," 679.
35. Yan Phou Lee, "Why I Am Not a Heathen," 311–12.
36. Wong Chin Foo, "Why Am I a Heathen?," 11.
37. Yan Phou Lee, "Why I Am Not a Heathen," 4.

Yan Phou Lee begins the essay by appealing to the social and racial equality that was the aim of the recent Civil War: "But now, looking at the actions of this generation of Americans in their treatment of other races, who can get rid of the idea that the Nation, which Abraham Lincoln said was conceived in liberty, waxed great through oppression, and was really dedicated to the proposition that all men are created to prey on one another?"[38] Yan Phou Lee holds that, despite Lincoln's argument that the nation "was conceived in liberty," no one can "get rid of the idea" that it "was really dedicated to the proposition that all men are created to prey on one another." Once again, Yan Phou Lee is writing during the driving-out era in which Chinese Americans continued to be lynched or spectacularly driven out of West Coast cities in other ways, en masse. However, Yan Phou Lee does not simply rest on the criticism of American racism in the essay. He goes on to dismantle several stereotypes and misconceptions of the Chinese. First, he addresses and demystifies the exceptional, model minority / yellow peril stereotype by stating,

> Chinese immigrants never claimed to be any better than farmers, traders, and artisans. If, on the one hand, they are not princes and nobles, on the other hand, they are not coolies and slaves. They all came voluntarily, as their consular papers certified, and their purpose in leaving their home and friends was to get honest work. They were told they could obtain higher wages in America than elsewhere, and that Americans were friendly to the Chinese and invited them to come.[39]

According to Yan Phou Lee, Chinese Americans fall prey to the promise and evasive myth of democracy: "They were told they could obtain higher wages in America [. . .] and that Americans were friendly to the Chinese." It is also clear that Chinese immigrants are neither exceptional, model minorities, for they "never claimed to be any better than farmers, traders, and artisans," nor yellow peril, "coolies and slaves." Instead, Yan Phou Lee enfleshes the Chinese Americans as merely human, wanting "honest work."

Yan Phou Lee goes on to assert his activism and protest of the status quo of Chinese exclusion by dispelling nine myths about the Chinese:

> I. *That the influx of Chinese is a standing menace to Republican institutions upon the Pacific coast and the existence there of Christian civilization* [. . .]
>
> II. *That the Chinese race seems to have no desire for progress* [. . .]

---

38. Yan Phou Lee, "The Chinese Must Stay," 1–2.
39. Yan Phou Lee, "The Chinese Must Stay," 2.

III. *That the Chinese have displaced white laborers by low wages and cheap living, and that their presence discourages and retards white immigration to the Pacific States* [. . .]

IV. *That the Chinese do not desire to become citizens of this country* [. . .]

V. *That the Chinese live in filthy dwellings, upon poor food, crowded together in narrow quarters, disregarding health and fire ordinances* [. . .]

VI. *The Chinese neither have intercourse with the Caucasians nor will assimilate with them* [. . .]

VII. *The Chinese come and go as pagans* [. . .]

VIII. *That the Chinese immigrants are mostly criminals* [. . .]

IX. *That the Chinese bring women of bad character to San Francisco, and that their vices are corrupting the morals of the city.*[40]

Yan Phou Lee responds to these myths with a great deal of sarcasm: "Surely the Chinese must be angels or devils! If angels, they would go without your bidding. If devils, you would not be able to drive them out."[41] He insists, instead, that they are merely human. Responding to the myth that Chinese do not desire progress, Yan Phou Lee claims that they, in fact, do appreciate Western notions of progress and they do not hesitate to show their appreciation to white Americans.[42] To the charge of cheap Chinese labor, he is quick to indicate that it is the fault of exploitative white American capitalists and that such cheap labor built the coveted railroads.[43] Again, Yan Phou Lee uses sarcasm to respond to the claim that the Chinese refuse American citizenship—"Why should they [accept citizenship]? Where is the inducement?"—as he reminds the liberal reader of all the exclusion laws that have been enacted against the Chinese since their arrival in the United States.[44] He continues to enflesh the Chinese Americans by emphasizing that the Chinese person "does not object to dainty food and luxurious belongings" as he responds to the accusations against their impoverished living conditions.[45] Moreover, he responds to the failure of Chinese Americans to assimilate into white American culture with sarcasm since it is clear, during the driving-out era, that white America's lack of acceptance of the Chinese has prevented their assimilation when there have been clear instances of assimilation in clothing, ideology, and education by the

---

40. Yan Phou Lee, "Chinese Must Stay," 3–6.
41. Yan Phou Lee, "Chinese Must Stay," 3.
42. Yan Phou Lee, "Chinese Must Stay," 3.
43. Yan Phou Lee, "Chinese Must Stay," 3–4.
44. Yan Phou Lee, "Chinese Must Stay," 4.
45. Yan Phou Lee, "Chinese Must Stay," 5.

figures mentioned in this study.[46] By the same token, Yan Phou Lee is quick to point out that over five hundred Chinese Americans have converted to Christianity since their arrival in the States and that only one in eighteen Chinese American has committed crimes.[47]

Even though he cited the numbers of Chinese American Christian converts, Yan Phou Lee debunked the exceptional minority stereotype, even while sometimes deploying the discourse to combat specifically the yellow peril stereotype—which was ironically part of the exceptional minority stereotype—that was, in part, responsible for the driving-out era in his graduate address at Yale College two years earlier: toward the beginning of his speech, he comments on the "nature" of the Chinese, "The Chinese are by nature and from habit gregarious, but not migratory. They dislike to cut adrift from the ties of kindred, the associations of home, and traditions of fatherland."[48] Here, he combats the exceptional minority image of the mechanistic and economically efficient Chinese American by enfleshing the Chinese as "gregarious, but not migratory." In response to the exceptional, model minority / yellow peril stereotype of industriousness and theft from America, which also traumatically plagues him, he states, "I admit both points: I admit that they do not come to America for the good of *their* fatherland and mother church, and that they *do* come to make money. So do Americans in China."[49] By comparing the Chinese to American aims in immigration, Yan Phou Lee claims that the aim of building wealth is universally human, not particularly racial.

As he enfleshes the Chinese in his speech later in his autobiography, Yan Phou Lee focuses on the "torrents of hatred and abuse which have periodically swept over the Chinese industrial class in America" and the horror of the driving-out era, which has spectacularly objectified Chinese Americans.[50] Remarking on the "catastrophe" of the driving-out era, which "was too terrible, and has made too deep an impression to be easily forgotten," he even uses lynching rhetoric to discuss the violence enacted against Chinese Americans in the last two decades: "Mob-rule knows no respect for persons; the Chinese were attacked first simply because they were the weakest. I do not deny that the anti-Chinese agitation has some *show* of reason. But its strength rests on three erroneous assumptions, by proving the groundlessness of which the whole superstructure of fallacy and falsehood can be made to totter."[51]

---

46. Yan Phou Lee, "Chinese Must Stay," 5.
47. Yan Phou Lee, "Chinese Must Stay," 5, 5–6.
48. Yan Phou Lee, "Graduate Address of Yan Phou Lee at Yale College," 270.
49. Yan Phou Lee, "Graduate Address," 272.
50. Yan Phou Lee, "Graduate Address," 269.
51. Yan Phou Lee, "Graduate Address," 270.

He goes on to discredit three yellow peril myths about Chinese immigration. Here, Yan Phou Lee recognizes the driving-out era as such and the humanity of the Chinese Americans when he states that "mob-rule knows no respect for persons." Although he seems to perpetuate some stereotypes of Chinese effeminacy—"they were the weakest"—he could have also meant their minoritization in numbers in the US and their vulnerability as an economic class.

He continues to document the driving-out era by commenting on the ways in which the 1882 Exclusion Act responded to and perpetuated the violence against Chinese Americans. Despite his tactical and *repetitive* exceptional minority rhetoric which responds to both his own trauma and his conservative, liberal US audience, at times, his stark activism comes through in the passion with which he writes his protest:

> Were it not for the tragic events which trod on the heels of the Chinese Immigration Bill, one might be inclined to laugh at the absurdities in the bill itself. If the law is faithfully executed (and to be worth anything it must be), all Americans born in China are disfranchised, and all Chinese natives of British colonies, like Hong Kong and India, have free access to this country. But who could laugh in the midst of indignant tears? By passing a discriminating law against any already persecuted class, the Central Government yielded to the demands of the mob, and to that extent countenanced its violence and lawlessness. The Anti-Chinese Act is a cause of all the outrages and massacres that have been since committed in Rock Springs and Denver, in Portland, San Francisco and other parts, which, if they had been perpetrated in China against Americans, would have resounded from Bedloe's Island (whereon stands the Statue of Liberty) to the Golden Gate. But the criminals in these cases were not punished, and even the pitiful indemnity was voted down until Congress could not withhold it from very shame.[52]

Despite the "absurdity" of the Exclusion Act, Yan Phou Lee holds that it is a very real, "discriminating," "shameful," and impactful law. He documents the otherwise subaltern, "indignant tears" of Chinese Americans during this driving-out era, which he references with such rhetoric as "the Central Government yielded to the demands of the mob, and to that extent countenanced its violence and lawlessness." Again, although he does not explicitly refer to the period as the "driving-out era," his rhetoric suggests that indeed it was. In his activism, he enfleshes Chinese Americans and memorializes the victims from the recent massacres at Rock Springs, Denver, Portland, and San Francisco.

---

52. Yan Phou Lee, "Graduate Address," 272.

While Congress failed to bring the white American "criminals" to justice, Yan Phou Lee once again turns to Christianity for social justice: as he does in "Why I Am Not a Heathen," he calls on Christians to dialectically become truer Christians, despite their failures in their "duties as lovers of justice and fatherland, in *not* enforcing your opinions in public and in private, as well in church as in State."[53] Despite Christian hypocrisy and failure, he turns to the "avenging Deity" for the retribution for "the cold-blooded murder of innocent strangers."[54] Yan Phou Lee's resounding insistence on the social justice of Christianity seemed to be received well by Christians and the scientific community alike, as his graduation speech was published in *The American Missionary* in September of 1887, redelivered at the annual American Association for Advancement in Science session the same year, which was reported on by the *Scientific American*.[55] The reception of Yan Phou Lee's Christian activism and call for organizing in his graduation speech suggests an unlikely overlap between Christianity and science. That is, the ways in which he enfleshes Chinese Americans in his activist writing, as "innocent strangers," is scientific insofar as his method is ethnography.

DEBUNKING THE OTHER IN ETHNOGRAPHY

Yan Phou Lee enfleshes Chinese Americans in his ethnographic articles and his most famous work, his ethnographic autobiography, *When I Was a Boy in China* (1887). *When I Was a Boy in China,* although a cohesive autoethnography, is not strictly an autobiography. Rather than describe Yan Phou Lee's life, explicitly, the text structures itself around ethnographic chapters: chapter 1, "Infancy," chapter 2, "The House and Household," chapter 3, "Chinese Cookery," chapter 4, "Games and Pastimes," chapter 5, "Girls of My Acquaintance," chapter 6, "Schools and School Life," chapter 7, "Religions," chapter 8, "Chinese Holidays," chapter 9, "Stories and Story-Tellers," chapter 10, "How I Went to Shanghai," chapter 11, "How I Prepared for America," and chapter 12, "First Experiences in America." The autoethnography does not really focus on Yan Phou Lee's life until the last three chapters of the text. Otherwise, bits and pieces of his life are strewn in with the ethnography of Chinese life. The fragmentation of his autobiography within his ethnography reflects the collective trauma he experiences during the driving-out era and his hardship as Yung Wing's mentee in witnessing Yung's own persecution as co-commissioner

---

53. Yan Phou Lee, "Graduate Address," 272–73.
54. Yan Phou Lee, "Graduate Address," 272–73.
55. Xu, 107.

of the Chinese Educational Commission on which Yan Phou Lee came to the United States. Herman writes that a "completed narrative [which] must include a full and vivid description of the traumatic injury"[56] is necessary for healing from PTSD. Although he discusses the driving-out era in his auto-biographical essays, he declines to mention it in his autoethnography even though it is a "completed narrative" of Chinese culture; the fragmentation of his autobiography bears witness to his trauma, which is also evidence of his enfleshment. Thus, inasmuch as his autoethnography helped Yan Phou Lee heal and make sense of being a Chinese American during the driving-out era, it also bears witness to the trauma he faced as an early Chinese American living in the late nineteenth-century United States.

As Xu points out, Yan Phou Lee published much of his autoethnography serially in advance for Daniel Lothrop's children's magazine *Wide Awake* between 1884 and 1887.[57] Lothrop also published his book. Mary Mapes Dodge, who edited for Lothrop, also published Yan Phou Lee's ethnographic articles, "A Chinese Market" (1888) and "The Boys and Girls of China," in her own children's magazine, *St. Nicholas.*[58] While it is true that Yan Phou Lee's ethnographies are not written in high literary style and thus were placed well in children's magazines, his activism in appealing to the social justice of the younger generations emerges in the publication venues of his choosing.

In contrast to Ling's claim about Yan Phou Lee that he took on "the 'tourist guide' role, in which the alien was asked to describe how things are done in his country with the expectation that he would provide titillation by his exotic and quaint revelations,"[59]I argue that Yan Phou Lee's ethnographies also attempt to draw parallels between Chinese and American cultures, particularly for the younger generations. In this way, he displaces the Chinese American from being the "alien" Other. In "The Boys and Girls of China," Yan Phou Lee writes, "the average boy of the country [China] or the other side of the globe and directly under us, is, I assure you, astonishingly like boys of more enlightened climes. He, too, is compounded of naughtiness and goodness, obedience and rebelliousness, love of play and thirst for knowledge, wearisome curiosity and wholesome respect for his elders."[60] Once again, Yan Phou Lee takes on an exceptional minority rhetoric of deferring to American culture by calling it a "more enlightened clime" than Chinese culture. Traumatized by the very stereotype that led to the driving-out era, he nevertheless strategically deploys

---

56. Herman, 177.
57. Xu, 92.
58. Xu, 92.
59. Ling, *Between Worlds*, 16.
60. Yan Phou Lee, "Boys and Girls of China."

the exceptional minority rhetoric to make his ethnographic activism more palatable to conservative liberal readers. For example, he once again draws parallels between Chinese and American boys, "The Chinese boy enjoys his games of running and jumping, and he can hop on one leg as long as the nimblest of American lads."[61] Nevertheless, he goes on, again, to defer to American games as superior to Chinese ones: in describing a bound ball game, he states, "This game is too simple to elicit anything but scorn from a Yankee lad. It would not be a bad idea for some young baseball enthusiast to go to China and teach the boys there the American game."[62] Witnessing the tokenism and poor reception, at times, of his predecessors, Yung and Wong Chin Foo, Yan Phou Lee once again deliberately takes on a more moderate tone and deploys the exceptional minority rhetoric in order to appeal to and enter into a healing community with a conservative liberal audience and convince them to embrace racial equality.

Although he makes comparisons between white American and Chinese boys, he nevertheless makes the proviso of the strict discipline that the Chinese boy must observe:

> It must be owned, however, that children in China, from their earliest days are taught to obey implicitly, never to question the propriety of commands laid upon them by their superiors, and never to contradict. [. . .] On no account should a boy walk side by side with his father, an elder brother, or an uncle,—and still less precede them. He should show his respect by always following in their footsteps.[63]

Despite his emphasis on Christianity in his overtly activist essays, he makes concessions of Confucian hierarchies and discipline in Chinese culture. However, Yan Phou Lee clearly values this difference from American culture with words such as "propriety" and "respect." Again, he runs the risk of simply reaffirming the exceptional minority stereotype in these ethnographic depictions and thus reaffirming Gilded Age conservatism.

On the other hand, he reflects Gilded Age reformism in his activism by disavowing the exceptional minority stereotype, which has led to his own psychic fragmentation, concerning Confucian discipline, when he makes a similar claim about a Chinese child's discipline and respect for elders in "How Chinese Boys Live":

61. Yan Phou Lee, "Boys and Girls of China."
62. Yan Phou Lee, "Boys and Girls of China."
63. Yan Phou Lee, "Boys and Girls of China."

Babyhood is the most enjoyable stage in the life of an Oriental. It is the only period when his wishes are regarded and when demonstrations of affection are shown him. The family regulations in China are such that so soon as a child begins to understand, he is not only taught to obey, but also loses his freedom of action: nor does he fully recover it till he is old and past the brief season of youthful enjoyment. Every person in China is in strict subjection to somebody. The child is subject to his parents or guardian. They, in turn, are subject to their parents, who are liable to be called to account by the elders of the clan. The magistrate is considered the father of the people he rules over; and the emperor stands in the same relation to his subjects as the father to his children.[64]

Yan Phou Lee clarifies his critique of the "strictness" of child-rearing when he admits that "babyhood is the most enjoyable stage in the life of an Oriental." In the rest of this excerpt, his tone is matter-of-fact and accepting of Confucian hierarchies: "Every person in China is in strict subjection to somebody." And yet, in his other essay, "The Boys and Girls of China," he suggests that such roles are merely performative:

Before his superiors he is as quiet, studious, and grave as you please; but out of their sight and among his comrades he is a different being altogether. Remember he has been acting a part; maybe his mother has promised him a mango or a moon-cake if he would be good; or perhaps his teacher is a ferocious tyrant, ready to use the rattan whip or walnut ruler on all occasions. Our boy abstains from play, frolic, and fun, only so long as he is watched. Out in the back yard, where none but indulgent mothers or sympathizing sisters are about, or at the street corners, you will find the Chinese boy lively and frolicsome.[65]

Yan Phou Lee highlights the performance of draconian discipline in a Chinese boy's life to, once again, draw parallels between the Chinese and Americans. This described performance, "acting a part," also enfleshes the Chinese, who have their flaws and "lively and frolicsome" nature; it also reveals his own performance in his exceptional minority rhetoric.

Likewise, in *When I Was a Boy in China*, published the same year as his "Why I Am Not a Heathen" and his graduate address, Yan Phou Lee continues to both perform and, to a certain extent, embody, the exceptional minority

---

64. Yan Phou Lee, "How Chinese Boys Live."
65. Yan Phou Lee, "Boys and Girls of China."

stereotype and to discuss the strict discipline under which the Chinese boy must go as a point of distinction from American culture: in the second chapter, he writes, "The boy attains to the ideal character only when he habitually checks his affectionate impulses, suppresses his emotions and is uniformly respectful to his superiors and uniformly dignified with his inferiors."[66] Chinese culture, according to Yan Phou Lee, is structured by hierarchies that organize people into "superiors" and "inferiors." As he does in his later ethnographic essays, he seems to critique the strictness of Chinese discipline in *When I Was a Boy in China,* when he woefully recalls, "The bamboo rod hung over my head like the sword of Damocles."[67] Comparing the "bamboo rod" to the Western Sicilian figure Damocles's sword again suggests Yan Phou Lee's attempt to draw parallels between Eastern and Western cultures. He continues to make distinctions, particularly between Chinese and American cultures, when it comes to academic discipline and sports:

> The active sports of Chinese boys are few. There are hardly any sports, so-called that develop the muscles and render a lad graceful and agile. [. . .] He thinks it work if his play entails much perspiration. His elders, too, frown upon boisterous games. They approve quiet, meditative lads who are given to study.[68]

Although he risks perpetuating the exceptional, model minority / yellow peril stereotype of Chinese male effeminacy in his performance of it, he is not afraid to delineate the cultural differences concerning physical activity between Chinese and American cultures. Again, inasmuch as there are differences, Yan Phou Lee is sure to relate Chinese to American culture, again, to both universalize and enflesh Chinese culture and Chinese Americans: "The names given on those occasions are not like your 'Jack,' 'Harry,' or 'Dick,' but are usually words chosen 'from the dictionary' for their lucky import, or because they are supposed to possess the power of warding off evil influences in the child's horoscope. You should know that in China a baby's fortune is told almost as soon as he is born, the events of his life being foretold with surprising particularity."[69] He specifically mentions American names, "Jack," "Harry," or "Dick," to bring familiarity to his liberal US readers as they read about what they have perceived as alien.

---

66. Yan Phou Lee, *When I Was a Boy in China,* 36.
67. Yan Phou Lee, *When I Was a Boy in China,* 39.
68. Yan Phou Lee, *When I Was a Boy in China,* 47.
69. Yan Phou Lee, *When I Was a Boy in China,* 30.

Critics have perceived Yan Phou Lee's moderate stance in relating cultural values between Chinese and white American cultures as "titillating"[70]
and pornographic, particularly when he discusses food. However, upon closer
examination, I argue that he once again attempts to appeal to common, universal interests in food among all people: "Roast pig is the national festal
dish in China, as you will learn. No occasion is complete without it, whether
it be a religious festival, the worship of ancestors, a wedding, or a birthday
celebration."[71] Exemplary of his food writing, this passage reveals that his
depictions of Chinese food are not actually very titillating. Rather than writing food pornography,[72] he matter-of-factly states that roast pig is a national
dish used in most celebrations. He also dedicates an entire chapter of *When I
Was a Boy in China* to "Chinese Cookery," in which he discusses how food is
prepared with attention to detail. In the same chapter, he begins to talk about
gender roles and the similar strict standards to which Chinese girls are held:
"We had a hired cook, several maid-servants and a man-servant, so that there
was never a need that the ladies of our family should soil their dainty hands or
weary their delicate feet. My grandmother, however, had her own ideas about
work, and used to arrange that her daughters should not be idle or ignorant."[73]
Although he does not expound on the contradictions here, the intersections
of class and gender would be relatable to the white American reader: that
is, on the one hand, Yan Phou Lee's household hired a cook and men and
women servants to preserve differences in social class; on the other hand, his
grandmother believed that the women in the household should work and be
educated. Likewise, during a period in which white, middle-class American
women were not yet allowed to vote, they faced the same contradictions of
class expectations and aspirations to work and education.

Yan Phou Lee continues to relate Chinese and American cultures in his
later ethnographic article about Chinese food, "A Chinese Market." In this
essay, he attempts to appeal to the white American reader: he begins the article by, once again, reframing the unfamiliar with the familiar, and using a
Western idiom: "Birds of a feather flock together."[74] He narrates himself as
comfortable "walking" the white American reader "through a long avenue in
my native place."[75] Again, his desire is for the white American reader to consider Chinese "native" rather than foreign. When he states that "the way the

---

70. Ling, *Between Worlds*, 16.
71. Yan Phou Lee, *When I Was a Boy in China*, 10–11.
72. See Thompkins and Mannur. I thank Shirley Wong for these references.
73. Yan Phou Lee, *When I Was a Boy in China*, 42.
74. Yan Phou Lee, "Chinese Market."
75. Yan Phou Lee, "Chinese Market."

meats are roasted may be of some interest" to white readers, he again attempts to appeal to their interests and subject positions.[76] Contradicting the yellow peril stereotype of Chinese filth, he emphasizes that the animals are "well cleaned."[77] He continues to draw parallels between Chinese and American cultures when he discusses methods of payment at these food markets: "Potatoes, cabbages, greens, melons, and the various cereals, are raised in great plenty and sold comparatively cheaply."[78] He writes that Chinese isolation from world commerce contributes to the cheapness of produce.[79] Yan Phou Lee uses logic to explain cultural differences: "The reason why things are sold so cheaply there, compared with prices in America, is because gold and silver, being wholly imported, are very dear."[80] He refuses to naturalize differences between Chinese and American cultures. For example, he writes,

> Dried fish of many kinds are sold in the stores, but fresh fish, and sea-food generally, are usually sold by men who bring them from a great distance, early in the morning or the afternoon, in baskets. Behind there they squat, and hawk their wares in loud tones. That is the reason why a Chinese market is so noisy and animated. [. . .] Beef is not often eaten by the Chinese, on account of their religious scruples, most of them being tinged, more or less, with Buddhism, but especially because the ox is used in ploughing.[81]

He explains that rather than being innate to Chinese character, marketplaces are environmentally "so noisy and animated" because people who travel "from a great distance" are attempting to "hawk their wares in loud tones." He also explains that the reasons for which people abstain from eating meat are religious and economical—"the ox is used in ploughing." His logical translation of Chinese culture disproves the "otherness" that liberalism attributes to Chinese Americans.

In addition to using logic to counteract stereotypes and expose the liberalism that essentialize the Chinese, Yan Phou Lee disproves myths that are perpetuated by the yellow peril stereotype of Chinese filth, disease, and impropriety in both "A Chinese Market" and *When I Was a Boy in China* during a period in which Chinese Americans were driven out owing to such notions. For example, in "A Chinese Market," Yan Phou Lee writes, "You

76. Yan Phou Lee, "Chinese Market."
77. Yan Phou Lee, "Chinese Market."
78. Yan Phou Lee, "Chinese Market."
79. Yan Phou Lee, "Chinese Market."
80. Yan Phou Lee, "Chinese Market."
81. Yan Phou Lee, "Chinese Market."

perhaps wonder why I have not described cats, kittens, and dogs, which are said to be the common food of the Chinese people. The reason is because no such things are to be found in the market."[82] Again, his activism against the yellow peril stereotype emerges in his ethnography. He makes such activism his mission in his ethnography when he states in *When I Was a Boy in China,*

> I still continually find false ideas in America concerning Chinese customs, manners, and institutions. Small blame to the people at large, who have no means of learning truth, except through newspapers or accounts of travelers who do not understand what they see in passing through our country. From the time of Sir John Mandeville, travellers (with a few noble exceptions) have vied with each other in relating the most wonderful stories about our ancient empire. Accordingly, what I tell in this series of articles about Chinese customs, manners and institutions may often contradict general belief.[83]

He places the blame of exoticizing travel writing on the European forefathers of the US. Unlike the Europeans who wrote about foreign cultures, Yan Phou Lee is particularly positioned to talk more accurately about Chinese culture since he grew up in China.[84] While there are "false ideas in America concerning Chinese customs, manner, and institutions," he makes it a point to "contradict general belief." Most critics have depoliticized and critiqued Yan Phou Lee's ethnographic, "travel writing"; however, one sees that he attempts to correct stereotypes and divulge "truth" about Chinese Americans in his ethnography during a period in which they were rampantly dehumanized, exceptionalized, and thus violently killed or expelled from the West Coast. This excerpt about discrediting "false ideas" begins his fifth chapter, which is on "Girls of My Acquaintance." Yan Phou Lee is particularly interested in this chapter and throughout his ethnographic autobiography in countering American gender assumptions about Chinese culture.

YAN PHOU LEE'S TRADITIONALIST GENDER POLITICS

In *When I Was a Boy in China,* and previously in *Wide Awake* and *The Christian Union* (1885), Yan Phou Lee wrote, "Women are subject to their fathers or husbands. All are subject to the national laws."[85] The tone is, once again,

---

82. Yan Phou Lee, "Chinese Market."
83. Yan Phou Lee, *When I Was a Boy in China,* 52.
84. I thank Jane Wessel for pointing this out to me.
85. Yan Phou Lee, *When I Was a Boy in China,* 36; and Lee, "How Chinese Boys Live."

matter-of-fact, particularly when he follows up the gender hierarchy with a universal subjection to national laws. And yet, Yan Phou Lee's repetition of this phrase in three different publications suggests the importance of gender in his writing. Like Wong Chin Foo, Yan Phou Lee addressed gender differences in China but in more traditional, masculinist terms and in defense of Chinese culture. From the outset of his autoethnography,[86] or ethnographic autobiography, *When I Was a Boy in China,* Yan Phou Lee emphasizes his "boyhood" but also acknowledges the gender inequality between men and women in China: "Being born a boy, there was a deal of rejoicing in the family, and among numerous relatives. If I had happened to be a girl, it would have been very different."[87] Yan Phou Lee goes on to elaborate on the "three obediences"[88] in which Chinese women are viewed as subservient to men as he once again states, "Women are subject to their fathers or husbands. All are subject to the national laws."[89] His only allusion to their sexuality is his subtle statement "I trust I must impress upon you that the house was divided into two portions; the front belonging to the men and the rear to the women. My grandfather's rule was that no lady of the family should pass the boundary line except on 'occasions.'"[90] It is implied that such conjugal occasions within a traditional household were, of course, matrimonial. In comparing the demureness of Chinese women to bold white American women, Yan Phou Lee writes, "I wish to call attention to the fact that Chinese girls—though you may think they lead a humdrum sort of life, though it may be true that they are strangers to the exciting gayeties enjoyed by American girls—are usually contented and think their lot a pleasant one."[91] His autoethnography here generalizes the modesty of all Chinese girls but emphasizes their "humdrum life" to counteract the discourse of Chinese female prostitution in the United States. He flips this stereotype on its head when he writes to his American audience, "You perhaps think of their existence a failure. They look upon the sort of life that American girls lead as very improper."[92] Without naming white supremacy or the white patronage of Chinese prostitutes, Yan Phou Lee declares that "impropriety" rests with white Americans rather than Chinese women, underhandedly critiquing the sovereignty of US liberalism and its gender inequalities.

---

86. Cheung, 26.
87. Yan Phou Lee, *When I Was a Boy in China,* 29.
88. J. Yung, 18; and Pfaelzer, 101.
89. Yan Phou Lee, *When I Was a Boy in China,* 36.
90. Yan Phou Lee, *When I Was a Boy in China,* 40.
91. Yan Phou Lee, *When I Was a Boy in China,* 57.
92. Yan Phou Lee, *When I Was a Boy in China,* 57.

Yan Phou Lee likewise disproves liberal US myths surrounding the treatment of Chinese girls. Although they are treated differently from boys, he defends the Chinese culture against charges of female infanticide: "I had two sisters who had died before my birth; by the course of nature, let me add, for the horrible practice of female infanticide was in our part of the empire only heard of in stories, and not without a shudder."[93] Although he and his fellow countrymen "shudder" at the thought of female infanticide, he later contradicts himself by admitting that poor people "'make way' with their babies rather than see them slowly starve to death. With them, girl-babies are more often sacrificed because boys are readily adopted by rich and childless persons, while the female infants rarely can be thus provided for."[94] Still supportive of other classes despite distancing himself from them by entering the middle class, he does not demonize the poor for killing their infant daughters but still recognizes the extreme structural sexism that would lead them to do so. During the concurrent period of exceptionalizing and dehumanizing Chinese American driving-out, Yan Phou Lee defends the nobility of the Chinese: "I am indignant that there should be a popular belief in America that Chinese girls at their birth are generally put to death because they are not wanted by their parents. Nothing can be further from the truth."[95] Even though he refutes the common belief of Chinese female infanticide, he admits and, to an extent, perpetuates ("for the very good reasons") the structural sexism in which "women do not appear in public life" and "sons are more to be desired."[96] His admission demonstrates his traditionalist gender politics, at the time, which more widely appealed to a conservative, Gilded Age liberal audience.

And yet, the reformism of the Gilded Age allowed for Yan Phou Lee to proceed with two interracial marriages with white women in Connecticut, one of the few states that did not enact antimiscegenation laws. For all its discussion of gender and gender roles, *When I Was a Boy in China* elides any mention of Yan Phou Lee's first marriage to a white American woman named Elizabeth Maud Jerome in 1887, the same year the ethnographic autobiography was published. The *New York Times* covered and spectacularized the marriage as "the first marriage in New-Haven of a native of China to an American lady."[97] It stated,

93. Yan Phou Lee, *When I Was a Boy in China*, 53.
94. Yan Phou Lee, *When I Was a Boy in China*, 53.
95. Yan Phou Lee, *When I Was a Boy in China*, 53.
96. Yan Phou Lee, *When I Was a Boy in China*, 53.
97. "Married to a Chinaman."

Yan Phou Lee of the Class of '87 at Yale, and a native of Fragrant Hills, China, was married to-day to Miss Elizabeth Maud Jerome, daughter of Mrs. E. Gilbert Jerome, of this city. [. . .] In the Summer of 1884 he returned to this country, despite the wishes of his relatives, determined to become an American citizen. He has already taken out his first papers. While in college he supported himself partly by lecturing in different cities. At graduation he was awarded the Larned Scholarship, and will spend one more year at Yale pursuing a post graduate course. His wife is heiress to a handsome fortune. Among those present at the wedding were Yung Wing, formerly of the Chinese embassy and now an American citizen living in Hartford, and several Yale Professors.[98]

Yan Phou Lee's achievement of graduating from Yale and having Yale graduates like Yung and many of the college's professors in attendance at the wedding is mentioned as if to legitimize the interracial marriage through accomplishments. This underhanded racism gets at the social damage and slippery slope of the exceptional minority stereotype—that one must overwork and achieve in order to be considered a racial equal. The article also mentions that Yan Phou Lee "has already taken out his first papers" toward citizenship and that Jerome "is heiress to a handsome fortune," thus perpetuating the yellow peril in suggesting Yan Phou Lee is taking advantage of Jerome through their interracial marriage. Again, it's unclear why Yan Phou Lee omits any mention of his first marriage, particularly when his moderate, exceptional minority activism includes assimilationist principles. However, other sources suggest that the marriage, which ended after the birth of their second child, Gilbert, only three years later, was unhappy from the start—in part, due to the liberal unacceptance of interracial marriages.

In concert with his own traditionalist, liberal gender politics, Yan Phou Lee seemed to have many conflicts with the women figures in his life. At the end of his marriage, the *Chicago Tribune* published a piece on his divorce which begins by giving Yan Phou Lee a voice only to disparage him as a "a tempest-tossed Chinaman."[99] The piece begins with his complaints about his mother-in-law:

In his own words, she began the work of "repression and suppression. Petty persecutions and constant fault-finding almost broke my spirit and unfitted me for work. By the time the first child was born things had grown so bad

---

98. "Married to a Chinaman."
99. "Yan Phon Lee and His Mother-in-Law." Misspelling in the original.

and I had so little money or chance of getting any that I accepted an offer to work in the Pacific Bank in San Francisco."[100]

The article directly interviewed him, citing him as saying that his marriage was already failing, because of his mother-in-law's "repression and suppression," by the time his first child, Jennie, was born in 1888—just a year after their marriage. He clearly blames his mother-in-law's "petty persecutions and constant fault-finding" for the limitations of his career. He goes on to explain why he did not publicly pursue a settlement and custody in court:

> (1) I do not want a wife who does not want me. (2) I wish to avoid publicity; I don't care to have my dirty family linen washed in court. (3) If I contest the suit I may be charged with mercenary motives; some one will say that I wish to keep a hold on her money—which I have no "use for." (4) I have suffered so much that I shall be glad to be free, no matter how bad the means to that end. (5) I have not the means to support my wife and children in the style she is accustomed to. (6) She would not leave a comfortable house in New Haven to follow my uncertain fortunes. (7) It may be that through much suffering I am to be free to do my country a great service. Who knows?[101]

Yan Phou Lee attempted to end his marriage with dignity, not "want[ing] a wife who does not want [him]" and declining "to have my dirty family linen washed in court," even though he ironically reports his story to the newspaper.[102] He nevertheless points out the predicament he has endured in having his mother-in-law sabotage his career and "not [having] the means to support my wife and children in the style she is accustomed to." As a liberal in the Gilded Age, despite being an activist, he expects to be the sole breadwinner in his household.

However, the journalist's ambivalence toward Yan Phou Lee explains Lee's liberal gender politics. The journalist cites Yan Phou Lee's conclusion with sympathy: "He closes his screed with a genuine bit of pathos: 'I am a poor, tempest-tossed creature. I will be glad to be free. What a fool I was to get married, anyhow!'"[103] And yet, the journalist proceeds to criticize Yan Phou Lee with racist epithets:

---

100. "Yan Phon Lee and His Mother-in-Law."
101. "Yan Phon Lee and His Mother-in-Law."
102. I thank Jane Wessel for pointing out this irony.
103. "Yan Phon Lee and His Mother-in-Law."

If such be the outcome of Yan Phou Lee's reflections, with how much more fervor may Mrs. Yan Phou Lee utter the same ejaculation. Will it ever occur to her what a fool she was to marry him? Should it occur to every American girl who goes out of her way to contract these unnatural, unwomanly, unpatriotic, and monstrous alliances that she is making a fool of herself and that her chickens will sooner or later come home to roost? And yet, in spite of just such warnings as this, there will not be wanting American girls eager and willing to marry a tempest-tossed Chinaman, a drunken Duke, a flat-footed Feejee Islander, or any other monstrosity that offers itself to their absurd fancies.[104]

Clearly, the liberal journalist was against "unnatural, unwomanly, unpatriotic, and monstrous" interracial marriages to begin with. He uses different iterations of the term "monstrous" twice in his description of Yan Phou Lee's marriage. The same article that begins by giving Yan Phou Lee a voice proceeds to denigrate him in a racist manner. Faced with the racism of nineteenth-century liberalism, Yan Phou Lee gives in to a patriarchal marriage in spite of his liberal sympathy toward women. Such was the way in which he critiqued and perpetuated nineteenth-century US liberalism.

Moreover, even though and because his first wife was also a contradictory liberal, she cast public racial accusations at Yan Phou Lee. His first wife, Elizabeth Jerome, condemned him for his divorce in newspapers in 1890 despite his achievements. Elizabeth leveled accusations of "adultery, deceitfulness, and theft" against him, which also demonstrate how quickly the model minority stereotype reverts to the yellow peril, since both exceptionalizing stereotypes objectify the subject even in one's personal life.[105] As a result, Yan Phou Lee lost custody of his children. Such a personal and public reception of interracial marriages is perhaps one reason why he omits any mention of it from *When I Was a Boy in China*. In addition to his first marriage, many important parts of his life such as his children were left out of his autoethnography, which reflects the many traumas and psychic fragmentations he experienced.

A COHESIVE NARRATIVE IN HONORING YUNG

Though a cohesive but hybrid autoethnographic narrative that protests the status quo of Chinese exclusion and both reflects and heals his experience of collective trauma, *When I Was a Boy in China* also elides any mention of his

104. "Yan Phon Lee and His Mother-in-Law."
105. R. V. Lee, 17.

birth in 1861 in Xiangshan [Fragrant Hills], China, and only briefly glosses his arrival in the United States in 1873 with the Chinese Educational Commission after having spent a year in preparatory school in Shanghai.[106] These omissions are due, in part, to his own trauma of living in the States during the objectifying and exceptionalizing driving-out era and hardship of witnessing Yung's persecutions. Yan Phou Lee, however, does go on to detail his own accomplishments such as passing the examination in Shanghai to pursue his studies in the United States.[107] Although the autoethnography does end in the United States, Yan Phou Lee avoids a teleological immigrant narrative of chastising the poverty and backwardness of a nation of origin and arriving in the progressive United States that is mythically paved with gold. Instead, *When I Was a Boy in China* ends subversively with Yan Phou Lee and his schoolmates running away in 1873 from the proselytizing church: "We did not stop till we got into our room, while our American friends, surprised at this move on our part and failing to overtake us, went back to the church."[108] However, the autoethnography concludes with Yan Phou Lee and his Chinese classmates industriously learning English and American culture—the same industriousness for which the eighteen Chinese men were lynched just a few years earlier in the Massacre of 1871 and for which Chinese were concurrently driven out in other ways from West Coast cities, suffering a social death:

> We learned English by object-lessons. At table we were always told the names of certain dishes, and then assured that if we could not remember the name we were not to partake of that article of food. Taught by this method, our progress was rapid and surprising.[109]

The rapidity and surprising nature of his learning contributed to Yan Phou Lee's academic achievements in the United States. He exposes the social coercion of Gilded Age liberalism that is used to perpetuate the traumatizing, exceptional minority stereotype.

His inclusive and cohesive honoring of his mentor Yung Wing protests the discrimination against Yung and also critiques the exceptional minority stereotype. Publishing before his mentor, who was socially tokenized and disciplined for being the earliest Chinese American activist of his time by a lack of interest in his writing, Yan Phou Lee purposefully describes and aspires to emulate his mentor Yung Wing in *When I Was a Boy in China*: "About forty years ago, there came to this country under the auspices of the Rev. Dr.

---

106. Xu, 80, 81.
107. Yan Phou Lee, *When I Was a Boy in China*, 93.
108. Yan Phou Lee, *When I Was a Boy in China*, 93.
109. Yan Phou Lee, *When I Was a Boy in China*, 98.

Brown, an American missionary in China, a Chinese youth who was destined to exert a potent influence on the future of the Chinese Empire. Many have heard of him or read about him; his name is Yung Wing."[110] That he has to introduce his mentor, who founded the Chinese Educational Commission on which he traveled to the United States, is humiliating for Yan Phou Lee, who is differently tokenized as the *repetitive* exceptional minority par excellence or the "good immigrant" who came after Yung. Yan Phou Lee chooses to include Yung both out of due respect for Yung and to critique the exceptional minority stereotype that objectifies and exceptionalizes Asian Americans disparately—the first wave as "bad" and the second wave as "good." And although he performs the exceptional minority stereotype to critique the contradictions and exceptionalism of Gilded Age liberalism, his activism is engulfed by his own conservative liberalism.

In his liberalism, in which he gives credence to those who have authority over him, he nevertheless proceeds to give a brief biography of Yung to enflesh and memorialize him:

> He went back to China soon after his graduation and engaged in business at Shanghai. But business with the incidental pleasure of moneymaking, did not entirely absorb his attention. China was at that time having troublesome diplomatic negotiations with foreign powers, and was being taken advantage of right and left for want of men in office who understood the customs, the laws and the civilization of Western countries.
>
> Dr. Wing, indignant at the wrongs which China had suffered and was suffering at the hands of so-called "Christian" and "enlightened" nations, sought for a remedy, and conceived the brilliant project of educating a number of Chinese boys in America for future service at the government expense.
>
> He made his plan known to prominent Chinese officials. At first he met with no sympathy, no encouragement. Still, he persevered; and after twelve years of patient waiting and active labor, he succeeded in convincing two of the most powerful ministers at the court of Pekin of the feasibility of his scheme. In consequence, an edict was issued by the emperor to enforce its execution.[111]

According to Yan Phou Lee, Yung also draws a distinction between the hypocritical "so-called 'Christian' and 'enlightened' nations" and true Christians. He also points out Yung's activism in his "indignance" at social injustice and

---

110. Yan Phou Lee, *When I Was a Boy in China*, 86.

111. Yan Phou Lee, *When I Was a Boy in China*, 86–87.

comments on Yung's good character in "persevering" for twelve years in starting the Chinese Educational Commission. However, Yan Phou Lee recognizes that Yung's career was subject to the tokenization of the exceptional minority stereotype when he states that Yung was "inspired by a lofty ambition[;] he worked his way through preparatory school and college, graduating from Yale in 1854 with high honors."[112] Dismissed as a sold-out, Christian assimilationist during the Civil Rights era,[113] Yung Wing has been an under-researched figure in Asian American studies and was an overlooked literary figure in his day. Even though Yung immigrated to the United States the earliest of all five figures I discuss in this book, he was the last to publish his voice in his only publication, *My Life in China and America*, in 1909. Born in the village of Nam Ping[114] in Xiangshan County in China, near Macao, on November 17, 1828, he immigrated to the States when he was eighteen years old in April of 1847.[115] He lived through the Opium Wars of 1839–42 and 1856–60, the first of which influenced his parents to send him to a missionary school.[116] Perhaps his parents felt it best to give him a social advantage by sending him to a missionary school since, during the Opium Wars, China inevitably fell to Western power in which Western mission work was synonymous to opening China to the West for trade; for example, Karl Gützlaff, the husband of Mrs. Gützlaff to whom Yung is indebted in his work, was one missionary who also worked for the East India Company.[117] He was also living in the United States during the Gold Rush that brought over Toy, and the Tianjin Massacre in 1870, which spurred the creation of Yung's famous Chinese Educational Commission (alternately referred to as the Chinese Educational Mission); he also lived through Tape's Supreme Court hearing in 1885, and the driving-out era of the 1870s and 1880s that all the writers of the study witnessed and to which they responded. Yung's academic achievements, as I discuss in the next chapter, helped him gain the quotidian status of citizenship but were absorbed and misrecognized by the exceptional minority stereotype.

Like Yung, Yan Phou Lee graduated with high honors—Phi Beta Kappa and summa cum laude—from Yale in 1887. He deployed and risked the traumatizing exceptional minority stereotype through his "celebrity" status from

112. Yan Phou Lee, *When I Was a Boy in China*, 86.

113. Chin et al., *Big Aiiieeeee!*, xxvii, xxviii.

114. Fred Gilbert Blakeslee, "Chinese Came Here to Study Western Ideas: Hartford Was Home of First Educational Mission to United States," *Hartford Daily*, Saturday, February 16, 1929, Yung Wing papers, Sterling Memorial Library, Yale University, New Haven, CT MS 602; Series Accession 1999-M-069, additional; box 1; 1878–1881; folders 1–4; 5; 6; 7; 8.

115. Worthy, 267.

116. Xu, 33–34; and Blakeslee.

117. Platt, 421, 275.

his accomplishments and publications, like his autobiographical ethnography, to enflesh himself and Chinese Americans, generally; however, both Yan Phou Lee and Yung were dismissed as and co-opted by Gilded Age liberalism and its symmetrical exceptionalisms of exemption from law and exceptionalizing Chinese Americans.[118] Nevertheless, Yan Phou Lee enfleshed himself by writing cohesive narratives in response to his collective trauma. And despite Yan Phou Lee's aims to subjectify and enflesh himself and his fellow Chinese Americans, he was objectified by the exceptional, model minority / yellow peril stereotype at the end of his life by the liberal discourse of the press and his family.[119] Yan Phou Lee eventually remarried another white American woman named Sophie Florence Bolles about ten years after his first marriage and raised their two sons on a farm with her in Lincoln, Delaware.[120] Although their marriage seemed happier than his first, he eventually left his family in the 1930s to go to China by himself and died there in a year that is unspecified.[121] Yan Phou Lee's tumultuous personal relationships with women and his criticism of structural sexism in China contribute to his traditionalist, liberal gender politics. But it was also liberalism that supported his marriage to white women during an era of state-specific antimiscegenation laws. As Cheung points out, there are also many times during his autoethnography that his liberal masculinism comes through despite his criticism of cultural sexism.

Nevertheless, despite his admission of the structural sexism in China and occasional masculinism, Yan Phou Lee aims to enflesh Chinese Americans and Chinese culture—a culture historically denigrated by the yellow peril discourse—in his autoethnography. Written for a white American audience, Yan Phou Lee's *When I Was a Boy in China* is a contact zone of hybridity[122] in which he deploys academic American English and engages with American values to convince white Americans that Chinese Americans are civilized humans rather than "aliens ineligible to citizenship." His ethnographies and activist essays overlap in his insistence on "true" and just Christianity and his criticism of the exceptional minority stereotype even as he sometimes uses the rhetoric to convince his conservative audience to rail against social injustice. His *repetitive* use and even embodiment of the exceptional minority stereotype was not just a political ploy but also evidence of his enduring trauma even as

---

118. Richard V. Lee, "Introduction," 16.

119. R. V. Lee, "Introduction," 16. Ten days after his death, Jennie Jerome enfleshed her father when she wrote to her brother Gilbert: "We had a brave father, even if he was not good" (R. V. Lee, "Afterword," 99).

120. Xu, 119.

121. Xu, 118–19.

122. Pratt, 7.

he tried to heal from the driving-out era through his cohesive narratives. Herman writes, "Resolution of the trauma is never final; recovery is never complete. The impact of a traumatic event continues to reverberate throughout the survivor's lifecycle."[123] Thus, in his writings, Yan Phou Lee deployed and remained plagued by the exceptional minority stereotype. As I mentioned, the same year he published *When I Was a Boy in China,* he published "Why I Am Not a Heathen," in the *North American Review* (1887), in direct response to Wong Chin Foo's famous essay, which, again, he made obvious by the subtitle: "A Rejoinder to Wong Chin Foo."[124] Although he seems to attack Wong Chin Foo, two years later, in his essay "The Chinese Must Stay" in the *North American Review,* he turns his political critique to Kearney's famous motto "The Chinese must go!" Although Wong Chin Foo's and Yan Phou Lee's politics were different insofar as the former's was radical and the latter's was liberal and moderate, both were activists in their own right. Wong Chin Foo's and Yan Phou Lee's circles also overlapped through the literary figure Mark Twain. While Twain was in the same speaking circuit and had the same manager as Wong Chin Foo, he was also a major supporter of Yan Phou Lee's work.[125] Ultimately, Yan Phou Lee, as well as Yung, attempted to deauthorize the yellow peril—ironically part of the exceptional minority stereotype—which stereotyped Chinese Americans en masse, by demonstrating their individual accomplishments and humanity through the exceptional minority rhetoric even as they also critiqued it. The tandem exceptional minority discourse, which they deployed and critiqued, nevertheless allowed liberalism to co-opt their moderate efforts since it ultimately suggested competition with and economic threats to white Americans in the nineteenth century. Yan Phou Lee's integration into the middle class through his elite education and his interracial marriages also heralded the middle-class liberal reforms of the Progressive Era in which Yung was finally recognized and published.

---

123. Herman, 211.
124. Seligman, 144.
125. Yan Phou Lee, *When I Was a Boy in China,* 11–12.

CHAPTER 4

Yung Wing

Exceptional Minority Discourse in the Plague Era

PLAGUE-WRITING IN RESPONSE TO THE EXCEPTIONAL MINORITY STEREOTYPE AND SOCIAL DEATH

Yung Wing is best known among the five figures studied in this book for his establishment of the Chinese Educational Commission (CEC), from 1872 to 1881, which educated 120 students from China in the United States, a feat in itself, during the driving-out era. However, Yung also had other aspirations to write, as evidenced in his publication of his autobiography, *My Life in China and America,* in 1909 and his unpublished writing in college. Although there is no evidence that Yung Wing necessarily failed in previous efforts to publish, he seemed to be heading toward a literary career in college but did not publish until his eighties: he went to Yale University, where he excelled at writing, winning several prizes in composition, wrote poetry, and graduated with an AB.[1] In 1876 he was also conferred an LLD by the Yale Law School.[2] Nevertheless,

---

1. Koh; and Bush, 43.

2. *When East Met West,* excerpted from *Yung Wing and the Young Chinese Students in America,* by Timothy Kao, Professor Emeritus-Economics, Gateway Community-Technical College, and President of the Chinese Students Memorial Society in Connecticut; and *The Story of the Chinese Educational Commission to the United States,* by Richard C. DeAngelis, Professor Emeritus, Fairfield University, 7; Yung Wing papers, Sterling Memorial Library, Yale University, New Haven, CT, accession 2000-M-097; group 602, box 1.

it is clear that at one point he aspired to be a writer, but he focused his time, upon graduating, on the Chinese Educational Commission. He was the first Chinese to graduate from an American university—and Yale, at that.[3] And yet, with the exceptional minority stereotype at his back, Yung overachieved by going to Yale just to qualify as a quotidian US citizen, which he became during his junior year, in 1852.[4] Although, as he also taught Yan Phou Lee to do the same, he tactically deployed the exceptional minority stereotype to advance his career but also railed against it, nineteenth-century US liberalism ultimately co-opted and misrepresented Yung's academic, modernist distinction between secular personal development and Christianity as the yellow peril in his day. The model minority / yellow peril stereotype catalyzed his loss of US citizenship in 1898[5] and obstructed what might have been a prolific writing career; the model minority, assimilationist stereotype also plagued Yung Wing's reception in the twentieth century after the Civil Rights era. Most significantly, it has dehistoricized and decontextualized Yung's activism during the driving-out era. Critics have also failed to contextualize his masculinism during the later, plague era of his book's publication in which the yellow peril stereotype deemed the Chinese unhealthy and contributed to the scapegoating of Chinese Americans for disease; this resulted in authorities quarantining Chinatown several times. Some critics have cited Yung as a masculinist in his writing.[6] He nevertheless reveals his traditionalist gender politics that were also sympathetic to women during the Page Act era through his personal letters. This chapter contextualizes Yung Wing's Chinese American activism and his traditionalist but sympathetic gender politics during the driving-out and the coincident and subsequent plague eras to better understand his gender politics, his modernist writing, his secularization of Christianity, and his work for the CEC.

Yung's work in enfleshing himself during the exceptional driving-out era is yet another form of "divine violence," which thus "deposes" "violence."[7] In exposing the sovereign violence of the driving-out era as an early Chinese American activist and universal humanist, Yung was discursively disciplined as one of the first "troublemaker[s] [who] is precisely one who tries to force [the invisible] sovereign power [that is, white supremacy,] to translate itself into actuality."[8] That is to say, Gilded Age American liberals ignored his

3. Blakeslee.
4. Koh; and Worthy, 270.
5. Xu, 59.
6. Cheung, 32.
7. Agamben, 64, 65.
8. Agamben, 47.

writing prowess and the US government eventually stripped him of his American citizenship. Yung wrote during the plague era, which preceded, coincided with, and followed the driving-out era—in which the liberals blamed the Chinese, as part of the yellow peril stereotype, as the source of epidemics and disease. Living and active through the plague era and the driving-out era, being stripped of his citizenship, Yung experienced a "social death": that is, what Cacho defines as "ineligibility to personhood refers to the state of being legally recognized as rightless, located in the spaces of social death where demands for humanity are ultimately disempowering because they can be interpreted only as asking to be given something sacred in return for nothing at all" and what Patterson defines as "general dishonor."[9] Yung was an "alien ineligible to citizenship" so much so that he lost his and was relegated to "the spaces of social death." To Cacho's definition, Grace Kyungwon Hong adds that liberalism, specifically neoliberalism, requires the death of minoritized subjects: "death can and indeed must be the basis of a politics in the contemporary moment, impossibly of life. The theoretical and political practice of 'difference' holds in suspension the ostensibly mutually exclusive states of life and death. In so doing, it remembers the exacerbated dispersal of minoritized death that neoliberalism disavows."[10] Yung, who was, as Hong describes, stripped of his rights of US citizenship because of his minoritized subjecthood, was finally published during the Progressive Era, in which neoliberalism was beginning to take root.[11] And thus Yung's "troublemaking" work, what I call his exceptional *plague writing,* exposes and tracks the literal deaths (lynchings) and the social death (other forms of driving-out) that the liberalism of the Gilded Age and the Progressive Era both required and disavowed. His plague-writing consists of his positivistic, enfleshing projects: his actual writing—his autobiography and his modernist poetry—his work with the CEC, his secularization of Christianity, and his masculinist politics, which he articulates in his autobiography. The positivism of his plague-writing, such as his autobiography, is an example of what Lowe calls "affirmation and presence"[12] and responds to the negating disavowals of the Chinese American exceptional, driving-out deaths—both lynching and social deaths—of contemporary liberalism.

As a strict autobiography rather than autoethnography, *My Life in China and America* allowed Yung, more so than Yan Phou Lee, to enflesh himself during the early era of Asian exclusion in which the discourse of the exceptional minority flourished. Despite his attempts to westernize China, he travels constantly between China and America in his book, demonstrating that

---

9. Cacho, 7; and Patterson, 13.
10. Hong, 8, 27.
11. Cohen, 226.
12. Lowe, 40.

neither country is the more favorable; on the other hand, in *When I Was a Boy in China,* Yan Phou Lee teleologically travels from China to the US, suggesting that the US is the ultimate end goal. In using the form of the autobiography, Yung enfleshes himself even though he never mentions any of his failures. His growing knowledge of Chinese exclusion and the enduring, liberal discourse of white supremacy in his studies at Yale make him unhappy, as he states,

> All through my college course, especially in the closing year, the lamentable condition of China was before my mind constantly and weighted on my spirits. In my despondency, I often wished I had never been educated, as education had unmistakably enlarged my mental and moral horizon, and revealed to me responsibilities which the sealed eye of ignorance can never see, and sufferings and wrongs of humanity to which an uncultivated and callous nature can never be made sensitive. The more one knows, the more he suffers and is consequently less happy; the less one knows, the less he suffers, and hence is more happy.[13]

Although none of his writing protested anti-Chinese sentiment in the US, his admission here of the "sufferings and wrongs of humanity to which an uncultivated and callous nature can never be made sensitive" indicates his disagreement with the contemporary hate crimes against and legal exclusions of Chinese Americans. Publicly responding to each other in newspapers, Yung and Wong Chin Foo disagreed on their Christian and heathen belief systems, respectively, but they both fought against the driving-out and dehumanization of Chinese Americans during the late nineteenth century in their writings.[14] Moreover, his focus on his own, healthy, vigorous manhood was both a way to harness the exceptional minority stereotype to discursively qualify as a Chinese *American* and to disprove the yellow peril stereotype of Chinese disease and pestilence during the plague era.

As demonstrated during the smallpox epidemics of 1868, 1876, 1880, and 1887 in San Francisco, plagues become politicized when they pose threats and inconveniences to people. Health and government authorities repeatedly blamed the Chinese for the smallpox epidemics and the bubonic plague in San Francisco in 1900 and sealed off Chinatown twice from the rest of the city.[15] Because traces of the plague began in the Chinese community in Hawai'i in 1899, the Chinese were discursively associated with this disease.[16] While experiencing stark yellow peril bias, Yung was writing *My Life*

13. Yung Wing, *My Life in China and America*, 14.
14. Seligman, 206, 207.
15. Trauner; and Shah, 120–21.
16. Randall, 1.

in China and America. Again, the Chinese were used as scapegoats when the disease was inconveniencing white American lives. After Chinatown was quarantined, Chinese Americans could not trust American health inspectors as "rumors of beatings and rape at the hands of health inspectors spread through Chinatown."[17] Moreover, during the bubonic plague era, California's governor, Henry Gage, accused federal authorities of overreacting to the epidemic and inducing panic at a national level.[18] Joseph Kinyoun, the founder of the Hygienic Laboratory, which became the National Institutes of Health (NIH), was placed in charge by Surgeon General Wyman of treating the bubonic plague in San Francisco through the Marine Hospital Service. Although Kinyoun went along with the quarantine of Chinatown, he warned Wyman against "overly stringent public health measures" because he felt that the enforced aggressive quarantine was unconstitutional[19] and because he understood the epidemiology of the plague and focused his efforts on killing rats and vermin instead of quarantine and isolation. As Shah points out, the bubonic plague in San Francisco in 1900, as has the recent coronavirus pandemic, exposed the rift between "scientific knowledge and government strategies."[20] Despite Kinyoun's expertise in the plague epidemiology, Governor Gage accused Kinyoun of "malicious intent, declaring plague a ruse concocted by Kinyoun and the San Francisco Board of Health to blackmail the city for public health funds."[21] Gage and Wyman also signed a pact of secrecy to prevent the news of the bubonic plague from spreading.[22] The press called Dr. Kinyoun "stupid and malignant" and declared the plague "fake."[23] Governor Gage eventually removed Kinyoun from the Marine Hospital Service, as he accused Kinyoun of importing and spreading the plague by implanting the plague bacteria in cadavers.[24] Instead, Gage placed Dr. Rupert Blue in charge of handling the plague. Blue, although not as adept as Kinyoun in epidemiology,[25] was not only able to address the rat infestation before and after the earthquake of 1906, he was also able to link the disease to the fleas that were spreading the disease between rats and humans.[26] Despite these scientific discoveries, scapegoating Asians, specifically the Chinese in the late nineteenth and early twentieth century, supported the fallacy that "public

17. Randall, 62.
18. Shah, 121.
19. National Institutes of Health, 2, 4.
20. Shah, 123.
21. NIH, 2.
22. Randall, 108; and *Plague at the Golden Gate.*
23. NIH, 3.
24. NIH, 4.
25. *Plague at the Golden Gate.*
26. Randall, 224; and *Plague at the Golden Gate.*

space—white space, citizens' space—could be cordoned off from the danger of contagion and the sound, smell, and sight of disease, all of which were carried flagrantly by the intruding, uncontained, unsightly foreign beggar."[27] Thus, one must understand Yung's *My Life in China and America* in this context of scapegoating Chinese for disease and poverty.

Yung wrote and published his autobiography during the events of the early exclusion era in which the Chinese were blamed for urban epidemics, anti-Chinese organizations such as the Anti-Coolie Association (1869) were created, and Chinese were driven out and experienced spectacularizing social deaths through legal discourse (1875, 1882). And thus, his focus on exceptional minority health and manly vigor was part of his activist resistance against the yellow peril. Yung's asserted masculinity is impossible to ignore in his autobiography. Demonstrating his subjectivity (rather than objectivity), Yung emphasizes his masculinity when he fights and defeats a Scotchman in a fight: "The Scotchman, after the incident, did not appear in public for a whole week. I was told he had shut himself up in his room to give his wound time to heal, but the reason he did not care to show himself was more on account of being whipped by a little Chinaman in a public manner."[28] Appealing to popular discourse about the effeminacy of Chinese men, Yung refers to himself as "a little Chinaman" who nevertheless defeats a white European in a fistfight. Cheung writes of this scene: "In this way, Yung begins to solve a peculiarly Chinese American problem. To avoid feminization, he fights, but to avoid association with the stereotype of the yellow peril, he invokes reason and acts with restraint."[29] At Yale Yung never hesitated to show his masculinity in participating in sports: Worthy writes,

Once each fall, the entire freshman and sophomore classes competed against each other, the only rule being that the first touchdown won the game. Yung of course took part and as one witness described him, he appeared in old clothes and wore a tall straw hat underneath which his queue was coiled and fastened with pins. [. . .] In the words of the observer: "Yung pounced upon the ball with no one to say nay, and like a flash was off, off around the end and toward Chapel Street. He had gone two or three rods before anyone knew it. Half the college was looking on from the sidelines. The movement caught their attention first and their sudden cheering gave the alarm. The players still struggling, looked around surprised. Then the mass burst into two hundred individual fragments went after that peculiar 'Chinese.' But it was too late. He had the start. He was fresher than most of them. It was the

---

27. Schweik, 170.
28. Yung Wing, *My Life in China and America*, 23.
29. Cheung, 93.

chance of his life, and he made the most of it. He bounded like a deer; he flew on the wings of the wind. His hat went off; his queue burst from the pins and streamed out behind him like a pump-handle. The whole college ran after him with yells of anger and delight. But he was in front and nothing could stop him till he had struck the iron fence and tossed the ball in the middle of Chapel Street."[30]

Described as "a flash," Yung never hesitated to show his physical prowess in football—a quintessentially manly American sport. Despite his demonstration of "fresh" American masculinity, the observer particularizes him as "that peculiar 'Chinese'" whose "queue burst from the pins" and elicited both "anger and delight" at his assimilation. Masculinity was also an essential part of a US imperialism that Roosevelt championed during the Progressive Era.[31] But for Yung, during the driving-out era, demonstrations of vigorous masculinity contradicted the yellow peril stereotype of Chinese disease and infirmity but did not guarantee assimilation.

During this period of rampant anti-Chinese sentiment, Yung and Yan Phou Lee,[32] whom Yung obviously influenced, are able to represent themselves and their masculinities as enfleshment. At times, they deploy "ethical manhoods" or inclusive "manhoods that care for others,"[33] and make efforts to represent Chinese women by enfleshing them as complex subjects at various moments; however, in keeping with the problem of discourse, their efforts to enflesh Chinese women are co-opted and reinterpreted by liberalism as gendered exceptional minority stereotypes of the Dragon Lady / Lotus Blossom, to which Ling's criticism attests. Despite the few outstanding examples of Ah Toy and Mary Tape, Chinese American women in the nineteenth century were largely unable to represent themselves. Their exceptional minority objectification as hyperfeminine, exotic and enslaved prostitutes was represented by the exceptional, driving-out rhetoric of the Page Act, which led to the forced and often fatal prostitution of Chinese women and the policing of all Chinese women as prostitutes. Reflective of Progressive Era contradictions of reform and the lack of woman suffrage, Yung's masculinism seems to support this problematic objectification of Chinese women, and, at other times, he displays his sympathy toward their social oppression. Nevertheless, his masculinism must also be contextualized during the plague era and is better understood as a response to the plague-era rhetoric of Chinese disease and unhealthiness.

---

30. Worthy, 271–72.
31. Clark, *Asian American Avant-Garde*, 42; and Bederman, 171.
32. Yan Phou Lee, *When I Was a Boy in China*, 51.
33. Shimizu, 4.

As a result, his masculinity countered some of his sympathies toward women exemplified by his descriptions of his teacher/mentor, Mrs. Gützlaff, his mother, and his wife, which I discuss in detail later. Since he worked closely with and mentored Yan Phou Lee, his gender politics likewise influenced Lee, who also demonstrates his traditionalist gender politics in his writings. And yet, as I mentioned in the last chapter, Yan Phou Lee as the token, "good immigrant," who arrived subsequent to and was mentored by Yung, succeeded in his writing career. On the other hand, Yung, who was considered the "yellow peril," despite his efforts to document his achievements, was stripped of his citizenship eleven years before he published his autobiography and had a very meager writing career. The personal hardships he endured and the collective trauma he experienced during the driving-out and plague eras contributed to his experience of what Jaime Castillo, LCSW, calls a "little t" trauma, a social death that is a denial of rights and general dishonor, which "was not [necessarily] life-threatening—but caused [one] to feel overwhelming distress, fear, or helplessness at the time, and the effects from it have lasted into adulthood."[34] Likewise, psychiatrist Jonathan Shay argues that "cohesion"[35] is the most critical factor in helping trauma recovery. As I discussed in the previous chapter, collective and personal trauma can create gaps in memory storage, which is why building cohesive narratives, such as autobiographies, is so important in healing.[36] Autobiographies were indeed typical literary forms at the time but also used by those who suffered from racial oppression, such as African Americans and their slave narratives, to creative cohesive narratives to heal. As Yung experienced the "little t" trauma of witnessing the driving-out and plague eras and the social death of his loss of citizenship and assimilation, he *plague wrote* and published his autobiography for both social activism and personal recovery; but, unlike Yan Phou Lee, his sparseness in publications shows that the liberal public disciplined him for his early Chinese American activism during the driving-out and plague eras.

WRITING CITIZENSHIP

Although he published *My Life in China and America* in 1909 when he was in his eighties, during the massive reforms of the Progressive Era, it seems unclear whether Yung aspired to be a writer in the first place. Previous to the publication of *My Life in China and America*, Reverend Twichell gave a

---

34. Castillo.
35. Shay, 57.
36. Rothschild, 29.

sermon about Yung's life, "What Hath God Wrought," and prefaced it by saying, "Mr. Wing had never been willing to tell the story of his life, or to have it told, but that he in this case had not positively forbidden it."[37] Yung clearly changed his mind by 1909. But he was not always sure he wanted to be a writer: in a letter to Williams over Christmas vacation in 1852, Yung writes,

> I shall take my degree of B.A. if I live in the summer of 1854. I shall be thinking of going home and study my profession afterwards. In relation to a profession, I have not as yet come to a definite conclusion. One thing is certain however that I am going to study agricultural chemistry. I may possibly study medicine and surgery. There are so many things, and every one of them is so valuable to a man who intends to benefit his country, that it is extremely trying to know which to choose. I shall rely upon my own judgement[,] not consult my own inclination to the choice. I hope God will direct me; with his aid I hope to decide satisfactorily.[38]

In the 1850s, Yung seemed to be "certain" that he would study agricultural chemistry and possibly medicine, although he never pursued these fields in his career. He did, however, succeed in "going home" and "benefiting his country" with the Chinese Educational Commission. And, again, he relies on his Christianity for direction in his career. As Worthy concludes, "Yung never was able to decide exactly what profession he would follow; however, he did have the intention of working for the betterment of China. He claimed in his autobiography that he conceived of his Chinese Educational Commission scheme during his senior year at Yale, but there is no contemporary documentary evidence to prove this."[39] Nevertheless, his focus, upon graduating Yale, was on the CEC and his Chinese American activism in bridging the two cultures, above his writing career, particularly during an era in which Chinese lives were threatened and lost.

While he was at Yale, Yung worked two jobs to support himself—the first as a waiter in his residential college and the second as a librarian in a college debating society called the Brothers in Unity.[40] For working as a librarian for the Brothers in Unity, he also received a small allowance from the Savannah Ladies' Association, which also "sent him occasional gifts of money, together with socks, shirts, and other articles of clothing."[41] While his work in the library demonstrated his interest in literature, he did not pursue a specifically

---

37. "Remarkable Career," 6.
38. Worthy, 274.
39. Worthy, 274.
40. Koh.
41. Harris, 94; and La Fargue, 22.

literary career after Yale. When he returned to China after graduation, he engaged in the silk and tea business and also became the private secretary to a US representative, Peter Parker.[42] La Fargue writes, "In 1859 Yung Wing made a trip to the T'ai P'ing headquarters at Nanking in order to ascertain the character of the T'ai P'ing leaders, but any illusions which he might have had that the rebellion would lead to the salvation of China were dispelled by what he was able to observe at first hand."[43] Thereafter he did some literary work and writing such as translations for commercial houses, and he also served as a traveling agent for the English in China.[44] In 1862 a viceroy and army generalissimo by the name of Tsang Koh Fan offered to make him a mandarin of official rank.[45] As an officially ranked mandarin, he went to England, France, and the United States to purchase arms for China.[46] The machines he purchased from the United States were from Putnam & Co. (Fitchburg, Massachusetts): "Those machines contributed to the founding of the Kiang-Nam Arsenal in Shanghai, China's first modern arsenal."[47] He continued his interest in arms when, in 1873, "he made a brief visit to China and induced the government to send large orders for Gatling guns, and while there he was appointed to visit Peru and investigate the condition of the Chinese coolies in that country."[48] Before his work with the CEC and the Gatling guns, he continued his literary work in translating schoolbooks, including Colton's atlas and geography books, for the next three or four years.[49] However, his main passion after Yale was the Chinese Educational Commission, which he began to plan while in college.[50] It took him two decades to see it come to fruition, which happened in 1872, just a year after the Los Angeles Massacre. The Tianjin Massacre occurred in 1970, when a mob killed French Roman Catholic missionaries, and, after years of planning, the Chinese Educational Commission, fruit of the liberal reform of the Gilded Age, was finally formed to ease tensions between China and the West. At first, Yung only "succeeded in persuading the viceroy to have a mechanical school annexed to the arsenal in which Chinese youths may be taught the theory and practice of mechanical engineering and thus enable China in time to dispense with the employment

---

42. Blakeslee; and "Remarkable Career," 6.

43. La Fargue, 23.

44. "Remarkable Career," 6.

45. "Remarkable Career," 6.

46. "Remarkable Career," 6; and Blakeslee.

47. *When East Met West*, 2.

48. Yung Wing Papers, Sterling Memorial Library, Yale University, New Haven, CT, Yung Wing, 1828–1912; MS 602; HM 18; Reel 1U; 1876–1877.

49. "Remarkable Career," 6.

50. "Remarkable Career," 6.

of foreign engineers and machinists."[51] In 1870 the viceroy of China was interested in Yung's idea of the commission. However, "before the first installment of boys had started for this country, the mission suffered a great loss in the death of Viceroy Tsang Koh Fan, its backer, but the work was carried on by his successor, Li Hung Chang."[52] When Yung set up the CEC, the commission stipulated that 120 young Chinese boys could be educated in any Western country—some sources specify US and the Northeast, specifically, while others do not.[53] La Fargue writes, "In the memorials relating to the establishment of the Educational Mission it was proposed that the United States be the country in which this initial experiment was to be carried on. Later, similar contingents of students could be sent to Europe, but all of the one-hundred and twenty students embraced in the original project were to be sent to the United States."[54] Despite these options, the boys began to arrive in the northeast of the United States in 1872 under the leadership of Chin Lan Pin, the commissioner, and Yung Wing, the co-commissioner, two Chinese teachers, and an interpreter.[55] All these details supported Yung's Chinese American activist belief in the possibility of a hybrid Chinese American culture, which was an aim of his plague-writing.

The students of the CEC, as Yung predicted, found a place for themselves In the United States upon arrival. From 1872 to 1875, the boys arrived in detachments of thirty and were placed in family homes, "where in most cases, they were not treated as boarders, but as members of the family."[56] In 1875 the CEC "moved into [their] new headquarters, which was a large, double three-story house spacious enough to accommodate the commissioners, teachers and seventy-five students at one time. It was provided with a schoolroom where Chinese was exclusively taught; a dining room, a double kitchen, dormitories and bathrooms."[57] In 1877

the Chinese Educational Commission erected its own building at 352 Collins Street in Hartford, to be used as a center for learning the Chinese classics. The facility provided classrooms and boarding for seventy-five students.

---

51. Blakeslee.

52. Blakeslee.

53. Xu, 43–44; Koh; and "Remarkable Career," 6.

54. La Fargue, 32.

55. Blakeslee.

56. Blakeslee.

57. "Chinese Ambassador Coming to Celebration: Will Attend Banquet in Observance of 50th Anniversary of Founding Here of Chinese School," undated, Yung Wing papers, Sterling Memorial Library, Yale University, New Haven, CT, accession 2000-M-097; group 602, box 1, folder 7; Newspaper Clippings Pertaining to Yung Wing 1929, 1970.

Students would gather as a group to listen to the Chinese instructor, who read the Emperor's instructions at regular intervals. The curriculum for Chinese studies included the classics, poetry, calligraphy and composition, which reflected Yung's own interest in literature. To the newly American-ized Chinese students, the Chinese studies soon became a burden, and they referred to the CEC building as "Hell House."[58]

The journalist Fred Gilbert Blakeslee, whose family had housed one such CEC student, wrote,

> When the boys arrived they were dressed in Chinese costume but they soon discarded this and appeared in American clothes. As it was a behead-ing offense to cut off the cue, they were obliged to retain their pig-tails but they made them as inconspicuous as possible by wearing them under their clothing.
>
> The boys took kindly to sports, being especially fond of baseball. Our home was then located on Sumner street and the lot where they played being across the street from our house, the boys kept their bats and balls in our vestibule.
>
> No Chinese boy ever rang our front door to inquire if any of our boys were at home. He opened the door and walked upstairs to see for himself.[59]

From Blakeslee's account, the CEC seemed to be successful in assimilating the Chinese students, who gravitated to American baseball and "discarded" their "Chinese costume" and "appeared in American clothes." They also clearly made themselves at home in the US, perhaps to the annoyance or amazement of the white American families: "No Chinese boy ever rang our front door. [. . .] He opened the door and walked upstairs to see for himself." At school the students seemed to assimilate well, which was the aim of the CEC: "From 1872 to 1881, the Chinese students' academic achievements were matched by their victories on the baseball diamond and in the ballroom. Their great 'south-paw' pitcher, Liang Tun-Yen, led the 'Orientals' to many victories (he later served as the last Minister of Foreign Affairs in the Qing Dynasty). When Zhong Monyu (Chung Mun-yew) called the strokes as coxswain for the Yale crew, they defeated Har-vard in the boat races in 1880 and 1881."[60] The CEC was a clear success insofar as Yung Wing was heralded as a "modernizer and a rebel," and "now, especially

---

58. *When East Met West*, 4.
59. Blakeslee.
60. *When East Met West*, 4.

in intellectual circles, Yung Wing is a national hero."[61] The achievements of the graduates of the CEC are legion: they became "railroad builders, engineers, medical doctors, diplomats, college presidents, and naval admirals."[62] It was clear that China appreciated Yung Wing's work and the achievements of the CEC. Nevertheless, politics led to the commission's early demise.

Despite the success of the commission, the Qing government decided to close the program five years before its planned conclusion.[63] Professors Timothy Kao and Richard C. DeAngelis have suggested the following reasons for its closing:

1. Confucian Conservatism vs. Liberalism

   To the old elite, any modernization scheme was viewed with suspicion and regarded as a threat to essential Chinese cultural and political values. [. . .] The Chinese students also began to adopt western manners. They stopped wearing the long Chinese gown and wore western suits instead. Some had cut off their queues and some converted to Christianity. They dated American girls and danced at parties. An American classmate, who went on to become a Yale faculty member, recalled the Chinese students' charm with the ladies in the ballroom: "at dances and receptions, the fairest and most sought-out belles invariably [. . .] accepted the attention of Chinese rivals with more than a yielding grace." Chen Lan-Pin was shocked at the degree of Americanization among the students. He believed that the educational process had resulted in the alienation of the youth from Chinese tradition.

2. *Chinese reaction to students being baptized Christian* [. . .]

3. *The military academy disappointment*

   Until 1880, no single Chinese student was admitted into an American military academy, despite several Chinese attempts. China became convinced that the United States had violated the pledge of the Burlingame Treaty by barring her students from the American military academies.

4. *The Anti-Chinese moods in America*

   [. . .] On May 12, 1881, the Chinese Ministry of Foreign Affairs condemned the CEC in a memorandum:

---

61. "Late Chinese Educator Is Remembered," *Hartford Courant,* Thursday, July 9, 1970, Yung Wing papers, Sterling Memorial Library, Yale University, New Haven, CT, accession 2000-M-097; group 602, box 1, folder 7, Newspaper Clippings Pertaining to Yung Wing 1929, 1970.

62. *When East Met West,* 8–9.

63. Worthy, 281.

Customs and etiquette in the foreign country are vicious and improper.
Confucian creed is lacking in all the young students. The best way to
solve the problem is to dissolve the Chinese Educational Commission in
America immediately.[64]

Despite the conservatism of Gilded Age liberalism, it seemed to pale in comparison to Confucian conservatism, and thus the Chinese government shut down the CEC. In protest of this decision, Yung asked Civil War hero and former president Ulysses Grant to write a letter to the Chinese government in support of the mission. During his presidency, Grant had "hosted a special reception for the Chinese students, during which he shook hands with each of them."[65] Yung made the request with great humility after being denied participation in fighting for the Union Army in the Civil War.[66] Yung had met Grant through Mark Twain and his friend Reverend Twichell.[67] Together, Grant, Twain, Twichell, and others signed the petition, which stated,

> with scarcely a single exception their morals have been good; their manners have been polite and decorous, and their behavior has been such as to make friends for themselves and their country in the families, the schools, the cities and villages in which they have proved themselves worthy of the confidence which has been reposed in them to represent their families and the great Chinese empire in a land of strangers. Though children and youths, they seemed always to understand that the honor of their race and their nation was committed to their keeping. As a result of their good conduct, many prejudices of ignorant and wicked men toward the Chinese have been removed, and more favorable sentiments have taken their place.[68]

Yung had high hopes for this petition, as he wrote a letter to Twichell stating, "General Grant's letter, the circular, and your note to Li Hung-chang ought to accomplish something. If the greatest general of the age and the whole might of American learning and Christian character are not heeded in their advice, then I say let China go to the dogs."[69] Like Toy, Tape, Wong Chin Foo, and Yan

---

64. *When East Met West,* 5–6.
65. *When East Met West,* 4–5.
66. Koh.
67. Xu, 217.
68. Blakeslee.
69. Worthy, 281.

Phou Lee, Yung was both oppressed by and solicited and received help and support from liberals such as "the greatest general of the age."[70]

Despite Grant's support, the mission was still aborted. Even the liberal journalists from the *New York Times* were in protest of the CEC's closure. On July 23, 1881, it published an editorial that stated:

> The educational scheme which the Chinese government has been trying in this country, for ten years has been, from our point of view, very successful! [. . .] It is unreasonable to suppose that the bright young men like those educated in the U.S. at the cost of the Chinese government should content themselves with absorbing the principles of engineering, mathematics and other sciences remaining, meanwhile, wholly unresponsive to the political and social influences by which they are surrounded. [. . .] China cannot borrow our learning, our science, and our material forms of industry without importing with them the virus of political rebellion. [. . .] Therefore she will have none of these things.[71]

The liberals at the *Times* supported Yung's "virus of political rebellion," or his desire to westernize China, which he fostered after the closure of the CEC. While many in the country protested the end of the CEC, Yung recovered and continued to serve his native country despite its abandonment of his program by focusing his concerns on such items as building railroads in China: in an April 1881 letter to his longtime friend Twichell, he writes, "Rail-roads in China would not be as some of the RRs in this country—where they have to wait for a population, & the produce of farming: both people & land are already there waiting for R.R.s."[72] Continuing to dedicate himself to his country of origin, Yung returned to China in 1882 but returned to the US in 1883 because of his wife's poor health. Mary died on May 29, 1886, and thereafter until 1895, he stayed in Hartford, Connecticut, raising his sons, Morrison B. and Bartlett G. Yung, on his own.[73] Both would go on to graduate from Yale's Sheffield Scientific School—Morrison in 1898 and Bartlett in 1902. In 1895 he was asked by the Chinese government to return to China without any specific reason.[74] In 1898, when he lost his US citizenship as a result of the Chinese

---

70. Yung Wing, *My Life in China and America*, 281.

71. "Chinese in the U.S."; and *When East Met West*, 7.

72. Letter from Yung Wing to Joseph Hopkins Twichell, 14 April 1881, Joseph Hopkins Twichell papers, Beinecke Rare Books & Manuscripts Library, Yale University, New Haven, CT, YCAL MSS 755; box 9; October 1967 acquisition.

73. Worthy, 282.

74. Worthy, 282–83.

Exclusion Act,[75] Yung was active in the Hundred Days Reform in China.[76] Journalist Edmund Worthy writes, during this time, "just how Wing managed to get into America is a mystery."[77] He returned to the States as an undocumented immigrant in 1902 and remained undocumented until his death in 1912.[78] As I mentioned earlier, Yung was writing and published *My Life in China and America* when he had been stripped of his US citizenship. Thus, as Worthy notes, "Even in his autobiography he made no mention of this significant act [his naturalization, which he eventually lost]; he only referred to America as his 'adopted country.'" With good reason, Yung writes about his belonging to the US with great ambivalence. Critic Paul W. Harris concludes that, by the end of his life, "he grew increasingly distrustful of government officials both East and West. He had become, not simply Chinese or simply American, but Chinese-American."[79] Despite his loss of citizenship, he still claimed his Chinese Americanness. His unpublished, archived plague-writing also contributes to Asian American modernism.

USHERING IN ASIAN AMERICAN MODERNISM
BY SECULARIZING CHRISTIANITY

Although, as Worthy puts it, the "manifestations of Yung's early leaning toward the West are his naturalization as an American citizen and his conversion to Christianity,"[80] Yung omitted his naturalization from and only briefly mentions his conversion in his autobiography.[81] Nevertheless, Yung's commitment and indebtedness to Christianity remain clear. After all, his early education took place in mission schools. Even though he refused to become a missionary in China as his friends expected him to,[82] Worthy writes,

> Yung's faith does seem to have been genuine, because in his letter he constantly alluded to God and His power. For example, in one letter he com-

---

75. Harris, 103.
76. Xu, 59.
77. Worthy, 284.
78. Xu, 59.
79. Harris, 107.
80. Worthy, 270.
81. Based on these elisions, Xu argues, "If the failure to mention his conversion signifies Yung's double consciousness toward missionaries, his deliberate ambiguity about his naturalization exhibits the writer's dilemma about finding his place in the world and his ability to situate himself as across lands" (56).
82. "Remarkable Career," 6.

mented: "How good a thing is to know and serve God." Be this as it may, Yung's Christianity was at that juncture in Chinese history a definite step away from China and especially his family. In the letter he wrote Williams his freshman year (1850) he revealed his family's antagonism toward Christianity when he said that his mother and uncle "are afraid that I will embrace the new religion or the gospel which is sent to all" if he were to stay in America for college education.[83]

Given his family's antagonism toward his Christianity, Yung secularizes and universalizes Christianity in his activism and political work in China. Yung attempted to use the Christian universalization of love from God in his politics of social equality: Worthy states, "As the deputy minister of China to this country, 1878–1881, he was an ardent advocate for the Chinese laborer in America against discriminatory legislation."[84] Worthy goes on to write about his political activities in China later in his life: "In the late 1890's, he returned to China and was such an active participant in the nascent reform and revolutionary movements that a reward was put on his head by the Ch'ing government in 1901, due to his implication in an ill-fated revolt staged by a group of reformers."[85] Forced to escape China because his life was at risk, Yung was clearly influenced by the martyrdom of Christ in his reformist and revolutionary activism in China.

Yung's reformist and revolutionary activism was reflected in his vacillation between Christianity and secularism. Yung considered himself neither Chinese nor American, and neither reformer nor revolutionary."[86] And yet, just as Yung was Chinese American, he was both reformer and revolutionary in his politics. In his analysis of Yung's "True Freedom" essay, Harris makes the link between Yung's Christianity and his secular politics: "The emphasis on action is another important link between Yung and the evangelicals. By emphasizing acts of 'disinterested benevolence' as the distinguishing marks of the truly godly, Edwards had helped to give American evangelicalism a powerful activist thrust which was still very much evident in the volatile world of antebellum reform. [. . .] As he states at the outset, 'True freedom is a perfected state of activity; activity as an end; not activity for an end.'"[87] Yung's secular "activism" was rooted and reflected in his Christianity. And yet, Yung was clear about his separation between his religion and politics: "Although Yung parenthetically

---

83. Worthy, 271.
84. Worthy, 265.
85. Worthy, 265.
86. Harris, 89.
87. Harris, 96.

inserts the comment that 'Divine Revelation' is 'the most perfect system of morality,' he makes no truly essential link between Christianity and the process of self-development he describes."[88] The notion of the healthy and vigorous, "self-made man" in the plague era was based on the "perfect system of morality" that the "Divine Revelation" prescribes.

As part of his positivistic plague-writing, Yung pursues this secular universalization of Christianity throughout *My Life in China and America*. When he returned to China after graduating from Yale, he had an interview with Kan Wong, the "Protecting Prince" of China. When asked what he thought about the Taipings and the Taiping Rebellion, Yung made the following suggestions to westernize China:

1. To organize an army on scientific principles.
2. To establish a military school for the training of competent military officers.
3. To establish a naval school for a navy.
4. To organize a civil government with able and experienced men to act as advisers in the different departments of administration.
5. To establish a banking system, and to determine on a standard of weight and measure.
6. To establish an educational system of graded schools for the people, making the Bible one of the text books.
7. To organize a system of industrial schools.[89]

Although he suggests the westernization of Chinese education by "making the Bible one of the text books," in the "educational system of graded schools for the people," the rest of his prescriptions remain secular. Likewise, when he proposed the Chinese Educational Commission to Governor Ting Yih Chang, he put forth four "Proposals" that were entirely secular in nature; that is to say, there was no mention of Christianity even though he was proposing a "mission."[90] Moreover, in his "Fourth Proposal," he writes,

No one who is at all acquainted with Roman Catholicism can fail to be impressed with the unwarranted pretensions and assumptions of the Romish church in China. She claims civil jurisdiction over her proselytes, and takes civil and criminal cases out of Chinese courts. In order to put a stop to such insidious and crafty workings to gain temporal power in China, I

---

88. Harris, 97.
89. Yung Wing, *My Life in China and America*, 33–34.
90. Yung Wing, *My Life in China and America*, 52–53.

put forth this proposition: to prohibit missionaries of any religious sect or denomination from exercising any kind of jurisdiction over their converts, in either civil or criminal cases.[91]

Despite his faith in Christianity, he proposes to secularize education here to universalize it. He goes as far as to call Roman Catholics "insidious and crafty."

At the same time, he believed that Christianity, although not enforceable, was important for the CEC students' characters. In the same letter to Twichell, during the closing of the CEC, he grumbles against "Mr. Woo who professing to be hostile to Christianity, & its influence over the students should employ a crazy & cracked Missionary to the Mission."[92] As he rambles here, he clearly resents being called "a crazy & cracked Missionary to the Mission" by Mr. Woo. In an earlier letter he wrote to Twichell, he emphasizes the importance of preserving the students' belief in Christianity:

> The Chinese officials who take an interest in the Educational schemes seemed to be much pleased with the way in which things are managed, & not a syllable was uttered against any thing that we have done. My associates in the work however are trying all they can to fortify the young minds against Christianity & a few external trifles of civilization. Poor benighted fellows! They might as well keep the youngsters from daylights as from the truth. When I go back, I mean to keep my temper, & behave like a stoic, & let their ways have full swing. I wish they could appreciate Christian patience & forbearance, then they would let good alone; but I am afraid that this petty interference could annoy people who have charge of the training of the students, which might lead them to give up this charge. For my part, I should not feel at all sorry for the teachers to make a simultaneous move of that kind just a few days before I arrive in Hartford. I could then step in & tell my Chinese friends that they must not interfere with the Education & management of the students as long as they are entrusted to responsible [tactics]. I could soon bring them to terms, about attending family prayers, Sunday schools, & church service. I tell you honestly & plainly that my Chinese friends need a move of that kind to teach them a good lesson that in America, the students must do as they are told by their teachers, & that they must abide by the rules & regulations of the families and public schools & institutions where they are. [...] If you should see Mrs. Laisun, & our mutual friend Mrs. Bartlett, you would do me a great favor to talk the matter over

---

91. Yung Wing, *My Life in China and America*, 53.
92. Letter from Yung Wing to Joseph Hopkins Twichell, 14 April 1881.

with them confidentially, & tell them the views that I have expressed, just as
though they came from you & not from me. This is taking it for granted that
you sympathize with me in these views.[93]

While he disagrees with his associates for warning the students against
Christianity, he pities them rather than chastises them: he calls them "poor
benighted fellows!" And although he "wish[es] they could appreciate Christian patience & forbearance," he deems this "interference" "petty." His true
focus is having "the students [. . .] do as they are told by their teachers." In this
way, Yung's focus on Christianity is as secular as it is religious.

Likewise, in his proposed description of the Chinese Educational Commission in his autobiography, he plague-writes that their preparation would
be strictly secular:

> As to the character and selection of the students: the whole number to be sent
> abroad for education was one hundred and twenty; they were to be divided
> into four installments of thirty members each, one installment to be sent
> each year for four successive years at about the same time. The candidates to
> be selected were not to be younger than twelve or older than fifteen years of
> age. They were to show respectable parentage or responsible and respectable
> guardians. They were required to pass a medical examination, and an exami-
> nation in their Chinese studies according to regulation—reading and writing
> in Chinese—also to pass an English examination if a candidate had been in
> an English school. All successful candidates were required to repair every day
> to the preparatory school, where teachers were provided to continue with
> their Chinese studies, and to begin the study of English or to continue with
> their English studies, for at least one year before they were to embark for the
> United States.[94]

Yung makes no mention of Christianity in these students' training. His prescription of age, "not to be younger than twelve or older than fifteen years of
age," and "proper" parentage or guardianship is consistent with his exceptional
minority discourse of the healthy, self-made, manly man during the yellow-
peril-induced driving-out and plague eras, which I later discuss. In keeping
with the exceptional minority notion of masculine physical and mental vigor
of Chinese Americans to combat the yellow peril stereotype, Yung applied for

---

93. Letter from Yung Wing to Joseph Hopkins Twichell, 4 February 1874, Joseph Hopkins
Twichell papers, Beinecke Rare Books & Manuscripts Library, Yale University, New Haven, CT,
YCAL MSS 755; box 9; October 1967 acquisition.

94. Yung Wing, *My Life in China and America*, 56.

the CEC students to be sent to the military academies, West Point and the US
Naval Academy, since he had stipulated at the start of the CEC: "*As the young
students grow up, those who are qualified should be sent to West Point and the
Naval Academy as cadets and midshipmen for their advanced training.*"[95] In
many ways, he modeled the CEC after West Point and the Naval Academy: in
a letter to Professor Noah Porter, requesting his help to set up the educational
curriculum of the CEC, he wrote of the CEC students, "They are not allowed
to become citizens of the United States nor to settle there permanently, nor
to leave in the middle of their courses with the view of following their own
fortune. As they are educated at the government expense, thus are under the
same obligations to it, as the Cadets of West Point or Annapolis are to the
United States government."[96] However, despite his interest in and inspiration
by these institutions, his request for the CEC students to go to West Point
and the Naval Academy was denied. In response, he chalked the denial up
to the yellow peril and plague stereotypes as he wrote, "The race prejudice
against the Chinese was so rampant and rank that not only my application for
the students to gain entrance to Annapolis and West Point was treated with
cold indifference and scornful hauteur, but the Burlingame Treaty of 1868 was,
without the least provocation, and contrary to all diplomatic precedents and
common decency, trampled under foot unceremoniously and wantonly, and
set aside as though no such treaty had existed, in order to make way for those
acts of congressional discrimination against Chinese immigration which were
pressed for immediate enactment."[97] Here, Yung's Chinese American activism
comes out most clearly in his writing when he decries the "race prejudice" and
contradiction of the Burlingame Treaty of 1868, which was "trampled under
foot unceremoniously and wantonly." The refusal to admit Chinese students
to military academies contributed to the contemporary discourse of Chinese
effeminacy, disease, and poor health.

The Chinese government and US liberals also disciplined Yung for his
Progressivist westernization of China and his Chinese American activism by
the closing of the Chinese Educational Commission and the lack of public
interest in his writing, respectively. Moreover, his secularization of Christianity, which Harris recognized as a critic later in the century, was poorly
received during an era in which successful Chinese Americans were either

---

95. *When East Met West*, 3.

96. Letter from Yung Wing to Professor Noah Porter, New College, New Haven, 17 February 1872, Yung Wing papers, Sterling Memorial Library, Yale University, New Haven, CT, MS
602; box 1.

97. Yung Wing, *My Life in China and America*, 63.

"heathen," like Wong Chin Foo, or strictly Christian, like Yan Phou Lee. Yung, incidentally, proclaimed himself to be a "heathen," with tongue in cheek, despite his Christian beliefs: when he traveled to Washington, DC, to visit the Japanese Minister, he writes, "I managed to be just as agreeable to them as a 'heathen Chinese' knows how: but I had to do an immense amount of talking before they would let me off."[98] Always aware of the plague-related, yellow peril stereotype, Yung recognizes that other Americans perceive him to be an unassimilated "heathen" despite his belief in Christianity. And thus, his strategy of replicating the exceptional minority stereotype in overachieving by being the first Chinese American to go to university—Yale University at that—gained him citizenship but only temporarily. The binary yellow peril stereotype ultimately obstructed his career as a Chinese American writer while the model minority stereotype has dampened his reception in literary history since. Even as he harnessed the discourse of the hardworking, accomplished model minority to fight its binary, the diseased yellow peril stereotype, Yung's activism during the overlapping and sequential driving-out and plague eras in his writing on Chinese American health, vigor, and masculinity undercut his assignment as the exceptional minority. However, his masculine activism and resulting traditionalist gender politics sometimes contradicted or compromised his sympathy toward women, which we see in his treatment of and descriptions of the women in his life in a section to follow. Yung's masculine activism is nevertheless significant during this period, since the quiet, demure exceptional minority is never expected to be dedicated to vociferous activism; indeed, the latter contradicts the former. Even though he was denied citizenship, Yung plague-wrote his way to democratic "true freedom." At the end of *My Life in China and America*, he writes of the Japanese governor of Formosa, Kodama, who warns him that his life is in danger even in Formosa after he has already left China. Moreover, "He said he would introduce me to the Japanese emperor and other leading men of the nation. I thanked him heartily for his kindness and invitation and said I would accept such a generous invitation and consider it a great honor to accompany him on his contemplated journey, but my health would not allow me to take advantage of it."[99] The "kind" and "inviting" solidarity he feels with the Japanese governor of Formosa coincided with the panethnicity we see just beginning before World War I in Asian American literature, starting with Sui Sin Far and moving to Carlos Bulosan after World War II.

---

98. Worthy, 276.
99. Yung Wing, *My Life in China and America*, 74.

YUNG'S LITERARY MODERNISM

In addition to reflecting the contemporary panethnicity of Asian American literature of his time, Yung's plague-writing also resonates with his reformism and dovetails with and traces the reformism of the contemporary Progressive Era. In his reformist activist days, Yung knew well the former Minister of Justice, Liang Qi Chao, whom he met during his involvement in the Hundred Days' Reform.[100] Likewise, Sui Sin Far, in her modernist writing, discussed the reformism of Liang Qi Chao in the *Los Angeles Express* in 1903.[101] As a Chinese American Christian, secularizing his faith in his politics during the driving-out and plague eras, Yung radically universalized the particularity of his identity in his only published work, *My Life in China and America*.[102]

Yung's gravitation toward the English language and literature demonstrates how closely he identified with being an American. Several critics note that when Yung returned to Hong Kong en route to China after graduating from Yale, he realized on the ship that he had lost his ability to speak Chinese even though he had retained some understanding of it. Koh states,

> When the Chinese pilot came on board in Hong Kong Harbor, and spoke to the passengers, Yung Wing was shocked to discover that he could understand what the pilot said only with great difficulty. When he himself spoke, he could not make the pilot understand him. Yung Wing found himself so changed by his Western experience that he now felt out of place everywhere, even in his own homeland.[103]

Despite the use of the term "homeland" here, it is precisely his loss of language that destabilizes Yung's sense of a homeland. A contemporary journalist likewise writes of Yung's estrangement from the Chinese after living in the United States for so long:

> He was all made over within—a New Englander. He belonged to us, was of our society, and China was as foreign to him as to us. When he went back to that country the native pilot who boarded the ship could not understand his attempts at the language. He had forgotten how to write it, and he was entirely ignorant of his native land; for he had lived all his Chinese life in a seaport town, and the inland country was unknown to him save as he

---

100. Harris, 104–5.

101. Chapman, 978.

102. Clark, *Asian American Avant-Garde,* 14–15.

103. Koh.

had read of it. He went back to China to meet a strong prejudice, stronger than we can appreciate, against people educated abroad. One thing took him back. He felt that being himself delivered, he must not remain here for mere enjoyment. He returned poor and friendless to no advantages, but with a single eye and heart to his great purpose.[104]

The very use of the term "makeover" or being "made over" harks back to the American self-made man of the nineteenth century. Here, the journalist claims Yung Wing as "belong[ing] to us." His assimilation to American society, however, was not without its costs: his westernization and loss of Chinese language skills caused him to be "[met with] a strong prejudice" by the Chinese. Thus, although Yung would eventually lose his American citizenship, he identified as a Chinese American through his language acquisition and interest in literature.

Although his autobiography does not document his longstanding interest in literature and lack of opportunities to publish, his papers at Yale's Sterling Memorial Library and Beinecke Rare Book & Manuscript Library contain many of his unpublished poems. The existence of these poems demonstrates that Yung was interested in a literary career but was disciplined for his early activism by a loss of opportunity and a lack of liberal public interest in his writing. His untitled and unpublished poems were written during his junior year at Yale; that he thought to document them as "Chinese poetry written by Yung Wing, a native of China & a Junior in Yale College, June 26th, 1853" suggests that he knew his poetry would otherwise not be published.[105] In the set of four poems, the first poem reads as follow:

There is
a morning
and
a day
when frost
& snow
fall.[106]

---

104. "Remarkable Career," 6.

105. "Chinese poetry written by Yung Wing, a native of China & a Junior in Yale College, June 26th, 1853," Yung Wing papers, Sterling Memorial Library, Yale University, New Haven, CT, group 602, box 1, folder 10.

106. "Chinese poetry written by Yung Wing."

I read this poem as Yung enjoying a different climate than that of southern China's Canton region, and pondering his New England existence where both the "frost" of the "morning" and the "snow" of the "day" fall together. In some ways, as plague-writing, the poem reflects the suspension of his literary career until 1909 through the conflation of the beginning "morning" "frost" and middle "day" "snow" of his literary career.

His second poem continues his meditation on wintry scenes:

We only
see
the evergreen
but
not the
flower.[107]

In this poem, he seems to admonish the reader for "only see[ing]" the sturdy, tall, and imposing "evergreen / but / not the / flower." In some ways, his classmates at Yale viewed him as a tall "evergreen," expected to bring Western knowledge back to China but failing to see the "flower" of his literary abilities. In his yearbook, his Yale classmates commonly addressed him as "Friend Wing" or "Dear Friend Wing" but would often refer to him as their "Celestial" classmate: for example, one of his classmates, W. G. Hagg, writes, "We shall always be proud and fond of our Chinese classmate and I for one shall hope that [. . .] I shall not be forgotten [. . .] in the far off regions of the Celestial Empire. You have the power of Knowledge in your hands. Use it to [. . .] your countrymen and mankind: may God be with you."[108] Like Hagg, many of his classmates expected his degree to be functional and instrumental in westernizing China; this expectation was a self-fulfilling prophecy of the CEC. At the same time, his classmates did not expect him to pursue a literary career. Perhaps Yung was influenced by such a prescription when he wrote his third poem:

The goat
resembles
the Evergreen
the wicked
resembles
the flower.[109]

---

107. "Chinese poetry written by Yung Wing."

108. Yung Wing papers, Sterling Memorial Library, Yale University, New Haven, CT, Yung Wing, 1828–1912; MS 602; HM 18; Reel 1U; 1876–1877.

109. "Chinese poetry written by Yung Wing."

I read this poem through the lens of his plague-writing about his exclusion from a literary career. Through this lens, we might see the sturdy, functional farm goat and the enduring evergreen as figures of his own perseverance. He compares himself to the sturdy, functional farm goat and the enduring evergreen; Yung perhaps gives in to the practical idea that a literary career, or a "flower," is for the idle and "wicked." And yet, in his final poem on the same sheet of paper, he concludes only that

> At present
> the one is inferior
> to the other.[110]

Yung insightfully concludes that only "at present" is the "wicked" and idle career of literary pursuit "inferior" to "the other" functional career of Chinese diplomacy, which he did succeed in pursuing as the co-commissioner of the CEC and one of the first diplomatic envoys to the United States, appointed by President Rutherford B. Hayes in 1878.[111] As a result, Yung's literary career was put on hold. Yung's four poems at the Sterling Memorial Library, which predate Ezra Pound's experimentation with the haiku form, are modernist in concision even though none of them are fourteen syllables. Thus, even before Yung modernized China by bringing Western knowledge back to his nation of origin, he was modernizing English poetry through his plague-writing.

In addition to the poetry held at the Sterling Memorial Library, the Beinecke Rare Books & Manuscript Library holds an untitled poem he wrote in 1854 to and perhaps for the poet James Gates Percival, who had also graduated from Yale decades earlier:

> A great man never forgets the
> heart he had when a child.[112]

Like the aforementioned four poems, this poem follows a modernist concision that predates the American modernists of the twentieth century. However, his plague-writing poetry was never published, and thus he never entered into debates about literary modernism even though his work predates Pound and other Asian American modernists such as Yone Noguchi and Sadakichi

---

110. "Chinese poetry written by Yung Wing."

111. *When East Met West*, 5.

112. Letter from Yung Wing to James Gates Percival, 1854, James Gates Percival collection, Beinecke Rare Books & Manuscripts Library, Yale University, New Haven, CT, YCAL MSS 703; box 13, folder 418; series IV, correspondence; letters to James Gates Percival 674.1, Yung Wing/ 1854.

Hartmann. Moreover, in this poem to a "great" poet, Yung identifies with Percival as a fellow poet and promises that even as he becomes "A great man" and a Chinese diplomat, who will "never forget[ ] the heart [for literature] he had when a child." He includes the evolutionary notes of the poem, as he does with the previous four poems, including the Chinese characters and their translations. In addition to his creative work, Yung thus also offers early literary criticism. The inclusion of his evolutionary notes also suggests the importance of his literary beginnings in shaping who he has and will become.

When he finally published *My Life in China and America* in 1909, it was well received by the public. He received a letter from Miss Susan Whedon that stated her appreciation for it. He responded by expressing his doubts about his career path of diplomacy: "It is doubtful whether I would live it over again. But such as it is, I have given in to the world for what it is worth."[113] He goes on to call his work in diplomacy and the CEC "plain." As his Yale classmates encouraged him to do, he "live[d] for China, & her highest welfare" instead of pursuing a literary career. He was, indeed, proud of his one publication, as he sent a copy of his book to the Yale library. In a letter to J. C. Schwab, the librarian at the time, he writes: "The book, 'My Life in China & America,' will be delivered to you either today, or tomorrow by Adam's Express, for the Yale University Library. as a slight token of my love of Yale."[114] Even in his later years of life, Yung dedicated his burgeoning literary career to his "love of Yale." In 1877 he donated 1,237 volumes of Chinese books to the Yale University Library. Thanks to Yung's donation, a year later, Yale made its first faculty hire in Chinese studies.[115] Yung lived a "checkered" life in becoming a diplomat while not realizing his long wished-for literary career of plague-writing until the end of his life.

His senior essay, "True Freedom," which was published in the *Yale Literary Magazine*, likewise demonstrated his early interest in a literary career. Harris writes that the essay "summarized and paid tribute to his American education":[116]

"True Freedom" describes a three-stage educational process that reveals the influence of evangelicalism through its structural similarity to a conversion

---

113. Letter from Yung Wing to Miss Susan Whedon, 13 January 1910, Yung Wing papers, Sterling Memorial Library, Yale University, New Haven, CT, MS 602; box 1.

114. Letter from Yung Wing to J. C. Schwab, Librarian, 13 December 1909, Yung Wing papers, Sterling Memorial Library, Yale University, New Haven, CT, group 602, box 1: Electrostatic copies of correspondence, poems and class book autograph, 1848–1910.

115. *When East Met West*, 8.

116. Harris, 95.

experience. The first stage, which Yung calls the Mechanical, is analogous to the stage of conviction in a religious conversion. In this stage individuals labor diligently but are frustrated because they are still outside the law and hence lack "power." In the second, or Philosophic, stage, individuals learn to impose a rigorous logic on their personal development. The culmination is then the Poetic stage, when the individual becomes "artistically skilled in the appliance of power" and enters into a state of "autonomic Spontaneity" in which action "costs him no struggle, no effort" because "he is so in the law, that there appears to be no law." This conception of true freedom as spontaneous action flowing from a kind of artistic intuition may be more directly related to the influence of Romanticism, but it also strongly resembles the evangelical conception of saving grace, particularly in the writings of Jonathan Edwards, the great eighteenth-century American theologian who remained a dominant figure in evangelical thought. Edwards had described grace as a kind of aesthetic taste—what he called a "holy relish"—that stimulates a "natural habit, or foundation of action."

In yet another example of plague-writing, Yung establishes genuine freedom through the literary arts: philosophy and poetry. Having just received American citizenship at this point in his life, before the driving-out and plague eras, Yung nevertheless recognized the instability of his citizenship. Therefore, he aimed to achieve "true freedom" through writing. Yung, again, showcases his activism here by prescribing the secularization of Christianity in order to achieve "true freedom." Yung's continual vacillation between Christianity and secularism adds to the sense of his "checkered life" and also reveals his Chinese American activist aims, his traditionalist gender politics, and his contributions toward Asian American modernism in *My Life in China and America*. Even though, as the earliest Asian American activist who contended with the exceptional minority stereotype, he was professionally held back by being published later than all of his contemporaries, Yung's writing did the important work of ushering in the modernist era of Asian American literature.

THE BURDEN OF THE EXCEPTIONAL MINORITY AND YUNG'S TRADITIONAL GENDER POLITICS

Like the other early Asian American literary figures—Tape and Yan Phou Lee—Yung Wing was considered an assimilationist figure by Asian American critics in the twentieth century: as Asian American literature was institutionalized in the 1970s, editors Frank Chin, Jeffery Paul Chan, Lawson Fusao Inada, and Shawn Wong promoted a cultural nationalist, Asian American "style of manhood" to which Yung Wing, as an "assimilative" "Christian" "missionary" autobiographer did not seem to subscribe.[117] In addition, the editors mention Yung Wing's *My Life in China and America* as model minority, assimilationist "Chinese" rather than Chinese American literature in their second anthology, *The Big Aiiieeeee!*, in 1991.[118] Critic Amy Ling also critiqued Yung's use of masculinity as a form of model minority assimilation—to appeal to white readers during the period of Chinese exclusion.[119] Following and responding to Ling, Floyd Cheung underscores Yung's activism in writing, "via autobiography Yung defends against assaults on the Chinese character made by Theodore Roosevelt and others during the late 1890s and early 1900s," referring to Roosevelt's reproduction of the discourse of manhood and manliness in the early twentieth century.[120] Xu, likewise, argues that Yung placed an emphasis on being a "self-made man" as it was in vogue in the nineteenth-century United States.[121] Critics Chih-Ming Wang and Patricia Chu recuperate Yung from the Manichean discourse of masculinity and femininity by reframing him as a "transnational actor whose engagements on both shores shaped the interactive cultural and political dynamic that I call 'Asia/America'" and a rhetorician who "discuss[es] the vulnerability of the Chinese people under the Qing [. . .] by drawing on the genres of the missionary travel narrative and the slave narrative,"[122] respectively. As I demonstrate, despite his emphasis on his masculinity, Yung was indeed sympathetic to women's oppression in his respect for and support of his mother and his first missionary schoolteacher, Mrs. Gützlaff. Moreover, his physically vigorous masculinity was produced by the exceptional minority expectation of good health. As critic James Kyung-Jin Lee argues, "Asian Americans must exemplify success, in the classroom and the workplace; by extension, they must also inhabit indefinitely healthy bodies that serve this success frame."[123] Inasmuch as Yung fought the exceptional minority stereotype through his, at times, revolutionary and reformist activism, he nevertheless deployed the discourse in his physically vigorous masculinity to qualify as an American citizen during a period in which Asian American citizenship was extremely unstable.

---

117. Chin et al., *Aiiieeeee!*, 37; and Chin et al., *Big Aiiieeeee!*, xxvii, xxviii.
118. Chin et al., *Aiiieeeee!*, xii.
119. Ling, "Reading Her/stories," 75.
120. Cheung, 25, 32.
121. Xu, 33–35, 38.
122. Wang, 38; and Chu, *Where I Have Never Been*, 30.
123. James Lee, 3.

Although Yung was traditional in his gender politics, he was clearly attached and owed his successes to the women figures in his life and was sympathetic to their social oppression. A journalist introduces Yung's high opinion of the two women who were formative in his upbringing and education—his mother and Mrs. Gützlaff—in an 1875 article, "A Remarkable Career," in the *New York Evangelist*. The article praises all of Yung's career achievements, including his education at Yale, his creation of the Chinese Educational Commission, and his further work for the Chinese government. Based on his conversation with Yung, the journalist concludes that it is either Mrs. Gützlaff, "the lady missionary who taught him his letters," or his mother, who is "the agent of this so great event," that is, the Chinese Educational Commission. In suggesting that Yung is "a fruit of the missionary work,"[124] the journalist attributes his greatness to the patience and wisdom of a woman, Mrs. Gützlaff, whose school he attended for three and a half years (1839–42), before the school was closed because of the Opium War.[125] Other sources suggest that he was placed in Mrs. Gützlaff's school slightly earlier, when he was seven years old.[126] Thereafter, Yung attended the Morrison Mission School, where he met the principal Mr. Samuel Robbins Brown, Yung's tutor and patron, who eventually brought him to the US with two other students, Wong Shin and Wong Foon, as Brown sought to improve his health in 1847.[127] Yung's gratitude to women, specifically, also emerges in his comments about his mother. He describes her in a feminist manner, as "a woman of strong native force, of great uprightness of character, a very religious woman in her way." Championing women, his emphasis is on his mother's strength and character and her own idiosyncratic religiosity.

Likewise, he demonstrates his support for women in his letters, where his focus on his family often centers on his mother. For example, in a letter to Monson, the head of the academy which he, Wong Shin, and Wong Foon attended in Massachusetts upon their arrival in the United States, he writes,

---

124. "Remarkable Career."
125. Xu, 40.
126. Blakeslee, *When East Met West*, 2.
127. Blakeslee also suggests that Yung entered the Morrison School in 1841. Blakeslee. Blakeslee writes of Wong Shin and Wong Foon, that upon graduating from Monson academy, "Wong Shing returned to China and Wong Foon went to Scotland where he attended the University of Edinburgh from which he graduated with honor as a surgeon. He returned to China and built up a fine practice in Canton." In *China's First Hundred*, La Fargue writes, "Wong Hsing, who had been forced to return to China because of ill-health, learned the art of printing in the office of the *China Mail*" (21). La Fargue, 20.

of course you are aware that my feelings would not allow me to leave my mother and the brothers and sister, since I promised them all when I left China to return in two or three years and you know ful [*sic*] well that the prejudice of the Chinese, how they misrepresent things, and that they are not able to see as you or any enlightened mind do, the object, the advantage, and value of being educated. Ignorance and superstition have sealed the noble faculties of their minds, how can they appreciate things of such worth.[128]

In this letter, a form of his plague-writing, he recognizes the intimacy he shares with his mother, whom he lists first, and then brothers, and sister even while recognizing that they are prey to the "ignorance" and "superstition" of their culture. His negative depiction of Chinese culture demonstrates his growing westernization. Nevertheless, owing to his love and devotion to them, he expresses his obligation to return to them.

In addition to his mother and Mrs. Gützlaff, Yung also demonstrates his admiration for other women, such as his wife Mary Golden Kellogg Yung, whom he praises for her strength of character: in a letter to his close friend, Reverend Joseph Twichell, he writes,

I am anxious to see China tho it will be difficult and painful for me to leave my family. Mary is brave and noble about my going. The pangs of separation have already been creeping over me, but duty is imperative and I have made up my mind to answer its call.[129]

While his attachment to his wife is clear—"The pangs of separation have already been creeping over me"—the letter focuses on Mary's bravery and nobility. In contrast with Yan Phou Lee's claim that white American women are more boisterous than Chinese women, Yung describes his white American wife, whom he declines to name in his autobiography, in much the same way as he describes his mother: demure, submissive, but enduring. It is possible that Yung only makes brief mention of his marriage because he knew that most white Americans disapproved of it; his friend Reverend Twichell wrote of the marriage in his diary: "The match was a good deal commented on. Some people feel doubtfully about it; some disapprove it utterly; some (like me) gloried in it (qtd. in Lafargue 42)."[130] Previously, Yung had felt "that there was no Chinese woman whom he would marry and no American lady who

---

128. Worthy, 273.
129. Worthy, 282.
130. Xu, 60.

would marry him."[131] However, the reformism of nineteenth-century liberalism provided him the opportunity to marry Mary, a white woman. Yung only makes mention of his marriage toward the end of the autobiography when he leaves Peking in 1882:

> I reached home in the spring of 1883, and found my wife in a very low condition. She had lost the use of her voice and greeted me in a hoarse low whisper. I was thankful that I found her still living though much emaciated. In less than a month after my return, she began to pick up and felt more like herself. Doubtless, her declining health and suffering were brought on partly on account of my absence and her inexpressible anxiety over the safety of my life. A missionary fresh from China happened to call on her a few days before my departure for China and told her that my going back to China was a hazardous step, as they would probably cut my head off on account of the Chinese Educational Mission. This piece of gratuitous information tended more to aggravate a mind already weighed down by poor health, and to have this gloomy foreboding added to her anxiety was more than she could bear.[132]

Although Mary is portrayed as mentally fragile because of his absence, her poor health is better understood when he conveys that she had been told he was likely beheaded because of his work in the Chinese Educational Commission. Thereafter, she spent two months at a sanitarium in Somerville, New Jersey, and eventually succumbed to Bright's disease.[133] Yung's tribute to his wife demonstrates the depth of his love and respect for her: "Her death made a great void in my after-life, which was irreparable, but she did not leave me hopelessly deserted and alone; she left me two sons who are constant reminders of her beautiful life and character."[134] Despite portraying his wife and mother as subservient figures, exemplifying his traditionalist gender politics, Yung is clearly indebted to both of them. In his plague-writing, Yung's similar depictions of his mother and wife demonstrate his belief in the behavioral virtue of and equality between Chinese and white American women.

In *My Life in China and America*, Yung attempts to give his mother a voice, but his depictions of her reinscribe the other gendered, exceptional minority stereotype of the hypersubmissive, gentle Lotus Blossom who mourns his departure to America: "My mother gave her consent with great reluctance, but

---

131. Worthy, 277.
132. Yung Wing, *My Life in China and America*, 67.
133. Yung Wing, *My Life in China and America*, 67.
134. Yung Wing, *My Life in China and America*, 67.

after my earnest persuasion she yielded, though not without tears and sorrow. I consoled her with the fact that she had two more sons besides myself, and a daughter to look after her comfort. Besides, she was going to have a daughter-in-law to take care of her, as my elder brother was engaged to be married."[135] Rather than depicting her as a matriarch whose permission he seeks to go abroad, Yung portrays her as a demure Lotus Blossom who "yields" to him "not without tears and sorrow" and requires comfort from her son. However, when he returns to China to visit his mother, she notices he has grown a mustache before his older brother has and asserts herself by ordering him to shave it off according to custom. It is significant that this is the only place in the autobiography where a woman is quoted and given speech:

> This interview seemed to give her great comfort and satisfaction. She seemed very happy over it. After it was ended, she looked at me with a significant smile and said, "I see you have already raised your mustaches. Yet you know you have a brother who is much older than you are; he hasn't grown his mustaches yet. You must have yours off."[136]

Despite previously framing his mother as a Lotus Blossom figure, per his masculinist rhetoric, Yung also enfleshes her in his plague-writing by powerfully giving his mother authoritative voice here ("You must have yours off") during a period in which Chinese and Chinese American women, largely, didn't have any. Yung's plague-writing about his mother demonstrates the Progressive Era contradiction of liberal reform and the social death of women who were denied voting rights until 1920, three years after the end of the Progressive Era.

Continuing to establish intimacy between him and his mother in his narrative when he visits his mother in China after graduating from Yale, Yung Wing also foretells Foucault's famous *Power/Knowledge* (1980) by telling her "'Knowledge,' I said, 'is power, and power is greater than riches. I am the first Chinese to graduate from Yale College, and that being the case, you have the honor of being the first and only mother out of the countless millions of mothers in China at this time, who can claim the honor of having a son who is the first Chinese graduate of a first-class American college. Such an honor is a rare thing to possess.'"[137] After graduating from Yale, Yung Wing became a mandarin of the fifth rank in the Chinese official system.[138] He was later

135. Yung Wing, *My Life in China and America*, 7.
136. Yung Wing, *My Life in China and America*, 17.
137. Yung Wing, *My Life in China and America*, 15.
138. Yung Wing, *My Life in China and America*, 79.

made the chief commissioner and, later, the associate minister of the Chinese Educational Commission, which educated Chinese scholars to be sent to the United States for further education.[139] And yet, despite all his visible plague-writing/projects and exceptional achievements, such as graduating from Yale, he is still despised by liberals as the exceptional minority that turns the luck of the boat on his return from the US to China when, as I mentioned earlier, the white American skipper calls him a "Jonah" on account of his race.[140]

In his plague-writing, Yung, as a Chinese American activist whose traditionalist gender politics still allowed for his sympathy toward women and their social oppression, nevertheless performed the vital work of modernizing Asian American literature in his own writing and secularizing Christianity through the CEC. His plague-writing, which included projects like the CEC and his gender politics, traced the lynchings and social deaths, including his own, that the contradictory liberal reformism of the Gilded Age and Progressive Era required and disavowed. His masculinist politics reflect the discursive sickliness attributed to Chinese Americans, and his traditionalist yet supportive attitudes toward women evince the contradictions of Progressive Era attitudes toward reform and suffrage. Although both Cacho and Hong have shown the intimacy between social death and neoliberalism, as Cohen has demonstrated, Progressive Era liberalism was the beginning of twentieth-century neoliberalism. As the CEC ended just one year before the Chinese Exclusion Act, Yung performed the extraordinary, "troublemaking" work of documenting and exposing the contemporary driving-out and the denial of Chinese American rights during the deathly plague era.

---

139. Yung Wing, *My Life in China and America*, 81–82.
140. Yung Wing, *My Life in China and America*, 16.

CONCLUSION

The Enfleshed Exceptions

On March 29, 2022, President Joe Biden signed the Emmett Till Antilynching Act, addressing the modern-day lynchings of African Americans that fueled the spectacular murders of George Floyd, Breonna Taylor, Ahmaud Arbery, and others in 2020. This law declares lynching a federal hate crime, in response to the historic increase of African American lynching after the emancipation of slavery through the Jim Crow era[1] and the ongoing forms of anti-Black hate crimes to the present day. If neoliberalism, as Cacho and Hong argue, relies on and disavows *mundane* Black death, the Till Antilynching Act is one step toward eradicating that toxic relation and addressing the inequities and racism of neoliberalism. The lynching era of African Americans, which also geographically spanned the South, the West, and the Midwest,[2] was at its height between the 1880s and the 1930s. In this study, I use the term *era* instead of *period* because era leaves open the possibility and actuality of ongoing violence against Black people (which Afropessimism encapsulates), Indigenous people, and people of color. Some scholars estimate that around 1,545 people were lynched between 1890 and 1900, of which only 438

---

1. Finnegan, 1–2. Finnegan writes, "The psychological, social, economic, and political elements of white racism merged in lynching, which dehumanized African American males so that whites could justify disfranchisement" (9).

2. See Pfeifer.

were white.[3] Other scholars have estimated that between 1880 and 1930, lynch mobs hanged 4,697 Americans, of which 3,344 were African Americans.[4] Many scholars assume that most nonwhite lynch-mob victims were Black.[5] Others acknowledge that white lynch mobs also targeted Latinx and Native American populations and that, moreover, Latinx and Native American mobs also lynched women who were blamed for witchcraft in their communities.[6] As this study has shown, Asian Americans, specifically Chinese Americans, were part of that number even though it is not well documented. However, different from other racializations, especially those of African Americans, in the case of which liberals problematically view and dismiss death and violence as quotidian and a matter of course, the exceptional minority stereotype of Chinese Americans correlated with and exposed the exceptional exemption of nineteenth-century liberalism from law and the founding principles of egalitarianism. Lynching itself is an exceptional—even if it is problematically viewed as mundane in the case of African Americans—spectacular act of racially motivated violence that nineteenth-century liberalism regularly disavowed and for which it shirked responsibility, even as liberalism encompassed white supremacy during the period. However, despite the driving-out era of the 1870s and 1880s, modern-day liberals do not usually associate Asian Americans with lynching, because of the reigning model minority stereotype in the twentieth and twenty-first centuries in which Asian Americans are discursively viewed as submissive, assimilative, and politically inactive based on their bourgeoisification. This study's focus on Chinese American lynching contributes to the triangulation of Blackness, whiteness, and Asianness in Lye's "Afro-Asian Analogy" and performs the work of drawing alliances between African American and Asian American histories and identities while also pointing out important differences of mundane and exceptional violence directed against each group, respectively.

The nineteenth-century exceptional minority stereotype, which encompassed both the submissive, hyperbolical, and economically efficient model minority and the invading, diseased, and competitive yellow peril, and which represented the "bare life" of nineteenth-century liberalism, is the root of the twentieth-century model minority stereotype that casts Asian Americans as assimilative but also submissive, academically achieving, and wealthy. Despite

---

3. Wexler, 76. Wexler goes on to say that between 1890 and 1946, three thousand African American people were lynched (77).

4. Madison, 13.

5. Wexler, 76.

6. McLure, 21–22, 36, 44.

the deceptively benign, reigning paradigm of the Asian American "model minority" in the American social imaginary since the late twentieth century, contemporary lynchings (spectacular deaths, although not always involving hanging) continue to occur, as in the 1982 case of a Chinese American man, Vincent Chin, who was murdered in front of a McDonald's by two white men—one a laid-off Chrysler auto worker and the other a plant supervisor— in part because they blamed him for the competitive success of the Japanese auto industry in the US. Hate crimes toward Asian Americans ramped up in the twenty-first-century United States after President Trump called the coronavirus the "Chinese virus"[7] on Twitter and during press conferences throughout March of 2020. After Trump ethnically labeled the virus as the "Chinese virus," the "China virus," or the "kung flu," three members of an Asian American family, including a toddler and a six-year-old, were stabbed by a white American teenager who believed they were Chinese and spreading the coronavirus in Midland, Texas, on March 14, 2020.[8] On April 5, 2020, an Asian woman in Brooklyn was assaulted with acid by an unknown assailant, resulting in chemical burns on her face and body.[9] These assaults on the Asian American community continued into 2021, culminating in the murders of six Asian American women in Atlanta, Georgia, on March 16, 2021; the brutal assault on a sixty-five-year-old Asian American woman in Hell's Kitchen, New York, on March 28, 2021; and the murder of Christine Yuna Lee in New York's Chinatown on March 16, 2022. With constant news and social media reports of anti-Asian sentiment during the 2020 COVID-19 outbreaks, people around the world were shocked at the discursive transformation of Asians and Asian Americans, more specifically, from the model minority to the yellow peril, or the anti-Asian sentiment that associated Asians with disease, overpopulation, and conquest of Western civilization. But it is precisely the exceptionalism with which Asian Americans continue to be racialized that has made these Asian hate crimes, on the whole, so invisible to the public and unimportant to the media. *Against Exclusion* traces this exceptionalist discourse back to the nineteenth century and points out that the tandem stereotypes of the model minority and the yellow peril have existed in the United States for centuries but surface in economic crises such as emancipation of slave labor or a global pandemic.

This book pays tribute to Foucault's theory of biopolitics, which he defines as "the attempt, starting from the eighteenth century, to rationalize the problems posed to [liberal] governmental practice by phenomena characteristic of a set of living beings forming a population: health, hygiene, birthrate, life

---

7. Brito.
8. Boboltz.
9. Lim.

expectancy, race."[10] In other words, biopolitics demonstrate liberal govern-mental control across all populations and their human bodies. This study con-tinues Agamben's claim that the exceptionalism of sovereignty relies on and disavows the exceptionalism of the homo sacer, the bare life that cannot be sacrificed but may be killed without penalty of murder. However, this study resituates race, specifically Chinese Americanness, at the center of Agamben's notion of exceptionalism in the nineteenth-century US. Although the figures of my study were very much ahead of their time, and for that reason often illegible to contemporary liberals, they did not yet reach the postliberal man, or the human as praxis stage that Sylvia Wynter endorses. In deploying the exceptional minority discourse in their activism, they very much relied on the power of nineteenth-century liberalism even as they sought to reconstruct it. As Foucault writes in various places, power emerges through different, orga-nized disciplines and is executed through epistemological discourse. In *Disci-pline and Punish*, Foucault invokes the quarantine of the prison system: "On the whole, therefore, one can speak of the formation of a disciplinary society in this movement that stretches from the enclosed disciplines, a sort of social 'quarantine,' to an indefinitely generalizable mechanism of 'panopticism.' Not because the disciplinary modality of power has replaced all the others; but because it has infiltrated the others, sometimes undermining them, but serv-ing as an intermediary between them, linking them together" through dis-course, that is, what is said.[11] In *The History of Sexuality*, Foucault clarifies that discursive power is perpetuated by "a determination on the part of the agen-cies of power to hear it spoken about, and to cause *it* to speak through explicit articulation and endlessly accumulated detail" through different people who reproduce such discourses of power.[12] A case in point: President Trump calls the pandemic coronavirus the "Chinese virus" and hate crimes against Asian Americans ensue. Moreover, in the 1870s labor leader Denis Kearney famously stated "The Chinese must go!," and Chinese Americans were lynched and vio-lently expelled from West Coast cities. According to Foucault, discourse—like liberalism—mutates, is difficult to escape, and, in the instances I cite, co-opts one's intentions to enflesh oneself against the dehumanizing rhetoric of the exceptional minority.[13] As this book shows, the exceptional minority stereo-type worked for and against Toy, Tape, Wong Chin Foo, Yan Phou Lee, and Yung Wing insofar as they harnessed it to gain political visibility, but their efforts were not recognized, often absorbed as, and undifferentiated from hegemonic liberalism.

10. Foucault, *Birth of Biopolitics*, 317.
11. Foucault, *Discipline and Punish*, 216.
12. Foucault, *History of Sexuality*, 18, 27.
13. Foucault, *History of Sexuality*, 27.

Toy, Tape, Wong Chin Foo, Yan Phou Lee, and Yung were contemporaries of each other insofar as they lived in the US in the second half of the nineteenth century and responded to a contradictory liberalism. Although it is unclear whether Tape personally knew Wong Chin Foo, Yan Phou Lee, or Yung Wing, as a literate and educated woman, she likely read about them or their works in newspapers and magazines through which they all also knew about the contemporary driving-out. There is no evidence that Toy and Tape knew each other, although they may have read about each other in the newspapers and were affected by sex work and sex trafficking. Wong Chin Foo, Yan Phou Lee, and Yung Wing, who spent their time mainly on the East Coast, also may have read about Toy and Tape on the West Coast in the newspapers; nevertheless, the three of them knew each other and responded to each other's work in other ways. Yung also likely read about Toy and Tape in the newspapers. Tape and Wong Chin Foo both knew Reverend Otis Gibson. All public figures and contemporaries of each other, some of whose professional circles overlapped, they were Chinese American activists and writers during the age of Chinese American driving-out. Their historical contexts of the different Chinese exclusion laws, the Massacre of 1871, and the West Coast purges of Chinese Americans in the 1880s allow us to understand the aims of their shared universal humanism and their activist aims of enfleshing the otherwise objectified, driven-out, and socially dead Chinese Americans at the time. While Toy, Tape, and Wong Chin Foo were protofeminists, Yan Phou Lee and Yung were masculinist in their rhetoric but often espoused ethical manhoods,[14] which sympathized with the plight of Chinese women in the nineteenth century and favorably represented them in their autobiographies. One also has to account for the individual hardships that Yung and Yan Phou Lee endured in relation to each other in American society to understand their avenues of traditionalist gender politics in rallying a conservative American audience. Taken together as Christians and heathens, these diverse figures further enflesh the Chinese American community in the US during the driving-out era of the 1870s and 1880s. However, as evident by their scant reception in twentieth-century literary criticism, liberalism co-opted their enfleshing efforts to dismantle and expand liberalism during an age in which liberals accepted Chinese exclusion and lynching as status quo.

Having endured, survived, and documented the driving-out era, these activists, are, instead, the founders of Asian America. And thus their enfleshed exceptionalism lies at the heart of Asian American studies. Refusing to recognize Wong's enfleshment during their famous debate, Denis Kearney scoffed at Wong's claim to the white founding fathers of the United States:

---

14. Shimizu, 4.

"I beg your pardon, they are not" was Wong's calm reply. "I'm an American citizen, and I've voted the good old Democratic ticket and sometimes for a good Republican. The Federal decisions you speak of are wrong and unconstitutional if they forbid the naturalization of Chinamen. They must be admitted to citizenship, as I was fifteen years ago, by the provisions of the Constitution made by our forefathers, and—"

"Your forefathers!" exclaimed Denis, wrathfully; "sure, what had your forefathers to do with it! Nothing at all. You can't call the framers of the Constitution your forefathers. Huh!" The great man of the sand-lots shouted violently and shoved back his chair from anything like proximity to Wong's, thus firmly proclaiming that there couldn't possibly be anything like common forefatherhood for them[.]

Wong smiled wrathfully, but coolly, and said: "I call them my forefathers, because politically they were—"

"I'm against that. That ain't so," shouted Denis.[15]

Despite Kearney's rejection of Wong's belonging to and cultural patrimony in the United States—"I'm against that. That ain't so"—and its body politic, little did Wong know that he was on his way to becoming a forefather of Asian American literature. Together, Wong Chin Foo, Yan Phou Lee, Yung Wing, Toy, and Tape demonstrate the earliest struggles of Chinese Americans and their use of their voices—whether civic or literary—to protest the social inequality Chinese Americans experienced during the driving-out era. They used their civic and literary voices to break out of their discursive objectification, to enflesh themselves, and to heal from the psychic fragmentation of trauma.

Chinese American exceptionalism transformed into the model minority stereotype in the twentieth century; hate crimes against Asian Americans continued and have continued precisely *because* the exceptional, model minority has always been part of the yellow peril, and Chinese American exceptionalism has become part of the Asian American exceptionalism that has continued in neoliberalism. Moreover, these figures and their stories demonstrate that, although it seems innocuous and congratulatory, the exceptional minority stereotype is damaging insofar as it spectacularly objectifies a *minority* of people within a general population as what Agamben calls sacred and thus sacrificed, "bare life." Toy, Tape, Wong Chin Foo, Yan Phou Lee, and Yung Wing provide genealogical snapshots of the exceptional minority insofar as it reveals that the exception is a type of exclusion; the exceptional minority is excluded even as it is a member of society; and it exposes the sovereignty of

---

15. "Wong Chin Foo and Denis," 26.

white supremacy through mimicry or divine violence, which "deposes" sovereign violence.[16] Many Asian American communities are influenced by the Confucian tenets of hard work and respect for hierarchy, which white Americans have historically exploited. The resulting, twentieth-century rendition of the exceptional minority stereotype, the model minority, thus objectifies the Asian American laborer and divorces them from their labor. Because of the exceptional minority stereotype in the nineteenth century, the Asian American subject, such as Wong Chin Foo, is relegated to *excessive* self-fashioning as if they were without history. The driving-out era of the 1870s and 1880s spectacularly objectified Chinese Americans as exceptional, model minority workers who became a yellow peril problem in purportedly stealing jobs from their white counterparts and spreading disease; to enflesh Chinese Americans during this period, Toy, Tape, Wong Chin Foo, Yan Phou Lee, and Yung sparked their activism through testifying in court cases and writing essays or books even as they, especially Toy and Tape, had to endure the spectacularizing and objectifying limelight to do so.

The driving-out era that resulted from the exceptional minority stereotype and the recorded voices of these figures, which responded to that discourse, demonstrates its great power. Kearney's motto "The Chinese must go!" rang throughout the driving-out era in which there is not even a complete body count of those lynched in and driven out of West Coast cities. One white California labor leader utters such words, and two decades of systemic violence follows suit. Likewise, the discourse of slavery surrounding Chinese Americans in a postbellum US contributed to Chinese exclusion. The first Chinese exclusion law, the 1875 Page Act, which persecuted all Chinese American women as illegal prostitutes, directly responded to such discourse. In this spirit, the exceptional minority discourse wreaked havoc on the lives even the earliest Asian Americans living in the continental United States.

Against Exclusion recovers some of the earliest Asian American activists whose lives were affected by the exceptional minority discourse that fueled the driving-out era of the late nineteenth century. This study makes sense of the earliest Asian American literature and activism as autobiographies and court cases by contextualizing them during the driving-out era. The five figures of my study form a cohort of the earliest Asian American activists who responded to the driving-out era and the exceptional minority gender exclusion of the Page Act. Toy, a sex worker, and Tape, a Christian Victorian Chinese American woman, were both influenced by the Victorian ideology of female moral reform, which disparately spurred the formation of Protestant mission homes

---

16. Agamben, 17, 25, 84, 64–65.

and suffragism. Although the Protestant mission homes attempted to homogenize the Chinese American community as Protestant and assimilationist to white American Victorian culture, and the suffragists did not include Asian Americans in their agenda, both Tape and Toy believed in the woman's ability to stand up for her own rights and the rights of those she represents. Wong Chin Foo was a bit of an anomaly as a Chinese American protofeminist man during a period in which Chinese American women largely did not have a voice in public spheres and in which white American women had not yet won the right to vote. He rescued trafficked sex workers and believed in feminist free love. He also refused to essentialize women in his writing. On the other hand, Yan Phou Lee and Yung demonstrate their traditionalist yet sympathetic gender politics in their writing. Yan Phou Lee's difficult personal relationships with women and his admission but documentation of structural sexism in Chinese culture in his ethnographic work contribute to his traditionalist gender politics. These politics also broadened his appeal to a conservative liberal audience. Yung's vigorous masculinity in his plague-writing responded to charges of sickness and infirmity leveled at Chinese Americans during the plague period. As a result, his sympathy toward women's oppression appears in his support and honor of the women who inspire his education and pursuit of writing even when he, at times, portrays them as submissive and demure. The respective protofeminism and gender sympathy of the five figures I discuss importantly respond to the Page Act, which excluded Asian women on the presumption of their sex work and was based on the yellow peril / model minority discourse of Asian American hypersexuality and hyperfemininity. Toy, Tape, Wong Chin Foo, Yan Phou Lee, and Yung Wing demonstrated their activism in their gender politics and in enfleshing themselves during a period in which Chinese Americans were spectacularly objectified through lynching in and expulsion from West Coast cities. However, their activism often relied on their collaboration with liberals.

As my second chapter on Wong Chin Foo demonstrates, there were liberals who capitalized on early Chinese Americans and objectified them in much the same way that white supremacists did. However, ideologically, they could not afford to be associated with white supremacists, and such disassociation kept them accountable. On the other hand, there were other liberals, like John Clark (at one point) for Toy, Florence Eveleth for the Tapes, William Lloyd Garrison Jr. for Wong Chin Foo, Allen Thorndike Rice for both Wong and Yan Phou Lee, Mark Twain for Wong and Yung, and Ulysses Grant for Yung, who genuinely supported these figures and their activist efforts. These liberals were, for the figures of this study, what the white leftist activist Eileen Odell was for Carlos Bulosan—"undeniably the *America* I had wanted to find in those frantic days of fear and flight, in those acute hours of hunger and loneliness. This America was human, good, and real."[17] During a period of extreme anti-Chinese violence and legislated exclusion, Toy, Tape, Wong Chin Foo, Yan Phou Lee, and Yung found solace in these individuals and the liberalism that was eagerly and ideologically separating itself from the inhuman white supremacy that was responsible for the driving-out. The constituting, sovereign power of liberalism, exemplified by "all men are created equal"—inevitably became a problem of potentiality for the actuality of white supremacy.

Together, Toy, Tape, Wong Chin Foo, Yan Phou Lee, and Yung faced the empiricism of white supremacy, documented the driving-out era, and provided a genealogy of the exceptional minority. In their work, they demonstrate that the exceptional minority stereotype, which existed more than a century before the term *model minority* was coined, ineluctably collapses the model minority into the yellow peril stereotype. This exceptional stereotype propelled the driving-out era and the attempt to exterminate Chinese Americans on the West Coast during the 1870s and 1880s. The figures of my study, especially Yung, who had the disadvantage of publishing the latest, also heralded Asian American modernism: they integrated progressive protest, before the Progressive Era, into the establishment of their voices—through court cases or literature—and many of them focused on the separation of secularism and Christianity, and some, like Yung, experimented with their writing. These five figures pioneered Asian American activism, literature, and protofeminism during an era in which Chinese Americans, particularly women, were legally excluded from citizenship and immigration on the bases of their race and sexualities. Hegemonic liberalism often co-opted their activist efforts, but their work did not entirely result in failure: their work and lives contributed to and traced the shift from conservative reform in the Gilded Age to progressive reform in the Progressive Era.

Always collapsing the model minority into the yellow peril stereotype, and constructed as a threat to either white America in the nineteenth century or other racial minority groups in the twentieth century, the seemingly benevolent discourse of the exceptional minority is insidious and pernicious, and led to the driving-out era. This book traces the genealogy of the exceptional minority stereotypes to the events and cultural productions of the early exclusion era in which the Chinese were blamed for urban epidemics, anti-Chinese organizations such as the Anti-Coolie Association (1869) were created, and in which Chinese were lynched, driven out in other ways in the 1870s and 1880s, and suffered social deaths through legal discourse (1854, 1875, 1882, 1892). The

---

17. Bulosan, 235.

first pieces of Asian American literature and these *infrastructures of activism* emerged during this period to protest such stereotypes of the yellow peril but were absorbed by the model minority discourse. In attempting to enflesh themselves and other Chinese Americans and exposing the contradictions and exceptionalisms of liberalism, thus proving that they were all eligible for citizenship, Toy, Tape, Wong Chin Foo, Yan Phou Lee, and Yung were dismissed by the liberalism that required and disavowed their exceptionalism. Toy, Tape, Wong Chin Foo, Yan Phou Lee, and Yung presciently argued during driving-out and plague periods of the nineteenth century that all races are susceptible to discursively objectifying stereotypes, disease, and quarantine. As these figures demonstrate, tactically deploying and resisting these objectifying stereotypes are what make us human, in the flesh.

BIBLIOGRAPHY

MANUSCRIPT COLLECTIONS

California Biographical Mss. '49 Experiences. Bancroft Library, University of California, Berkeley.

Chan, Gertrude. Immigration Papers. San Francisco National Archives.

Garrison Family Papers. Sophia Smith Collection, Smith College, Northampton, MA.

Grover Cleveland Papers, Library of Congress, Washington, DC.

Walter Hines Page Papers. Houghton Library, Harvard University, Cambridge, MA.

James Gates Percival Collection. Beinecke Rare Books & Manuscripts Library, Yale University, New Haven, CT.

San Francisco Vigilance Committee. Bancroft Library, University of California, Berkeley.

Sorbier Papers. Box 7: Newspaper Clippings 1893–1928 Bulk: 18981921. *California Historical Society*, San Francisco, California.

Special Collections. Magill Library, Haverford College, Haverford, PA.

Statement of events in California as related by Elisha Oscar Crosby (1878). Bancroft Library, University of California, Berkeley.

J. P. Stuart Papers. Academy of the New Church Archives, Bryn Athyn College, Bryn Athyn, PA.

Joseph Hopkins Twichell Papers. Beinecke Rare Books & Manuscripts Library, Yale University, New Haven, CT.

Yung Wing Papers. Sterling Memorial Library, Yale University, New Haven, CT.

SECONDARY SOURCES

Aarim-Heriot, Najia. *Chinese Immigrants, African Americans, and Racial Anxiety in the United States, 1848–82.* Urbana: University of Illinois Press, 2003.

Agamben, Giorgio. *Homo Sacer: Sovereign Power and Bare Life.* Translated by Daniel Heller-Roazen. Stanford, CA: Stanford University Press, 1998.

"Anti-Chinese Demonstration." *Seattle Daily Call,* October 26, 1885.

Barnhart, Jacqueline Baker. *The Fair but Frail: Prostitution in San Francisco, 1849–1900.* Reno: University of Nevada, 1986.

Barth, Gunther. *Bitter Strength: A History of the Chinese in the United States, 1850–1870.* Cambridge, MA: Harvard University Press, 1964.

Bataille, Georges. *Visions of Excess: Selected Writings, 1927–1939.* Translated and edited by Allan Stoekl. Minneapolis: University of Minnesota Press, 1985.

Baudrillard, Jean. "Death in Bataille." In *Bataille: A Critical Reader,* edited by Fred Botting and Scott Wilson, 139–45. Oxford: Blackwell Publishers, 1998.

Bederman, Gail. *Manliness & Civilization: A Cultural History of Gender and Race in the United States, 1880–1917.* Chicago: The University of Chicago Press, 1995.

Bell, Duncan. "What Is Liberalism?" *Political Theory* 42, no. 6 (2014): 682–715.

Benjamin, Walter. "Critique of Violence." In *Selected Writings,* vol 1., 1913–1926, edited by Michael W. Jennings, 236–53. Cambridge, MA: Belknap Press of Harvard University Press, 1996.

Brito, Christopher. "President Trump Uses Term 'Chinese Virus' to Describe Coronavirus, Prompting Backlash." *CBS News,* March 19, 2020. https://www.cbsnews.com/news/president-trump-coronavirus-chinese-virus-backlash/.

Boboltz, Sara. "Stabbing of Asian American Toddler and Family Deemed a Hate Crime, Reporting." *HuffPost,* April 1, 2020. https://www.huffpost.com/entry/stabbing-of-asian-american-toddler-and-family-deemed-a-hate-crime-report_n_5e84b65fc5b6871702a84cob.

Boessenecker, John, ed. *Against the Vigilantes: The Recollections of Dutch Charley Duane.* Norman: University of Oklahoma, 1999.

"The Buddhist Religion." *New York Times,* April 30, 1877.

Bulosan, Carlos. *America Is in the Heart.* New York: Harcourt, Brace, 1943.

Bush, C. P. "Notes of Travel." *New York Evangelist,* September 19, 1872, pp. 43, 48.

Cacho, Lisa Marie. *Social Death: Racialized Rightlessness and the Criminalization of the Unprotected.* New York: New York University Press, 2012.

Cándida Smith, Richard. Correspondences, May 18, 2023.

Carey, Tom. Librarian/Archivist. San Francisco History Center, San Francisco Public Library. August 18, 2022.

Caruth, Cathy. *Unclaimed Experience: Trauma, Narrative, and History.* Johns Hopkins University Press, 2016.

Castillo, Jaime, LCSW. "What Is a 'Little t' Trauma?" *A Happier, Healthier You,* June 15, 2022.

Chang, Iris. *The Chinese in America.* New York: Viking, 2003.

Chapman, Mary. "A 'Revolution in Ink': Sui Sin Far and Chinese Reform Discourse." *American Quarterly* 60, no. 4 (December 2008): 975–1001.

Cheng, Anne Anlin. *Ornamentalism.* Oxford: Oxford University Press, 2019.

Cheng, Wendy. *Island X: Taiwanese Student Migrants, Campus Spies, and Cold War Activism.* Seattle: University of Washington Press, 2023.

Cheung, Floyd. "Early Chinese American Autobiography: Reconsidering the Works of Yan Phou Lee and Yung Wing." In *Recovered Legacies: Authority and Identity in Early Asian American Literature,* edited by Keith Lawrence and Floyd Cheung, 24–40. Philadelphia: Temple University Press, 2005.

"Childlike and Bland." *New York Times,* July 28, 1877.

Chin, Frank, Jeffery Paul Chan, Lawson Fusao Inada, and Shawn Wong, eds. *Aiiieeeee!: An Anthology of Asian American Writers.* New York: Mentor, 1991.

———. *The Big Aiiieeeee!: An Anthology of Chinese American and Japanese American Literature.* New York: Meridian, 1991.

"China Mary, Widely Known Clam Seller, Dies at Age of 99." *San Jose Mercury Herald,* February 2, 1928.

"The Chinamen Organizing." *New York Times,* July 30, 1884.

"Chinese in a New Role: Wong Chin Foo Intends to Found a New Political Party." *Chicago Daily Tribune (1872–1922),* July 12, 1896.

"Chinese in the U.S." *New York Times,* July 23, 1881.

"The Chinese School." *Daily Alta California,* April 14, 1885. Newspaper and Microforms Library, University of California, Berkeley.

Chon-Smith, Chong. *East Meets Black: Asian and Black Masculinities in the Post–Civil Rights Era.* Jackson: University Press of Mississippi, 2015.

Chou, Rosalind, and Joe R. Feagin. *The Myth of the Model Minority: Asian Americans Facing Racism.* 2nd ed. New York: Routledge, 2015.

Chu, Patricia P. *Assimilating Asians: Gendered Strategies of Authorship in Asian America.* Durham, NC: Duke University Press, 2000.

———. *Where I Have Never Been: Migration, Melancholia, and Memory in Asian American Narratives of Return.* Philadelphia: Temple University Press, 2019.

Chuh, Kandice. *The Difference Aesthetics Makes: On the Humanities "After Man."* Durham, NC: Duke University Press, 2019.

———. *Imagine Otherwise: On Asian Americanist Critique.* Durham, NC: Duke University Press, 2003.

Clark, Audrey Wu. *The Asian American Avant-Garde: Universalist Aspirations in Modernist Literature and Art.* Philadelphia: Temple University Press, 2015.

———. *Asian American Players: Masculinity, Literature, and the Anxieties of War.* Columbus: The Ohio State University Press, 2023.

Cohen, Nancy. *The Reconstruction of American Liberalism, 1865–1914.* Chapel Hill: University of North Carolina Press, 2002.

Coolidge, Mary Roberts. *Chinese Immigration.* 1909. New York: Arno Press, 1969.

Craddock, Susan. "Sewers and Scapegoats: Spatial Metaphors of Smallpox in Nineteenth Century San Francisco." *ScienceDirect, Social Science Medicine* 14, no. 7 (1995): 957–68.

"Demonstration." *Tacoma Daily Ledger,* October 26, 1885.

Duane, Charles P. "The First Chinawoman." *San Francisco Daily Examiner,* February 2, 1928.

DuBois, Ellen Carol. *Feminism & Suffrage.* Ithaca, NY: Cornell University Press, 1999.

———. *Suffrage: Women's Long Battle for the Vote.* New York: Simon & Schuster, 2020.

———. *Woman Suffrage and Women's Rights*. New York: New York University Press, 1998.

DuBois, Ellen, and Richard Cándida Smith. *Elizabeth Cady Stanton, Feminist as Thinker: A Reader in Documents and Essays*. New York: New York University Press, 2007.

Espiritu, Yen Le. *Asian American Women and Men: Labor, Laws, and Love*. 2nd ed. Lanham, MD: Rowman & Littlefield, 2008.

Fabian, Johannes. *Time and the Other: How Anthropology Makes Its Object*. New York: Columbia University Press, 1983.

Finnegan, Terence. *A Deed So Accursed: Lynching in Mississippi and South Carolina, 1881–1940*. Charlottesville: University of Virginia Press, 2013.

Fitzmaurice, Andrew. "Liberalism and Empire in Nineteenth-Century International Law." *AHR Forum. American Historical Review* 117, no. 1 (February 2012): 122–40.

Foucault, Michel. *Birth of Biopolitics*. 1979. London: Picador, 2010.

———. *Discipline and Punish: The Birth of the Prison*. 1975. New York: Vintage Books, 1995.

———. *The History of Sexuality: An Introduction*. Vol. 1. New York: Vintage Books, 1990; 1976.

———. "Nietzsche, Genealogy, History." *Aesthetics, Method, and Epistemology*. New York: New Press, 1998.

Gamble, Leland. "What a Chinese Girl Did." *San Francisco Morning Call,* November 23, 1892.

Garraty, John A., and Mark C. Carnes, eds. *American National Biography*. Oxford: Oxford University Press, 1999.

Gentry, Curt. *The Madams of San Francisco: An Irreverent History of the City by the Golden Gate*. Garden City, NY: Doubleday, 1964.

Gerstle, Gary. "The Protean Character of American Liberalism." *American Historical Review* 99, no. 4 (October 1994): 1043–73.

Ginzberg, Lori D. *Elizabeth Cady Stanton: An American Life*. New York: Hill and Wang, 2009.

Girard, René. *Violence and the Sacred*. Translated by Patrick Gregory. Baltimore: Johns Hopkins University Press, 1972.

Gyory, Andrew. *Closing the Gate: Race, Politics, and the Chinese Exclusion Act*. Chapel Hill: University of North Caroline Press, 1998.

Haney López, Ian F. *White by Law: The Legal Construction of Race*. New York: New York University Press, 1996.

Harris, Paul W. "A Checkered Life: Yung Wing's American Education." *American Journal of Chinese Studies* 2, no. 1 (April 1994): 87–107.

Hart, James D. *A Companion to California*. Berkeley: University of California Press, 1987.

Hart, Jerome Alfred. *In Our Second Century: From an Editor's Note-Book*. San Francisco: The Pioneer Press, 1931.

Hartman, Saidiya. *Scenes of Subjection: Terror, Slavery, and Self-Making in Nineteenth-Century America*. New York: Oxford University Press, 1997.

Hayot, Eric. "Chinese Bodies, Chinese Futures." *Representations* 99 (Summer 2007): 99–129.

"A Heathen Missionary." *Shaker Manifesto,* November 1879, p. 259.

Herman, Judith. *Trauma and Recovery: The Aftermath of Violence—from Domestic Abuse to Political Terror*. New York: Basic Books, 1997.

Hirata, Lucie Cheng. "Free, Indentured, Enslaved: Chinese Prostitutes in Nineteenth-Century America." *Signs: Journal of Women in Culture and Society* 5, no. 11 (1979): 3–29.

Hofstadter, Richard. *The Age of Reform*. New York: Vintage Books, 1955.

Hong, Grace Kyungwon. *Death beyond Disavowal: The Impossible Politics of Difference*. Minneapolis: University of Minnesota Press, 2015.

Howe, Daniel Walker. *What Hath God Wrought*. Oxford: Oxford University Press, 2007.

Hsu, Madeline Y. *The Good Immigrants: How the Yellow Peril Became the Model Minority*. Princeton, NJ: Princeton University Press, 2017.

"The Imported Chinese Females in Court on Habeas Corpus." *Daily Alta California* 20, no. 6679, June 28, 1868.

Jun, Helen Heran. *Race for Citizenship*. New York: New York University Press, 2011.

Jung, Moon-Ho. *Coolies and Cane: Race, Labor, and Sugar in the Age of Emancipation*. Baltimore: Johns Hopkins University Press, 2006.

Kanazawa, Mark. "Immigration, Exclusion, and Taxation: Anti-Chinese Legislation in Gold Rush California." *Journal of Economic History* 65, no. 3 (September 2005): 779–805.

Kim, Elaine. *Asian American Literature: An Introduction to the Writings and Their Social Context*. Philadelphia: Temple University Press, 1982.

Kim, Jodi. *Ends of Empires: Asian American Critique and the Cold War*. Minnesota: University of Minnesota Press, 2010.

Koh, Dean Harold Honju. "Yellow in a White World." Speech delivered at Yale Law School, September 24, 2004.

La Fargue, Thomas. *China's First Hundred*. Pullman: State College of Washington Press, 1942.

Lee, James Kyung-Jin. *Pedagogies of Woundedness: Illness, Memoir, and the Ends of the Model Minority*. Philadelphia: Temple University Press, 2022.

Lee, Lily Xiao Hong, and A. D. Stefanowska. *Biographical Dictionary of Chinese Women: The Qing Period, 1644–1911*. Armonk, NY: An East Gate Book, 1998.

Lee, Rachel C. *The Exquisite Corpse of Asian America: Biopolitics, Biosociality, and Posthuman Ecologies*. New York: New York University Press, 2014.

Lee, Richard V. "Afterword." In *When I Was a Boy in China*, by Yan Phou Lee. 1887. Bloomington, IN: Xlibris Corporation, 2003.

———. "Foreword." In *When I Was a Boy in China*, by Yan Phou Lee. 1887. Bloomington, IN: Xlibris Corporation, 2003.

———. "Introduction." In *When I Was a Boy in China*, by Yan Phou Lee. 1887. Bloomington: Xlibris Corporation, 2003.

Lee, Robert G. *Orientals: Asian Americans in Popular Culture*. Philadelphia: Temple University Press, 1999.

Lee, Yan Phou. "The Boys and Girls of China." *St. Nicholas; an Illustrated Magazine for Young Folks* 17, no. 4 (February 1890): 362.

———. "A Chinese Market." *St. Nicholas; an Illustrated Magazine for Young Folks* 15, no. 7 (May 1888): 546.

———. "The Chinese Must Stay." *North American Review* 148, no. 389 (April 1889): 1–6.

———. "How Chinese Boys Live." *Christian Union*, March 5, 1885, p. 31.

———. "Graduate Address of Yan Phou Lee at Yale College." *American Missionary* (September 1887): 269–73.

———. *When I Was a Boy in China*. 1887. Bloomington: Xlibris Corporation, 2003.

———. "Why I Am Not a Heathen: A Rejoinder to Wong Chin Foo." *North American Review* 145, no. 370 (September 1887): 306–12.

Lew-Williams, Beth. *The Chinese Must Go: Violence, Exclusion, and the Making of the Alien in America*. Cambridge, MA: Harvard University Press, 2018.

Lim, Clarissa-Jan. "A Man Attacked an Asian Woman Taking Out Her Trash at Night. She Now Has Chemical Burns on Her Face and Body." *BuzzFeed News*, April 8, 2020. https://www.buzzfeednews.com/article/clarissajanlim/asian-woman-chemical-burns-brooklyn-new-york-attack.

Ling, Amy. *Between Worlds*. New York: Pergamon, 1990.

——. "Reading Her/stories Against His/stories in Early Chinese American Literature." In *American Realism and the Canon*, edited by Tom Quirk and Gary Scharnhorst, 69–86. Newark: University of Delaware Press, 1994.

——. "Yan Phou Lee on the Asian American Frontier." In *Re-Collecting Early Asian America: Essays in Cultural History*, edited by Josephine Lee, Imogene L. Lim, and Yuko Matsukawa, 273–87. Philadelphia: Temple University Press, 2002.

Loomis, Rev. A. W. "Chinese Women in California." *Overland Monthly and Out West Magazine* 2, no. 4 (April 1869): 344–51.

Low, Victor. *The Unimpressible Race: A Century of Educational Struggle by the Chinese in San Francisco*. San Francisco: East/West Publishing Company, 1982.

Lowe, Lisa. *The Intimacies of Four Continents*. Durham, NC: Duke University Press, 2015.

Lum, Kathryn Gin. *Heathen: Religion and Race in American History*. Cambridge, MA: Harvard University Press, 2022.

Lye, Colleen. "The Afro-Asian Analogy." In "Comparative Racialization," special issue, *PMLA* 123, no. 5 (October 2008): 1732–36.

——. *America's Asia: Racial Form and American Literature, 1893–1945*. Princeton, NJ: Princeton University Press, 2005.

Madison, James H. *A Lynching in the Heartland: Race and Memory in America*. New York: Palgrave, 2001.

Mannur, Anita. *Intimate Eating: Racialized Spaces and Radical Futures*. Durham, NC: Duke University Press, 2022.

"Married to a Chinaman." *New York Times*, July 7, 1887.

Mbembe, Achille. "Necropolitics." Translated by Libby Meintjes. *Public Culture* 15, no. 1 (Winter 2003): 11–40.

McCunn, Ruthanne Lum. *Chinese American Portraits: Personal Histories, 1828–1988*. Vancouver: Raincoast Books, 1988.

McKittrick, Katherine, ed. *Sylvia Wynter: On Being Human as Praxis*. Durham, NC: Duke University Press, 2015.

McLeod, Alexander. *Pigtails and Gold Dust*. Caldwell, ID: The Caxton Printers, 1947.

McLure, Helen. "Who Dares to Style This Female a Woman?: Lynching, Gender, and Culture in the Nineteenth-Century U.S. West." In *Lynching beyond Dixie: American Mob Violence Outside the South*, edited by Michael J. Pfeifer, 21–53. Urbana: University of Illinois Press, 2013.

Miller, Charles. Archives Specialist. National Archive at San Francisco. San Bruno, California. August 15, 2022.

Mills, Charles W. *Black Rights / White Wrongs: The Critique of Racial Liberalism*. Oxford: Oxford University Press, 2017.

Mulvey, Laura. "Visual Pleasure and Narrative Cinema." *Visual and Other Pleasures*. Bloomington: Indiana University Press, 1989.

Myers, Peter C. *Frederick Douglass: Race and the Rebirth of American Liberalism.* Lawrence: University Press of Kansas, 2008.

National Institutes of Health. "Plague in San Francisco: 1900, the Year of the Rat." August 28, 2012. https://www.niaid.nih.gov/about/joseph-kinyoun-indispensable-man-plague-san-francisco.

Ngai, Mae. *The Lucky Ones: One Family and the Extraordinary Invention of Chinese America.* New York: Houghton Mifflin Harcourt, 2010.

Ninh, erin Khuê. *Passing for Perfect: College Imposters and Other Model Minorities.* Philadelphia: Temple University Press, 2021.

Novicow, Jacques. *Le Péril Jaune.* Paris: V. Giard et E. Brière, 1897.

Okihiro, Gary Y. *Common Ground: Reimagining American History.* Princeton, NJ: Princeton University Press, 2001.

Ong, Paul, Edna Bonacich, and Lucie Cheng, eds. *The New Asian Immigration in Los Angeles and Global Restructuring.* Philadelphia: Temple University Press, 1994.

"Our Chinese Edison." *San Francisco Examiner,* August 4, 1889.

The Page Act of 1875. 2019. https://immigrationhistory.org/item/page-act/.

Pascoe, Peggy. *Relations of Rescue: The Search for Female Moral Authority in the American West, 1874–1939.* Oxford, UK: Oxford University Press, 1990.

Patterson, Orlando. *Slavery and Social Death: A Comparative Study.* Cambridge, MA: Harvard University Press, 1982, 2018.

Peden, W. Creighton. *From Evolution to Humanism in 19th and 20th Century America.* Newcastle upon Tyne: Cambridge Scholars Publishing, 2015.

Peffer, George Anthony. *If They Don't Bring Their Women Here: Chinese Female Immigration before Exclusion.* Urbana and Chicago: University of Illinois Press, 1999.

Petersen, William. "Success Story, Japanese-American Style." *New York Times Magazine,* January 9, 1966.

Pfaelzer, Jean. *Driven Out: The Forgotten War against Chinese Americans.* Berkeley: University of California Press, 2007.

Pfeifer, Michael J., ed. *Lynching beyond Dixie: American Mob Violence Outside the South.* Urbana: University of Illinois Press, 2013.

Plague at the Golden Gate. July 15, 2023. https://www.pbs.org/wgbh/americanexperience/films/plague-golden-gate/.

Platt, Stephen R. *Imperial Twilight: The Opium Wars and the End of China's Last Gold Age.* New York: Vintage Books, 2018.

"A Plea for the Chinese: Wong Chin Foo Describes the Woes of His People in America." *New York Times,* January 27, 1893.

Pratt, Mary Louise. *Imperial Eyes: Travel Writing and Transculturation.* New York: Routledge, 2007.

Pryor, Alton. *The Bawdy House Girls: A Look at the Brothels of the Old West.* Roseville, CA: Stagecoach Publishing, 2006.

———. *Fascinating Women in California History.* Roseville, CA: Stagecoach Publishing, 2003.

Rabiee, Robert Yusef. *Medieval America: Feudalism and Liberalism in Nineteenth-Century U.S. Culture.* Athens: University of Georgia Press, 2020.

Randall, David K. *Black Death at the Golden Gate: The Race to Save America from the Bubonic Plague.* New York: Norton, 2019.

Reichley, A. James. *The Life of the Parties: A History of American Political Parties.* New York: Rowman & Littlefield, 1992.

"A Remarkable Career." *New York Evangelist,* February 4, 1875, pp. 46, 5; and ProQuest pg. 6.

Rogers, Henry. *The Greyson Letters: Selections from the Correspondence of Greyson, Esq.* Boston: Gould and Lincoln, 1858.

Rothschild, Babette. *The Body Remembers: The Psychophysiology of Trauma and Trauma Treatment.* New York: Norton, 2000.

Rutter, Michael. *Upstairs Girls: Prostitution in the American West.* Helena, MT: Farcountry Press, 2005.

Saxton, Alexander. *The Indispensable Enemy: Labor and the Anti-Chinese Movement in California.* Berkeley: University of California Press, 1971.

Schweik, Susan M. *The Ugly Laws: Disability in Public.* New York: New York University Press, 2009.

Seligman, Scott. *The Remarkable Life of Wong Chin Foo.* Hong Kong: Hong Kong University Press, 2013.

Shah, Nayan. *Contagious Divides: Epidemics and Race in San Francisco's Chinatown.* Berkeley: University of California Press, 2001.

Shay, Jonathan. "Moral Injury." *Psychoanalytic Psychology* 31, no. 2 (2014): 182–91.

Shimizu, Celine Parreñas. *Straitjacket Sexualities: Unbinding Asian American Manhoods in the Movies.* Stanford, CA: Stanford University Press, 2012.

Sinn, Elizabeth. *Pacific Crossing: California Gold, Chinese Migration, and the Making of Hong Kong.* Hong Kong: Hong Kong University Press, 2013.

Skowronek, Stephen. "The Reassociation of Ideas and Purposes: Racism, Liberalism, and the American Political Tradition." *American Political Science Review* 100, no. 3 (August 2006): 385–401.

Stephens, Autumn. *Wild Women: Crusaders, Curmudgeons, and Completely Corsetless Ladies in the Otherwise Virtuous Victorian Era.* Coral Gables: Conari Press, 2020.

"Susan B. Anthony Receives an Ovation." *San Francisco Chronicle,* Tuesday, May 21, 1895.

Takaki, Ronald. *Strangers from a Different Shore.* New York: Penguin Books, 1989.

Tape, Mary. "Chinese Mother's Letter." *Daily Alta California,* April 16, 1885.

Tebbel, John, and Mary Ellen Zuckerman. *The Magazine in America, 1741–1990.* Oxford: Oxford University Press, 1991.

Thompkins, Kyla Wazana. *Racial Indigestion: Eating Bodies in the 19th Century.* New York: New York University Press, 2012.

Thompson, Richard Austin. *The Yellow Peril: 1890–1924.* New York: Arno Press, 1978.

Trauner, Joan B. "Chinese as Medical Scapegoats, 1870–1905, Historical Essay." *California History Magazine,* 1978, https://www.foundsf.org/index.php?title=Chinese_as_Medical_Scapegoats,_1870-1905.

Tseng, Timothy. "History of Chinese Christianity in North America: The Christian World They Made Together: 1850–1911." In "Chinese American Christianity in History and Today," edited by Andrew Lee and Sam George, special issue, *ChinaSource Quarterly* 22, no. 3 (Winter 2020). https://www.chinasource.org/resource-library/articles/the-christian-world-they-made-together-1850-1911/.

UPM staff. "Ersula J. Ore on Lynching." University Press of Mississippi, October 23, 2019. https://www.upress.state.ms.us/News/2019/Ersula-J.-Ore-on-Lynching.

Urbansky, Sören. "A Chinese Plague: Sinophobic Discourses in Vladivostok, San Francisco, and Singapore." *Features: Conference Reports: GHI News,* https://perspectivia.net/servlets/ MCRFileNodeServlet/pnet_derivate_00002122/75_urbansky_plague.pdf.

van der Kolk, Bessel. *The Body Keeps the Score: Brain, Mind, and Body in the Healing of Trauma.* New York: Penguin Books, 2014.

Waldrep, Christopher. "The Popular Sources of Political Authority in 1856 San Francisco: Lynching, Vigilance, and the Difference between Politics and Constitutionalism." In *Lynching beyond Dixie: American Mob Violence Outside the South,* edited by Michael J. Pfeifer, 54–80. Urbana: University of Illinois Press, 2013.

Wang, Chih-Ming. *Transpacific Articulations: Student Migration and the Remaking of Asian America.* Honolulu: University of Hawai'i Press, 2013.

Weheliye, Alexander G. *Habeas Viscus: Racializing Assemblages, Biopolitics, and Black Feminist Theories of the Human.* Durham, NC: Duke University Press, 2014.

Wellman, Judith. *The Road to Seneca Falls: Elizabeth Cady Stanton and the First Woman's Rights Convention.* Chicago: University of Illinois Press, 2004.

Wexler, Laura. *Fire in a Canebrake: The Last Mass Lynching in America.* New York: Scribner, 2003.

White, Richard. *The Republic for Which It Stands: The United States during Reconstruction and the Gilded Age.* Oxford: Oxford University Press, 2017.

Wilderson, Frank. "An Afropessimist on the Year since George Floyd was Murdered." *The Nation,* May 27, 2021. https://www.thenation.com/article/society/george-floyd-afropessimism/.

Wong Chin Foo. "A Celestial Belle." *Harper's Bazaar,* July 26, 1884, p. 475.

———. "The Chinese in Cuba." *New York Times,* August 17, 1874, p. 2.

———. "The Family in China and America." *Christian Advocate,* October 22, 1885: 679.

———. "Fashions in China." *Harper's Bazaar,* August 18, 1883.

———. "A Heathen in New York: Why Americans Should Embrace Confucius." Reproduction of "Why Am I a Heathen?" *North American Review,* 1887.

———. "Plans of a Chinese Manager." *New York Times,* March 10, 1884.

———. "Poh Yuin Ko, the Serpent Princess." *The Cosmopolitan* 6, no. 2 (December 1888): 180–90.

———. "The Story of San Tzon." *Atlantic Magazine,* August 1885, p. 258.

———. "The Wail of Wong Chin Foo." *Puck,* April 22, 1885, p. 117.

"Wong Chin Foo." *The Evangelist,* December 17, 1874: 2.

"Wong Chin Foo and Denis: The Sand-Lots Orator and the Mandarin Meet." *Chicago Daily Tribune,* October 23, 1887: 26.

"Wong Chin Foo Assaulted." *New York Times,* May 21, 1885.

"Wong Chin Foo Assaulted." *New York Times,* July 15, 1884.

"Wong Chin Foo Assaulted." *New York Times,* June 10, 1883.

"Wong Chin Foo in Danger." *New York Times,* May 7, 1888.

"Wong Chin Foo Protests against Class Legislation." *Chicago Daily Tribune,* December 27, 1897.

"Wong Chin Foo's Troubles." *New York Times,* October 16, 1887.

Wong, Edlie. *Racial Reconstruction, Black Inclusion, Chinese Exclusion and the Fictions of Citizenship.* New York: New York University Press, 2015.

Wong, Lily. *Transpacific Attachments: Sex Work, Media Networks, and Affective Histories of Chineseness.* New York: Columbia University Press, 2018.

Worthy, Edmund H., Jr. "Yung Wing in America." *Pacific Historical Review* 34, no. 3 (August 1965): 265–87.

Wu, Ellen D. *The Color of Success: Asian Americans and the Origins of the Model Minority.* Princeton, NJ: Princeton University Press, 2015.

Xu, Ying. "Across Lands: Double Consciousness and Negotiating Identities in Early Chinese American Literature, 1847–1910s." PhD diss., University of New Mexico, 2011.

"Yan Phon Lee and His Mother-in-Law." [Misspelling in the original.] *Chicago Daily Tribune,* May 11, 1890, p. 12.

Yin, Xiao-huang. *Chinese American Literature since the 1850s.* Chicago: University of Illinois Press, 2000.

You, Palma. Gallery Coordinator. Chinese Historical Society of America, San Francisco, California. August 16, 2022.

Yung, Judy. *Unbound Feet: A Social History of Chinese Women in San Francisco.* Berkeley: University of California Press, 1995.

Yung, Judy, Him Mark Lai, and Gordon Chang, eds. *Chinese American Voices: From the Gold Rush to the Present.* Oakland: University of California Press, 2003.

———. *My Life in China and America.* 1909. Middletown, DE, 2020.

Zellinger, Elissa. *Lyrical Strains: Liberalism and Women's Poetry in Nineteenth-Century America.* Chapel Hill: University of North Carlina Press, 2020.

Zesch, Scott. *The Chinatown War: Chinese Los Angeles and the Massacre of 1871.* Oxford: Oxford University Press, 2012.

Zimering, Rose, and Suzy Bird Gulliver. "Secondary Traumatization in Mental Health Care Providers." *Psychiatric Times* 20, no. 4 (April 1, 2003). https://www.psychiatrictimes.com/view/secondary-traumatization-mental-health-care-providers.

Zinn Education Project. "Oct. 24, 1871: Los Angeles Chinatown Massacre." zinnedproject.org, https://www.zinnedproject.org/news/tdih/la-chinatown-massacre/.

INDEX

www.ingramcontent.com/pod-product-compliance
Lightning Source LLC
Chambersburg PA
CBHW020352270326
41926CB00007B/406